Mooncake
Man

Mooncake
Man

John R. Fischer

iUniverse, Inc.
Bloomington

Mooncake Man

iUniverse books may be ordered through booksellers or by contacting:

iUniverse
1663 Liberty Drive
Bloomington, IN 47403
www.iuniverse.com
1-800-Authors (1-800-288-4677)

Because of the dynamic nature of the Internet, any web addresses or links contained in this book may have changed since publication and may no longer be valid. The views expressed in this work are solely those of the author and do not necessarily reflect the views of the publisher, and the publisher hereby disclaims any responsibility for them.

Any people depicted in stock imagery provided by Thinkstock are models, and such images are being used for illustrative purposes only.

Certain stock imagery © Thinkstock.

ISBN: 978-1-4759-2769-6 (sc)
ISBN: 978-1-4759-2768-9 (e)

Library of Congress Control Number: 2012909151

Printed in the United States of America

iUniverse rev. date: 6/26/2012

Do not judge yourself harshly. Without mercy for ourselves we cannot love the world.
Buddhist Teachings

Contents

Foreword

This book is not intended to be a chronological history of DHL Corporation in the Far East. In order to promote reader comprehension and consistent flow of the story I took the liberty of condensing the element of time in many of the events.

This is the story of a naïve young American raised with middle class values that clashed with the realities of life in Asia during the turbulent 1970's. Driven to success at any cost, he becomes like the people he despises as his life spirals out of control into a series of unpredictable events, strange adventures, war and romance.

I would also like to take this opportunity to recognize some of the very early employees of DHL who have never been given due credit in making the company successful. This includes the employees of the early Hawaiian Inter-island services, Andrew Johnson, Paul Kimoto, Marilyn Corral, Sandy Phillips, Bill Robinson and Grant Anderson.. The Guam operation with Bob Camp and George and Mary Sato running Cocos Island, Bruce Walker for taking over Singapore from me. And to the early employees of the USA operations, Sheldon Warren in Chicago, Jack Atwood in Seattle, Joe Wrechter in Texas and our attorney Wayne Alsop. And of course, I save the best for last. Lee Frazier, my sidekick selling DHL services in the USA after my return from Asia. I will always remember your opening line when we sold the service together in Texas,

"Were not here to shell peanuts." God bless you Lee wherever you are.

The person that should be recognize the most and has unfortunately been overshadowed for many years by the press and lifestyle of his partner Larry Hillblom, is the founder and my father in-law Adrian Dalsey. He was the guy that made it all happen, it was Adrian that camped on the doorstep of the Bank of America headquarters in San Francisco and persuaded them to give a little known company the chance to carry their documents. It was Adrian that secured our early key accounts Seatrain, Matson, and Sealand that generated the revenue and propelled our expansion into the Far East.

As I wrote this book and looked back at my experiences so many years ago I realize how fortunate I have been to be a part of it. This company not only survived but has evolved into one of the largest shipping companies in the world.

I would also like to thank my Concord Reading Group for their critiques of my writing, and Kristine Mietzner for her expert editing and suggestions. Finally, and most important, to the person who helped me immensely with the content, encouraged, and believed in me, thank you, Christina for making a dream come true.

John R. Fischer
AKA Mooncake Man

Chapter 1 Staying Alive

Guam. I hate this place. It's where God sends bad people when hell gets backed up. Like it or not, I'm waiting for the Pan Am flight to arrive from Honolulu so I can make the last hop to Hong Kong as a courier for a small start-up firm called DHL. I work for a company owned by an older guy named Adrian Dalsey who started it with his Visa credit card. Employees called it Dewy, Huey, and Louie after the Disney characters. No one knows how long we were going to be around.

In the small cinder block terminal the night air felt hot and humid. The steady hum of the overworked air conditioner droned as water steadily dripped to the tile floor. At 1:30 in the morning, the flight finally arrived, pulled into the gate, and started to dislodge its passengers.

Forty-five minutes later, I boarded the aircraft and settled into my usual seat in the rear, next to the window, and just a few seats away from the emergency exits. My routine was always the same: first a drink, a snack, and then I hoped to sleep through the next ten hours. I would arrive at Hong Kong the next morning. Maybe I'd feel rested. Getting there should be no problem as the weather is good and only a few passengers are on the flight.

As soon as all the passengers were seated, I felt the aircraft getting pushed back onto the tarmac and the engines starting with number one on the left, to numbers two, three and then four. Within a few minutes we were moving under our own power and heading for the runway at the far end of the field. Slowly, the giant plane turned toward the air strip, locked its brakes, and waited for final clearance from the tower.

The engines burst to life with a thunderous roar and as we hurtled down the runway the rapid acceleration pushed me down into the seat. As the aircraft picked up speed the roaring engines started to sound like a high pitched whine from the spinning turbines. I knew that any second the plane would climb upward to begin its long journey to Hong Kong. Only then would I relax. The nightmare of yesterday's failed takeoff played through my mind like an endless bad dream.

BANG. What the hell was that? An explosion of flame, fire, and thick black smoke swept the engines and window next to my seat. I felt the heat on the fuselage. God, I don't want to die here. I am not burning to death in goddamn Guam. Are we airborne or still on the ground?

In a spilt second, the aircraft nosed down, and we hit the runway with a hard, abrupt thud. I looked out the window and saw that the pilot had activated the engine fire extinguishers. Foam streamed out of the engine cowlings and spread over the wing. But the plane was still rapidly moving. How much runway was left? Was the pilot going to abort the takeoff or gun the other three engines to take off?

Suddenly I was pushed forward into the seat in front of me just as the oxygen mask came down from the overhead console. The pilot had made his spilt second decision. The brakes squealed and the engines screamed at maximum reverse thrust. Every screw and bolt in that plane strained to survive the sudden deceleration.

I looked out the window as far forward as possible and saw buildings rapidly coming into view. Oh, no, we're not going to make it. The airplane is still going too fast. We're going to hit those buildings. The aircraft left the runway and hit the grassy infield. The force of the impact jerked my head violently to the left and compressed my body into the seat.

All at once mud and grass sprayed on to the plane and covered the window as we rapidly came to an abrupt stop with the wing still on fire. This thing could blow up at any minute. I looked down the aisle, thick black smoke filled the cabin but I could still make out the exit signs in the dim light.

I unbuckled my seatbelt and made my way to the rear exit, my eyes burning. I could make out the stewardess standing next to the open door. The emergency chute had been activated and she said very calmly, "You're the first. Fold your hands across your chest and jump into the slide.

Mooncake Man

The next thing I remembered was feeling the hard ground beneath my feet. I had made it. I was alive.

On this flight, I felt a gentle touch on my shoulder. When I opened my eyes, the bright interior lights momentarily blinded me. I slowly recognized the small Asian stewardess smiling as she said, "We're an hour out of Hong Kong and it's time for breakfast."

"Just bring me coffee, please. I can never eat those rubber omelets." I gazed out the frosted window as the dawn broke over the deep blue ocean with tiny little whitecaps. It felt good to be finally on my way after the crash and inconvenience of waiting in Guam an additional day for a replacement aircraft.

Luckily no one had died in the crash. The pilot had made the right decision to abort the takeoff. I had no remorse about being the first one out the plane. I had made up a mind long before that I would survive the endless hours of flying throughout Asia in mostly third world passenger airlines.

I quickly learned it's every man for himself as the masses could be overpowering and unforgiving. Good intentions could cause unintended consequences, like what happened on my first trip to Jakarta, Indonesia.

After an evening of drinking I walked back to my hotel and casually gave some coins to a woman beggar who held a small emaciated child on a busy highway overpass. Almost immediately the local beat policeman starting arguing with her because she would not give him the money. After several minutes of shouting back and forth the policeman kicked the mother and child off the overpass into the busy traffic below. I was stunned.

I couldn't believe what was happening. The woman screamed, car horns blared, and tires skidded. I didn't look down, neither did the people on the overpass. They just walked away and so did I. What a cruel place. Indonesia was not my country and not my culture.

I was now a day late delivering the five big green courier bags. Each one weighed between 70 and 100 lbs. and survived the crash intact. Inside the large green canvas bags were individual company pouches containing such things as canceled checks, credit card receipts, bank letters of credit, legal documents, ship manifests, bills of lading, and other urgent documents.

In the days before faxes and the Internet this was the fastest and most secure way to send documents around the world. It was precisely for this reason and the anticipated loss of revenue that the Hong Kong Post Office had declared our operation illegal and in violation of their postal monopoly.

The courier service handled many large Hong Kong companies and even several agencies within their own government. We were an embarrassment to the Hong Kong Post Office and I had been warned by my own people there was a good chance I would be detained or arrested upon my arrival.

Suddenly a ring sounded and the seat belt light came on as the aircraft started rapidly descending for our approach to Hong Kong's Kai Tak Airport. This was always one of the hairiest landings in Asia. The runway looked like a postage stamp in the middle of Kowloon harbor. I looked out the window and saw the familiar green hilltops of the islands that ring Hong Kong Bay. The huge 747 aircraft started its slow turn toward the city getting lower and lower.

I glanced down at the multitude of apartment buildings below as the plane continued to descend to only thirty or forty feet above the buildings. I could clearly see women hanging their clothes attached to ropes on the tops of the buildings. How much lower can we go without hitting those buildings?

I could just imagine the co-pilot calling out the airspeed with the engineer glued to his engine thrust dials as the pilot tightly gripped the vibrating yoke and turned the giant plane to line up on the runway. I had seen this performance several times while sitting in the jump seat behind the pilot on cargo planes.

All of a sudden the aircraft jerked itself out of its steep right turn. We were over the runway and almost instantly as the plane touched down the engines screeched into reverse thrust as the brakes squealed and the plane shook and vibrated to a halt only yards from the end of the runway and the harbor's edge. I looked over at the arrival terminal. I hope Customs is not waiting for me.

Chapter 2 The Arrest

After landing in Hong Kong, my job was to recover the courier pouches at the baggage carousel and turned them over to my ground crew that waited just outside the restricted area. Once the bags had cleared Customs they would be separated by customer, loaded into a fleet of small vans, and delivered throughout Hong Kong.

As I approached the rotating stainless steel carousel, out of the corner of my eye I noticed movement in my direction. Several uniformed Chinese Customs officers and a tall plainclothes Englishman rapidly walked toward me. As I turned to face them, the Englishman in the lead inquired, "Are these green bags your property? Do you have a claim receipt for them?"

"Yes," I said, showing him the nine claim tags for the bags.

He said, "You're under arrest for violation of the Hong Kong Private Express Act and for bringing in undeclared financial instruments. Turn around and put your hands behind your back."

Someone slapped the hard steel handcuffs around my wrists and I felt the cold metal as the rings clamped shut. As I stood there by the baggage carousel two uniformed Customs agents grabbed me by each arm. I tried to walk but I got half dragged to a room adjacent to the baggage area. Other passengers simply stared and moved away from our procession. Once inside the room, the agents told me to sit on one of the small chairs next to a large table. After I was seated, they took off the cuffs and without a word turned abruptly, exited, and closed the heavy door with a thud. The lock snapped into place.

I looked around the small holding room. The walls were painted light green and it had a table in the middle with three chairs. There were no windows and the only light came from one bulb in the center of the room. If ever there was a cookie cutter design for standard interrogation rooms, this one was cut from it. How the hell did I get myself into this situation?

It really wasn't surprising if I thought about it. I had ended up in strange and unusual places most of my life. I was born into a military family and we moved every couple of years like a band of gypsies. I was always the new kid coming into a new school in the middle of the year. I can always remember the teacher saying, "Johnny tell us about yourself."

I hated that. Even as a ten-year-old, I felt like saying, "Screw you bitch. I'll be out of here in a couple of months and who the hell cares anyway." I guess I became an introvert who could not have cared less about people and their problems. What better qualifications for a courier job, flying from country to country, always on the move, never being anywhere for long, but eventually being everywhere?

After about an hour the locked door opened and in walked the tall Englishman who had arrested me. Following him came Adrian Dalsey, my boss and founder of the courier company, and Po Chung, our local manager. The Englishman spoke first and said we had to wait for the senior postal inspector before we could start the meeting.

I nodded to Adrian and he said, "Don't worry kid. We'll get you out of here." Adrian was an unforgettable character. I had first met him several years earlier when I was dating his daughter during my last year in college. He was in his mid 50's, Jewish, short, bald, and overweight with a round face. His suit fit tightly around his shoulders and stomach. His feet were exceptionally small so he took small steps to balance himself as he walked. Most of his life he had lived in Chicago, the city where he was born.

Adrian had moved to California in his early 40's. He would say he was a salesman by trade, and had sold everything from real estate to truck mud flaps and finally trucking transportation services. It was Adrian who had convinced Bank of America and several large ocean shipping companies to use a small, unknown courier service to transport their sensitive and confidential documents throughout Asia.

Standing next to Adrian was Po Chung, the manager of our Hong Kong office. At first glance he looked like any of the millions of young Chinese businessmen in Hong Kong, short, small in stature, and dressed in the standard dark Chinese business suit. But Po was different; he was educated at Cal State Humboldt in Northern California and had received a degree in fisheries. His father was a leading toy designer for a large American toy company. After graduating from college Po decided he didn't really want to commercially raise fish. Adrian recruited Po through a mutual friend that worked for one of the airlines.

Suddenly the door opened and the senior postal inspector appeared. He was British, in his mid 40's, and wearing a casual open sweater. He stated that all the courier bags would be held at the airport and that each customer would be contacted and instructed to come to the airport and sign for their property.

He looked directly at me and said, "You are no longer under detention but you are not allowed to leave Hong Kong pending the outcome of this case." With that proclamation we left for our hotel and a meeting with the attorney that Adrian had hired to prepare our case. The reality of the situation was that we did not have the resources for a long protracted legal battle; we had to win quickly as Hong Kong was our largest customer base and also a hub for shipments to all of Southeast Asia.

We all agreed that the Hong Kong Post Office had made a fatal mistake, instead of just closing a small courier company down they had seized all the documents and arrogantly demanded that corporate officers come to Customs at the airport and personally sign for their company property.

The Hong Kong Post Office could not provide a comparable service yet they were insistent that we were responsible for the loss of postal revenue as well violating numerous postal statues. The Hong Kong business community was incensed at the high-handed action to shut us down. Getting their property seized without any notice or discussion brought instant protests and threats of legal action.

The Hong Kong and Shanghai Bank, the largest and most prestigious bank in Asia, demanded that their property not be opened by Customs and be immediately returned to them. The battle lines had been drawn. The Hong Kong Chamber of Commerce, The American Chamber and various business organizations along with our customers would not allow a bunch of government workers to decide how they would run their businesses. Business was the lifeblood of Hong Kong, its very existence depended on their ability to innovate and adapt as the gateway to China for the rest of the world.

It was decided that a meeting would be held by all concerned parties that evening to discuss and petition the government to cease and desist their actions at the airport. It was now late afternoon. Exhausted from the long flight and arrest, I took a welcome nap so that I could be awake for the meeting that evening.

After having dinner with Adrian, Po, and the lawyers, we arrived at the Peninsula Hotel in Kowloon for the Chamber of Commerce meeting. I loved the Peninsula; it was built in the 1850's during the British colonial era. The entry had huge columns and opened up into an elegant reception area. The floors were teak, the chairs and couches were all overstuffed Victorian pieces, and the ceiling fans that slowly circulated were attached to cut glass chandeliers.

The staff wore immaculate uniforms and greeted each guest with attentive smiles. Tea was served promptly at two p.m. every day; I made myself a promise to attend the next one. We took the stairs to the designated meeting room on the second floor and were pleasantly surprised to see the large number of people standing around and talking in small groups. They all looked like professional business types and in the mix were Chinese, English, and Indian men and women. Po seemed to know everyone and introduced me to the director of the Hong Kong Chamber of Commerce, George Chen.

George was a retired executive of the Hong Kong and Shanghai Bank and was adamant that the Hong Kong Postal action was political and the Chamber would be presenting their position at the meeting which would start promptly at seven p.m. Po insisted that I meet all of the attendees. After all, he said, I was a celebrity after my arrest at the airport. We went from group to group telling the sordid story to each one.

The last group was at the far end of the room. As we approached it, one of the women turned and looked at us. I stopped in my tracks on seeing her beautiful face. Why hadn't I noticed her before?

She was young, English, above average in height, thin with a well developed figure and long slender legs. Her face had fine features and her eyes were deep brown and piercing when she looked at me. She wore a dark blue business suit and her long brown hair flowed over her shoulders.

Po introduced me as the guy who had been arrested with the courier bags that morning. She held out her hand and said, "My name is Jenny; I hope they didn't torture you at the airport." I assured her that I had not been hurt and then the meeting bell rang. We were instructed to take a seat. I started to follow Jenny but Po grabbed my arm and insisted we had to sit at the attorney's table.

The meeting started promptly at seven. George Chen the Chamber Director started talking about the Hong Kong postal action that morning. I didn't hear what he said or even cared. I look at the seated crowd and found Jenny's face; she caught my stare, smiled and then looked away. She took my breath away and I had to see her again.

Chapter 3 The Hong Kong Resolution

*T*he Hong Kong Chamber of Commerce meeting droned on for another hour with representatives of several companies testifying to the negative impact of the postal action. On a unanimous vote, the membership approved a resolution demanding the immediate release of their documents and requesting that a special license be issued to our courier service to handle documents only.

First class letters, according to our lawyers, were in violation of the postal monopoly. When the final vote was announced, and the meeting was adjourned, everyone started for the exits. I caught up with Jenny and touched her arm. As she turned and smiled, I said, "I would like to see you again. How can I reach you?"

Jenny looked directly at me and with a faint smile said, "I don't think so, but thank you anyway." She turned abruptly and started to walk through the open door.

I quickly called, "Wait Jenny." She moved slightly toward me and with a slow motion of her hand waved good-bye. I just stood there as the crowd left the meeting room. I couldn't believe she had rejected me with such a passive, unemotional movement of her hand.

Hell—Wasn't I single, twenty-six, good-looking with a steady job, witty, and fun to be with? I hadn't even gotten to first base with her. What was her story?

The next morning I slept in until the phone rang at 10 a.m. Po said that he and Adrian were waiting in the hotel restaurant to have breakfast and discuss the latest developments in our situation. I was staying at the

Prince Hotel on the Kowloon side of the bay just down the street from the famous Peninsula Hotel.

After a quick shower and shave, I went downstairs and spotted Po and Adrian at a table in the far corner of the restaurant. They felt confident the case would be resolved within the next 24 hours as the Hong Kong and Shanghai Bank was presenting our case to the governor in the afternoon.

With nothing left to do but wait, I decided to spend the day as a tourist and then meet George Chen and Po for dinner in the financial district of the island. Hong Kong was a crazy place. Some eight million souls crowded into thousands of apartments that seemed to hang perilously from 18 square miles of hills and mountains.

The population density was one of the highest in the world. Most of Hong Kong's residents were Chinese, but every race and color of human being could be found within the British Colony. It was July and it was another hot, humid, and muggy day as I walked down the crowed sidewalk on Nathan Road. Each side of the street was ringed by storefronts selling everything from pineapple sticks to cameras.

Hundreds of window air conditioners in a steady drone, dropped water on the crowded streets below as people scurried about shopping or queuing up for buses or taxis. Hong Kong was not a place for a claustrophobic; the crowds were endless in the stores, restaurants or in the streets.

Within a few short blocks, I was sweating from head to toe as I finally reached a shopping mall that had indoor air conditioning. In the cool air my strength returned in a matter of minutes. The indoor mall had hundreds of small luxury stores selling European and American goods with designer labels, high-end watches, and jewelry. Making the rounds, I saw the same items at different prices in various stores.

Next I headed for the Star Ferry to take the short ride across the harbor to the Hong Kong side. The Star Ferry was an institution: cheap, efficient, and consistently on time. Star vessels carried thousands of tourist and workers back and forth across the harbor, seven days a week, 24 hours a day.

The boats were painted white with a dark green hull and looked like they had been in service for the last one hundred years, steadily plowing from one side of the bay to the other. I deposited my 25 cents in the turnstile and waited patiently for the sounds of the diesel engines and the ferry to appear.

Within minutes, the vessel slowly came alongside the terminal and was secured to the dock. The side ramp in the front of the boat was lowered and the passengers queuing on the deck exited the boat. At almost the same time, the loading ramp at the rear of the boat was lowered and the boarding passengers quickly found their seats for the short ride across the bay.

It was a very efficient system as the entire unloading and loading of the passengers took less than 10 minutes and the engines were never turned off. I found a seat in the front of the boat and felt the cool breeze of the harbor as I looked at the multitude of gaudy colorful signs and logos of the Hong Kong Corporate world on the buildings and skyscrapers of the opposite shore.

As soon as the ferry landed, I headed for the Hong Kong Garden hotel just a few blocks away from the ferry terminal. It was almost five p.m. as I entered the hotel lobby and saw George and Po seated in the lounge area having drinks.

George Chen was an interesting guy. Born in Canton and educated in London, he had worked at the Hong Kong and Shanghai Bank in Canton until the communist revolution in 1948. The communists had put a price on George's head as they considered him a capitalist banker and an enemy of the state.

George and his family barely escaped. First they were smuggled off the mainland in a fishing boat to Macao and then to Hong Kong. He had worked for the bank in Hong Kong until his retirement and then shortly after became the director of the Hong Kong Chamber of Commerce.

As I spotted George, he immediately held out his hand and said, "We've won. The governor and the council have overridden the post office and will grant a special license to operate the courier service." George was ecstatic. This was a major victory for him and the Hong Kong Chamber of Commerce. He motioned us to the bar and said, "The drinks are on me."

After about five vodka tonics for each of us, I asked George who was the gorgeous woman named Jenny that I had met at the first Chamber meeting at the Grand Hotel. George replied, "Oh, you must mean Jenny Burgess. Yes, she is beautiful, isn't she?"

"Yeah," I said, "tell me everything you know about her."

George looked at me with a sympathetic smile and said, "You don't have a chance with her."

I replied, "Just tell me about her."

George looked down at the floor and finally said, "Okay." He told me that Jenny was the daughter of Sir James Burgess and the family that owned the largest insurance company in Hong Kong, API, Asia Pacific Insurance. The company went all the way back to the Tai Pan days, the early 1800"s when the British first established themselves in Hong Kong.

API insured most of the commercial ships and terminals on the island and was worth hundreds of millions of dollars. No one really knew its actual worth, as it had been a family business for the last 150 years. Jenny was the sole surviving child of Sir James. His only son had been killed in a military airplane crash years before and his wife had died within a few years of Jenny's birth.

Jenny had worked for her father in Hong Kong after graduating from business school in England about three years ago. She had been at the Chamber meeting to represent API as the company used the courier service to transport documents between the U.S., Hong Kong, and Singapore. George paused and asked, "Do you really want to hear the rest?"

"Yes," I said, "of course, of course."

What George told me next was like a dagger to my heart. "Jenny is engaged to Robert Walker, the son of a wealthy owner of a Hong Kong shipping company." He concluded by saying, "Well, that's the story."

I just sat there for a moment and waited for the full impact of what George had just told me and finally asked, "Is this an arranged marriage?"

George sighed and said, "Is there any other kind for the wealthy?"

"I don't give a damn about that. I will somehow get her to go out with me."

"Why bother?" said George. "There are hundreds of other exquisite women in Hong Kong: white, Chinese, Indian, whatever you want. Why waste time with Jenny? She's taken."

I just looked at George. How could I tell him I was crazy about her?

After a couple more drinks, both George and Po decided to call it a night and signaled the barman to get them a cab. I decided to walk back to the ferry and visit the Wan Chi District on my way back to the hotel. The Wan Chi was made famous by the movie "The World of Suzie Wong." It was portrayed as having nice friendly bars and young, pretty, and innocent-looking women everywhere.

I knew the area well. The company's first office was only a few blocks away and I had worked there for six months before leaving to start the Singapore office. Our local guys gave me the grand tour of the Wan Chi every Friday night after work.

The place was actually several hundred small seedy bars, each brightly lit up and right next to each other with names like the 007 Club, Pussycat, Cowboy Club, Cowgirl Club, Hollywood East and so on and so on, the names were endless. At night, the district teemed with locals, tourists, G.I.s on R&R from Vietnam and the usual assortment of pimps, dope dealers, pickpockets, prostitutes, transvestites, and other weird characters. Whatever you wanted, you could find it in the Wan Chi.

The bars made their money by having scantily clad young girls standing by the entrance and hustling all the white guys by flashing their eyes and their tight little butts and yelling, "Hey handsome, come in and check it out, hot chicks, really hot chicks in here."

If a guy went in he had to go through a draped doorway which led to a dimly lighted bar area. The young women were lined up to literally grab him by the ass or balls and lead him to a table in a booth. A girl would convince the guy to buy her a drink, which was usually tea or cola at double or triple the price of a normal drink.

The longer the guy stayed, the more drinks he had to buy the girl. The head hostess or manager recorded a meticulous count of each drink, the type, and the commission due to the girls at the end of the night. If you really liked the girl, you could buy her for the night, subject to serious negotiation with the management.

This scenario went on every night, usually until four or five in the morning. I felt sorry for the young G.I.s on R&R. The suckers didn't stand a chance. On the other hand, everyone had to make a living.

Chapter 4 Out of Hong Kong

The next morning, the phone rang on the night stand just a few inches from my pounding head as a result of the previous night's drinking and carousing in the Wan Chi. It was Po and he excitedly told me the company was back in operation and this evening the Hong Kong Chamber would be putting on a dinner to celebrate the victory over the post office. I told Po I wasn't really interested and he immediately replied, "All of our key customers will be there."

I said, "Do you mean API?"

Po replied, "Yes, I'm sure Jenny will attend."

"Great," I said, "I'll be there." As I looked into the mirror and started to shave, I thought to myself, what an unexpected break, this is fate, this is really supposed to happen. I also thought of George, the Hong Kong Chamber director. George was going to get as much mileage and notoriety out of this victory as he could. The next thing I know, he would be running for the governor of Hong Kong.

After a quick breakfast, I decided to take a late morning stroll along the newly created esplanade that ran for almost a mile along the Kowloon Bay. It was a beautiful tile walkway slightly elevated above the bay and crowded with a mix of young and old tourists, joggers, and locals. It was one of those hot, muggy July days and I could see the squall line of rain and mist slowly approaching from the harbor opening and the sea beyond.

As the rain entered the harbor, I could see the heavy mist slowly obscure the colorful lighted company logos that were perched high on the tops of the buildings on the opposite shore. As I looked out into the bay, I saw the faint outline of a large moving object. It looked like a large building coming directly at me. What the hell is that?

I kept my eyes glued to the object and very slowly it started to reveal itself as the bow of a very large ship. The vessel's superstructure seemed to be twice the size of its bow and was lighted up from stem to stern. As it came closer, I could see little dark objects that looked like ants scurrying about throughout the ship in preparation for docking at the Ocean Park Shopping Complex located near the harbor walkway.

The ship slowly edged its way to its final berth. The passengers were lined up to disembark as soon as the gangplank was in place. The ship flew the Chinese communist flag, the red flag with the yellow star that was seldom seen in Hong Kong. The vessel was not as large as the European ships that plied the world's oceans. Who were these people and where were they from?

I had to find out, so I wandered over to the docking area to get a better look. They were all Chinese, mostly older men and women. There was something odd about their appearance. Their clothes were old and just seem to hang on their bodies. They moved from one luxury store window to the next, always pointing and talking in high pitched excited tones.

None of the little groups ever entered the stores. They seemed content and satisfied to view the merchandise at a safe distance. Suddenly. the ship's horn blasted and all the men and women quickly made their way back to ship still talking and pointing at all the luxury items in the storefronts as they retreated back to their temporary home.

The shopkeepers seemed to accept these people and paid little attention to them. My curiosity was killing me as I walked into one of the shops and asked the young sales girl,

"Who are these people and where are they from?"

She told me they were visitors from Mainland China and several times each month a special cruise ship would dock in Macao and Hong Kong. This was their first experience seeing Western society and the many luxury items in the stores. They could not afford to buy any of the items or even eat in the restaurants and most of these people could not communicate with Hong Kong People as they spoke a different dialect of Mandarin Chinese.

One of the older shopkeepers told me that most of the Hong Kong people felt sorry for these mainland people as they were poor and uneducated and lived under a controlling communist government which would never tolerate wealth or capitalism. As I walked back to my hotel, I couldn't help but think about an ancient philosopher who said, "Let China sleep, for when she awakens the world will never be the same".

At 7:30 p.m. that evening, I arrived at the Sheraton Hotel function room and immediately saw George Chen greeting the guests at the door. As soon as George saw me he smile and said, "She's here."

The room was full of people talking in little groups. At the far end of the room was an open bar and a long buffet table with fresh oysters, shrimp, and various plates of appetizers and local delicacies. I immediately spotted Jenny near the bar talking to several people. As I approached she saw me and quickly turned and said, "John, I would like you to meet my fiancé, Robert."

I stopped cold in my tracks and held out my hand. Robert shook my hand and said,

"So you're the guy who got arrested. I guess someone had to take the rap."

"Yes," I said, "I was the lucky one." I immediately didn't like the guy. How could I?

Robert was a small, frail, skinny looking guy with a weak handshake and a high-pitched voice like a little girl. As soon as I pulled my hand back from the handshake, he looked away and started talking to the person standing next to him like I didn't exist.

This guy was not only a wimp but also an arrogant rude asshole. I looked at Jenny and her face told me she was sorry as she slowly turned away. I headed for the bar to numb myself for a while, thinking at the same time what the hell was a girl like Jenny doing with a jerk like that, then I remembered George saying the night before it was an arranged marriage. That was the only part that made any sense.

At the appointed time, George got to the podium and thanked everyone for their support on making the Hong Kong Chamber a powerful voice for the business community. I looked over to Jenny and she met my stare and started to walk toward the veranda. I followed her and saw her standing alone at the far end, looking out at the beautiful lighted Kowloon Harbor. She turned to me and said, "I apologize for Robert. He was rude to you."

I looked directly at her and said, "Do you really love that guy?"

She replied, "Excuse me?"

I said, "I think you are the most beautiful woman I have ever seen. I would hate to see you spend your life with someone you do not love."

Her face tightened up and her spine became erect as she said, "What business could this possibly be of yours?"

I looked straight into her brown piercing eyes and said, "I can tell by the way you look at him that you not only don't love him, you don't even like him. Why would you do this to yourself?"

Her face went blank and she said, "This conversation is over."

"Okay," I said, "but under one condition. You meet me tomorrow at the Peninsula Hotel for the two p.m. tea.

She looked at me with a surprised expression of incredibility and said, "Good evening." She began to turn on her heels to leave.

I immediately said, "You're crazy to marry a man you don't even like, so meet me at the Peninsula at two. No one will recognize you, only the tourists hang out there on Saturday." She turned away from me for a moment then looked back. Time stood still for me as her impossibly perfect form swelled with one breath. And then she left.

The next morning the damn phone rang early again. Shit this was Saturday. What the hell was going on? It was Adrian and he was downstairs at the restaurant and wanted me to come down right away. He said, "Kid, we're in deep shit again."

I jumped into my clothes without shaving and took the elevator down, all the while thinking it can't be Hong Kong, what else could it be? As soon as I entered the restaurant, I spotted Adrian looking dejected and worried as he slowly sipped his coffee. As I sat down, he looked up and said, "They closed us down early this morning in Korea. They arrested all our guys, padlocked the office, and confiscated all the vans and equipment."

I said, "What the hell for?"

Adrian shook his head, "I'm not sure. All we know is that according to the U.S. Embassy Commercial Officer I spoke with this morning, it is a security issue not a postal matter.

"Po can't go. He is a CI holder, a Certificate of Identity isn't even a passport, so you must go. Po has already booked you on a two p.m. flight to Seoul. Larry, my partner, and Ken, our station manager in Tokyo will meet you there. Find out what's going on and get us back up and running. I need to stay here and finish up with the lawyers, good luck and be careful."

With that Adrian got up and headed for the door. I sat there for a few minutes and thought to myself, this is Korea not Hong Kong, the government is run by a dictator with an iron hand, and those Koreans are tough little bastards and paranoid as hell about everything. This could be bad, really bad.

I went upstairs and started packing and then all of a sudden I remembered, Oh shit, I was supposed to meet Jenny at two p.m. at the Peninsula today. What if she actually showed and I wasn't there? I don't even know how to reach her.

I called Po and made him promise to be there and explain my "emergency" and tell her I would be back soon and also to get a number where I could reach her. By now it was close to noon and I checked out of the hotel and headed for the airport.

As I sat in the taxi and watched the crowded streets of Kowloon slowly disappear behind me, I thought to myself that this could be the dumbest thing I have ever done. I had no idea what was waiting for me at Seoul's Kimpo Airport. I was scared.

Chapter 5 The first 24 hours in Korea

As Korean Airlines Flight 47 slowly made its descent to Seoul's Kimpo Airport, I looked out the window and saw the enormously wide and dry Han River come into view. It was late July and the river had contracted into a narrow band of water flanked on each side by large yellow sand dunes.

It was now four p.m. in Hong Kong and I couldn't help but wonder whether or not Jenny had shown up at the Peninsula. As soon as I could, I would call Po and find out what happened. When the aircraft's wheels touched the runway, the Korean passengers instantly released their seat belts, stood up, and started taking down their bags from the overhead compartments.

With the aircraft still racing down the runway at well over 100 miles per hour, the stewardess shouted something in Korean to the passengers standing in the aisle. Suddenly, the pilot reversed the aircraft's engines and applied the brakes, scattering both passengers and baggage throughout the cabin.

Sitting in my seat with my seatbelt still fastened, I could hardly believe what I had just witnessed. Later I found out this was perfectly normal on Korean Airlines flights coming into Seoul. The FAA in the U.S. would have nightmares about this exhibition of chaos.

When the aircraft finally came to a stop on the tarmac, the pilot informed us that it was standard procedure for the plane to be escorted to the gate by a military vehicle. We waited on the taxiway with the engines still running. I nervously considered what was ahead. Would I be arrested upon entering the airport?

In less than a year, our Korean operation had acquired some excellent clients who depended on the courier service for their daily business. Our first customers were large American banks, followed by Asian shipping lines, and, finally, Korean banks and trading companies. Within the last several months, we began handling documents for both the U.S. Air Force and Army base exchanges scattered throughout Korea.

How had a profitable and successful operation come to such an abrupt halt and total shutdown? From what Adrian had told me, everyone had been arrested. Our manager in Korea, David Jensen, was married to a local Korean woman. He had lived in Seoul for the past 12 years and operated his own import-export trading company. I had never met David as he was hired by and reported to Ken, our Toyko-based Japan country manager.

I would meet Ken later in the day. I already knew he was an interesting guy. He was actually a Japanese-American, born and raised in Southern California. He learned Japanese after he moved to Tokyo.

The other person who was with Ken in Seoul was Larry, Adrian's partner, and co-owner of the company. Larry was from a small farming town in the central valley of California. He went to law school at UC Berkeley, passed the bar, and then went into business with Adrian. Larry and Adrian were exact opposites in almost everything. That's probably why the partnership worked as well as it did.

The plane jerked forward and we were finally on our way to the arrival gate. I stepped off the aircraft and entered a long corridor, which ended with a queue of people waiting to enter through Korean Customs and Immigration. As I inched my way up the line, I could see the immigration officer first examine the passenger's passport and then look into a large book propped up to his left that had names in alphabetical order. If the name was not in the book, the officer slammed the entry stamp into the passport and motioned the person away. I hoped my name was not in that book.

Within a few minutes, I stood in front of the immigration officer and I dutifully handed over my passport. The officer quickly looked at the photograph and asked in perfect English, "What are you doing in Korea and how long are you staying?"

I replied, "I'm here on business and will be here about one week."

He asked, "Where are you staying?"

I looked at the note on my ticket from Po and said, "The Chosen Hotel."

The agent turned around and looked into the large book. I looked around and saw two uniformed police officers staring directly at me, stationed at the exit just a few feet away. I started to sweat as I realized there was no escape route, no place to run. I told myself to be cool, look straight ahead. I hoped like hell they wouldn't arrest me. The officer quickly turned and looked directly at me, slammed the entry stamp on the passport, slid it across to me, looked at the person beside me in the line, and said, "Next."

I quickly put the passport in my top pocket and walked away feeling like my body was crumbling from the release of the stress and tension. I headed directly for the baggage claim area feeling relieved. This time I had no courier bags to recover because we had halted our operation into Korea; the documents were being held in Tokyo.

Grabbing my one suitcase off the carousel, I headed for the green line, the lane for no goods to declare. The Korean Customs agents looked on with indifference. As soon as I exited the restricted area into the main terminal, I was confronted by massive crowds waiting for the arriving passengers. There were people and signs everywhere, old people, young kids, Koreans, and foreigners all jammed together yelling names and frantically searching for a face they recognized.

As I walked into the crowd, Korean guys looked directly at me and called, "Come with me. I take you anywhere. Show you good time. Come on. Over here. Let me take your bag."

All of a sudden I almost walked into a sign that spelled my last name. I walked up to the young Korean guy holding the sign and said, "I'm Fischer. Who are you?"

He immediately replied in English, "I'm Kimmey. Mr. Larry and Mr. Ken are waiting at the hotel. I take you there now." Within a few minutes, we were on our way to the hotel, located about 20 kilometers away.

Kimmey was a young Korean guy about twenty-five years old, short, with black hair and a green shirt, a matching sport coat, a smile permanently painted on his face. As we sped along the motorway headed to the central business district of Seoul, Kimmey looked into his rearview mirror and asked, "Where are you coming from?"

"Hong Kong," I replied. Looking into the mirror, I saw a surprised look on the driver's face.

He replied, "Not from the states? First time in Korea?"

I replied that I had been in Korea about year ago but only for a few days. "Oh," Kimmey replied, "lots of good things to do in Korea. I tell you what! You already have long day flying. I take you to my special massage parlor. We get some good Scotch, have good massage with two or three nice Korean girls. Much better than Chinese girls. Korean girls screw your brains out. If you like girls, I put them in the limo and take to your hotel. We have good time, okay, boss?"

I replied, "Kimmey, you're a great guy, but I got to take care of business today. Maybe tomorrow."

Kimmey smiled and gave me thumbs up from the driver's seat. I thought to myself, "I like this guy; he can be useful in Seoul." As we drove up to the Chosen, I could tell it was a four star hotel. Supposedly one of the best accommodations in Seoul, it had the uniformed doorman, the red carpet, fountains and the whole deal. As I walked up to the reception desk, the clerk smiled and said, "Welcome to The Chosen. May I have your passport, please?"

As I handed over the green passport, I felt a hand on my shoulder and then a low voice that said, "It's about time you got here, thought you might chicken out." I turned and recognized Ken, our manager from Tokyo. Ken was a handsome guy in his early 30's, stocky and short and looked more Korean than Japanese. He spoke fluent Japanese but not Korean.

No matter where he went in Korea, whenever the locals spoke to him in Korean, Ken replied in English, "I don't speak Korean," then started talking in Japanese. The locals just walked away shaking their heads.

He said, "I'll buy you your favorite drink, a double shot vodka tonic." Upon entering the hotel bar, I spotted Larry at a table talking to the young cocktail waitress. He loved the young women, always tried to find young virgins working in the hotels, and never understood why he was usually disappointed. He always looked the same in his white tee-shirt, faded jeans, and black scuffed shoes. His entire traveling wardrobe could fit in a small gym bag.

In his mid 30's, Larry was average in height and weight with light brown hair. He had a receding hair line on the left side of his face caused by constant nervous scratching in the same spot. Larry was a smart guy, a lawyer, and a thinker, but you could not take him into our customers' offices. He refused to change his attire and would come off like some kind of misfit. Ken and I would deal with the customers. We needed Larry to work the legal side of our problems.

As I approached the bar, Larry saw me and broke into a cheerful smile and said, "Glad you're here, we've got to do a Hong Kong."

I replied, "You're right, except this is Korea. What is the deal with all this security bullshit? What is it all about."

Larry smiled and said, "I'll let our new manager fill you in. His name is Bae and he will be here in a few minutes."

"What the hell happened to the old manager, David Jensen?"

Ken said, "David is still in jail and charged with currency exchange violations. The Korean government has very strict laws on money changing, only the banks and licensed money changers are allowed to change foreign currency into Korean won notes. David was using the courier service to get the foreign currency out of the country and he and several of his guys got caught at the airport.

I turned to Ken and said, "Great hire, Ken. This guy risked our entire operation. Did we get a cut of the action?"

Ken looked down and with a solemn voice said, "No."

I turned to Larry and said, "Well then screw David. Let him rot in jail." I looked directly at Ken and Larry. They both nodded. As we ordered another round, I turned to Larry and asked him to tell me about this new manager, Bae.

Larry smiled and said, "I'll let Ken tell you about him. It's his deal but this one will work."

I turned to Ken and said, "Okay, Ken, you got a chance to redeem yourself. Let's have it."

Ken anxiously explained that he had done business with Bae and his freight company at the start of our service in Korea. Bae had helped us import the nylon courier bags into the country. Upon hearing our operation had been suspended, Bae had offered to try to reestablish the company as a joint venture with his Korean shipping company.

With an annoyed expression I interrupted Ken and said, "Wait a minute. Why would this guy risk his business for us, and how in the hell can you trust him?"

Ken smiled like he was anticipating my questions and responded that Bae saw how fast we had expanded and the kind of customers we had acquired in such a short time. "He sees the opportunity and he wants to be part of it."

I replied, "How can you trust him? He's Korean?"

Ken broke into a wide smile and said, "He's family."

I laughed and said, "What the hell do you mean by family?"

Larry looked over to me with a smirk on his face and said, "Fish, you'll love this."

Ken explained, "Bae's sister is married to one of my cousins and they both live in Tokyo." That's where he got the contact information on Bae's company to help us import the pouches into Korea. Ken said that he and Bae had become good friends prior to our current problems in Korea and that he trusted Bae like his own brother.

I looked over to Larry and said, "I hope you're right. Korean jails really suck."

Before he could reply, Ken looked over to the bar entrance and said, "There's Bae now." Bae was a typical looking Korean business guy-- medium-build, well-groomed, short, in his mid 30's, and wore slacks with a blue shirt and sport coat. Ken immediately introduced me as one of the guys who had saved our Hong Kong operation.

Bae spoke perfect English and told us that we would need to convince both our customers and the government to start the operations back up again as soon as possible. With an agitated expression, I asked Bae what the security issue was about as I had already heard the story on the currency violations.

Bae explained the currency issue was bad but the real serious problem was that during the routine inspection of our document pouches at the airport, one of the pouches from an American engineering company contained a blueprint of an underground tunnel from North Korea into South Korea. The blueprint was found among other architectural drawings and was discovered purely by chance in airport Customs.

The airport authorities immediately called in the Korean Central Intelligence Agency, the KCIA. The government security people and everyone involved in the courier service and its customers were being investigated. This incident was considered a very serious matter as North Korean assassins had attempted to kill the South Korean president numerous times in the last several years by using tunnels underneath the DMZ to enter South Korea.

With that Bae reached for his drink and said, "That's the short version of the story."

I replied, "How in the hell do you know all this? If what you said is true, why are we not in jail?"

Bae slyly smiled and explained that his brother worked for the KCIA and if they thought any of us were involved, we would have never made it out of the airport.

I turned and said, "Ken, why do I feel I just missed getting hit by a Mack truck?"

Everyone laughed and as I looked at my watch and noticed that it was getting close to seven p.m., I excused myself and headed upstairs to my room to call Po at home and find out if Jenny had actually showed up or not.

The hotel operator dialed the long distance number and when Po answered, he immediately started asking questions about Korea. I cut him off and said, "Po you know why I am calling, did she show?"

He laughed and said, 'Well, sort of."

I anxiously said. "What the hell does that mean?"

Po explained that he had waited at Peninsula's Hotel's reception area until well after the two p.m. meeting time. As he was about to leave he spotted Jenny looking in the storefront windows of the Cartier store in the hotel lobby. Po said he approached Jenny and apologized for my not being there because of an unexpected emergency. I interrupted Po and asked, "What exactly did she say?"

Po replied, "She said, 'What are you talking about? I'm not here to meet anyone. I'm just looking at the latest Cartier watches to buy for Robert's birthday.' With that she turned and walked away.

Po said, "Why don't you give up. She's a hard case."

I replied, "Po, she showed up. I knew she would. I knew it." With that I said goodbye and promised I would call him in a couple days about the Korea situation. I decided to go downstairs to the bar and finish my sixth vodka tonic and then find Kimmey the limo man and find out what this town was all about.

Chapter 6 Korea and the General

After Larry and Ken left the bar, I lingered over the last of my vodka tonics. "Where can I find Kimmey?" I asked the bartender. He looked over at the cocktail waitress and said something in Korean.

The woman replied in English, "Kimmey went to the airport to pick up some guests and he'll be back in about an hour."

Sitting at the end of the bar, I watched the other customers finish their drinks and leave. The more I thought about the whole Korea deal, the more questions I had; it didn't make sense. What was this guy Bae all about? Why was he so eager to have a partnership? Was he part of the KCIA or secret police?

If we were allowed to resume the courier service, what was in it for the KCIA or the security people? What did they really want from us? Was there really a drawing of a tunnel under the DMZ, or, was this just a ruse, a way for the Korean security people to control or use our service in some way to benefit them? If there was a secret tunnel drawing, who sent it and how did they get access to our document pouches?

The familiar voice of Kimmey brought me back to the reality of the hotel bar. When I turned and faced him, he said, "Hey boss, you ready for the massage girls? I shook my head and replied, "Jesus, isn't there something different in Asia than the inevitable massage parlor?"

Kimmey laughed, looked up at the ceiling and replied, "I got it! How about disco? I know a great place with plenty of girls. These are real girls, office workers and college students."

"Okay," I replied, "let's go."

After about 20 minutes of driving along winding roads in the hills above Seoul, we arrived at the entrance of a large building perched on a plateau overlooking the city. The sign in the front with large letters said, "Welcome to the Tower Hotel." Kimmey dropped me at the lobby entrance, parked the limo, reappeared a few minutes later.

He motioned for me to follow him. As we approached the entrance to what looked like a ballroom, he turned and said, "You'll love this place. Best disco in the world. Beautiful chicks."

I thought, "Boy, have I heard that before, from every limo and cab driver in Asia." But once inside I decided Kimmey was right. The place knocked me out. I felt as if I was back in the states at an awesome disco. I stepped into a huge ballroom with at least 100 tables circled around a large dance floor with a rock band in the middle. Strobe lights flashed and rainbow colors slowly moved on the walls. On each side of the band there were young women, decked out in lighted panties and bras, dancing inside spinning cages that were suspended from the ceiling.

The musicians jumped up and down while singing the lyrics of the Animals song, "We Gotta Get Outta This Place."

The disco was starting to fill up as Kimmey flashed the floor manager a won note and we were promptly seated at a table a just a few feet from the dance floor. As Kimmey ordered our drinks I looked around and could see in the dim light given off by the flickering table candles that the place was filled with mostly young Korean women, not couples.

Kimmey saw me looking around and said, "See I told you! Many good looking single Korean women here. They are looking for a rich American businessman like you. They hate American G.I.s. You show them your business card and they will become like gum on your shoe."

"What the hell," I thought, "let's see if Kimmey is bullshitting me." I walked up to a table of three girls, looked at the prettiest one, and said, "I'm John, an American businessman from San Francisco. Would you like to dance?" Without hesitation the girl smiled and took my hand. Wow. That was easy. Within an hour I had danced with six girls and each one had wanted to come to my table.

I turned to Kimmey and said, "This place is great. I could do this all night."

Kimmey laughed and replied, "Cannot do. Curfew starts at midnight. Everything closes down; everyone must be off the streets until six a.m."

"What?" I asked, "you're kidding, right? So what happens, everyone just leaves? How do they all get home?"

"Indeed," Kimmey explained, "it is a problem. All the taxi drivers line up outside and everyone bargains with the taxi drivers. People hold up two fingers which means they will pay double, three fingers means triple, and so on."

I turned to Kimmey and declared, "This place is a gold mine and all the chicks have to leave because of curfew. Larry, Ken, and I will move in here tomorrow and then we can pick out the best looking girls to stay with us in the hotel. We'll get the penthouse. Larry will go nuts over this place."

The next morning back at the Chosen Hotel the phone rang and it was Ken who said he and Larry were downstairs at breakfast. I told them I would join them in a few minutes. As I hung up the phone I heard the morning paper sliding under the door, picked it up for my morning reading, and headed for the john.

It was a Korean English language paper with the usual headlines about the Korean economy but as I scanned down the bottom of the front page I couldn't believe my eyes. There in bold print was my name under a section of the paper titled, "Foreigners arriving in Korea."

It listed my name, arriving flight from Hong Kong, and my hotel. Farther down the column were Ken and Larry's names. The information must have come from the Customs arrival form I had filled out and given to the immigration officer. There was no such thing as confidentially in Korea. The government controlled everything and released information at its own discretion. I could hardly wait for the phone to start ringing in my room with Koreans selling everything from ballpoint pens to plumbing fixtures. The timing was good to move to the Tower Hotel.

As I seated myself next to Ken, Larry looked up and said, "Missed you last night." I told him I would get to that in a minute and asked if they had read the paper this morning. They both shook their heads.

I replied, "Well you should because you're both in it. Shit! This place is scary. I'll get back to that later, but first, let me tell you what happened last night." I gave Larry and Ken a detailed report of my experience at the Tower Disco. When I got to the part about the girls having to leave because of the curfew, Larry nearly choked on his coffee as he said, "Let's go check out the hotel now. If it's halfway decent we can move in today, Sunday. We won't have time tomorrow. Bae called and said we are scheduled to meet the director of the American Chamber of Commerce and the U.S. Embassy Commercial Officer tomorrow morning." We packed our bags and piled into Kimmey's limo for the ride up to the Tower Hotel. After a few minutes talking to the desk manager we decided to get the penthouse with three bedrooms and a large living room. Divided among the three of us, the rate was cheaper than our hotel in downtown Seoul.

As we checked in, I noticed a sign on the counter that read, "If you are an American soldier who fought for our freedom please tell the desk clerk." I turned to the clerk and asked as I pointed to the sign, "What is this all about?"

"Oh," he said, "if you are an American soldier who served in the Korean War show us your Korea campaign ribbon and your first week's stay at the hotel is free."

I thought, "This if the first place I've ever been that doesn't hate American soldiers."

Bright and early Monday morning Kimmey was waiting for us in the lobby to take us to our meeting with the American Chamber and the US Embassy official in downtown Seoul. We pulled into the underground parking garage of a large 20 story building, took the elevator to the top floor, and found ourselves outside a door with a small American flag and the words, "Serving the needs of American business in Korea."

"We'll see about that," I thought. Once inside, we were ushered into a large office; an American sat at a huge mahogany desk.

The man immediately held out his hand and said, "I'm Daniel Green, the chamber director, but you can call me the General. Please take a seat."

This guy Green was in his mid 50's and had short cropped gray hair. He was a large man with a huge neck and a face that looked like a bulldog. The General looked mean and tough. After the introductions he turned to us and said, "Any of you boys been in the military?"

No one said anything. Finally I said, "Yeah, I have."

Daniel looked squarely at me and said, "What branch and where?"

I replied, "Combat engineers. Trained at Fort Leonard Wood."

"Oh," he replied, "I know it well. Fort Lost in the Woods. I was the base commander there some years back. I'm retired now. Glad someone here has served their country."

I replied, "Gee thanks, Dan, but I was drafted and I hated every fucking minute."

Daniel laughed and said, "At least you went, not like those chicken shit guys who went to Canada." He added that his last assignment was with the American army in Korea and that he married a local Korean woman and decided to retire in Korea. Then his face tightened up and his jaw got rigid as he told us that the courier service was in serious trouble. He had heard about our success in Hong Kong but emphasized that this was not Hong Kong. "The Korean government, not American or Korean business, will decide if you ever operate again," he said.

Just then a tall thin white guy walked into the office and nodded to Dan. He turned to us and said, "Good morning. I'm Ed Chambers, the US embassy commercial officer. I thought, "I love the way these guys in Asia pretend they are here to help American business, but that is just their cover. They're really CIA agents attached to the embassy."

Ed briefed us as to what had occurred within the last 48 hours which was pretty consistent with what Bae had told us at the hotel bar the night before, except for one development. The Korean security people had just this morning arrested the person who was supposed to receive the tunnel drawing. I turned to Ed and said, "Okay, I give up. In what company pouch was the DMZ tunnel drawing found?"

Ed replied, "It was Bechtel, the San Francisco engineering firm. It has a contract with the Korean government to build a new airport. Ed went on to explain that the FBI in San Francisco was on the case and trying to find out who was responsible for putting the tunnel drawing in the document pouch. The American and Korean CIA would work together on this case as it could involve a possible assassination attempt of a foreign leader that was an ally of the US government.

Larry turned to face Dan and asked, "Where do we go from here Dan"?

He replied, "Well, the first thing you have to learn is don't call me Dan, just call me the General.

Larry raised his eyebrows, "Okay, General, where do we go from here?"

The General, with Ed nodding in agreement, explained that we had to convince the Korean security people that this could never happen again, that we would agree to intensive inspections of all documents.

Larry said we had no problems with additional screening as every one of our customers was told that these pouches would be subject to Customs search all over the world. Ed then explained that we would be contacted by the Korean security people shortly to discuss the case and our future in Korea. In the meantime the best thing for us to do was to lay low and not get into any trouble. Ed than turned to me and said, "By the way what hotel are you staying at?"

"The Tower," I answered.

Ed laughed, slapped his hand on the General's desk, and exclaimed, "Oh, yeah, that place is nothing but trouble."

Chapter 7 The Tower Disco

We met at Bae's downtown office, just a few blocks from the American Chamber of Commerce, to decide what customers needed visits to explain our current situation and gain their support to restart our operation. We all agreed I would handle the American banks, Ken would take the shipping companies, and Bae would deal with the Korean manufacturing and trading companies.

Larry would coordinate our activities and work with the General at the American Chamber to present our position to the Korean Government. I immediately contacted our largest bank customer, Bank of America, and the management agreed to see me that afternoon. Kimmey dropped me off in front of the bank located in Seoul's downtown financial district. Entering the bank's executive offices, I was met by a young, gracious Korean woman who spoke perfect English and asked if she could be of assistance. After I explained that I had an appointment with the American manager, she asked for my business card and led me into a large corner office overlooking the busy streets below.

In a few minutes, a well-dressed American appeared who introduced himself as Gregg Scott, the bank's vice president. Gregg looked like a typical banker, wearing a three-piece gray suit, white dress shirt, and a silk tie. He was in late 40's, average in height, and overweight, with little round glasses teetering on the edge of his nose.

I explained that the courier service had been temporary halted but we felt confident that we could convince the Korean Government to resume our operation. I gave Gregg a form letter that would support our position and indicate to the Korean Government the importance and necessity of our services to the banking community. I requested that the bank put the contents of the letter on its company stationary and send it to the American Chamber where we would organize the letters by different businesses and present them to the Korean Ministry of Trade.

Gregg replied that he had heard we had some type of security issue at the airport but he was encouraged that we were working with the General at the American Chamber.

As I started to leave Gregg said, "You know the General's last assignment was as head of U.S. military intelligence in Korea. He's well-connected to the government security people. If anyone can help you it's the General. The real question is how far he wants to stick out his neck."

As I waited for the elevator on the 20th floor I thought how everyone but us seemed to know what was going on with our case. Finally, the crowded elevator arrived and when the doors opened the overpowering putrid smell of kim chee almost knocked me off my feet. Somehow I would have to hold my breath for the entire ride down to the ground floor.

The smells of Asia never ceased to amaze and confuse my brain, I thought of my early morning treks to deliver bank documents in Singapore. I had to walk through a multitude of dimly lit alleyways and at each turn my senses were invaded by combinations of fish, steaming rice, tropical fruits, vegetables and the inevitable disgusting smells of the open sewer that ran parallel to the food stalls and tables.

All the scents blended into a mixture that I could not comprehend until I would finally ask myself, "What did I smell? What was this?" As I continued my walk into the abyss of the narrow alleys I came upon a huge vat spewing steam and bubbles and a very distinct sweet smell of some type of meat. I looked into the vat and saw small whole monkeys floating and bobbing on top of a boiling, spicy mixture; it looked like small children being boiled to death.

One of my favorite scents was the aroma in the night markets in Malaysia when the food vendors cooked satay over an open flame and served it on a bed of streamed rice. The marinated peanut sauce, ginger, and peppers all mixed into a delicious combination of taste and texture.

For the rest of the week our day began by meeting the General promptly at 0800 hours in his office for what he named our "situational briefing." He updated us on any of the form letters he had received from customers and his suggestions to gain support from the American business community.

By mid-morning we retreated to Bae's office where he briefed us on what was going on at the Korean CIA according to his brother the KCIA agent and various other unnamed informants. Bae enthusiastically talked about how the different government agencies were at odds about who had jurisdiction in our case. The KCIA was adamant that the case belonged to them. The Korean army intelligence people, however, said this was an army security issue because it involved a tunnel under the DMZ. Customs at the airport wanted part of the action and so did the Ministry of Communication and the post office. Bae always ended his daily sessions with the word, "Unbelievable."

As the end of the week and Friday evening approached, we were all anxious for the start of the weekend disco night at the Tower ballroom. Larry could hardly contain himself as I had been feeding him stories of unattached young virgins all week.

By eight p.m. we had our front row table adjacent to the dance floor. The strobe lights kicked in, the girls in the cages began dancing, and the band started moving around and singing in a Korean accent the Rolling Stones song, "Satisfaction."

I ordered three vodka tonics and started to check out all the young Korean women seated all around us. I looked over at Larry and he had a grin like a kid in a candy store that had just been given a $20.00 bill.

He turned to me and yelled over the music, "Fish, you're a genius. This place is great. I am promoting you to the position of corporate procurement officer." Ken came along but stayed at the table as he was still in love with his girl friend in Tokyo. Larry and I danced like maniacs with all the girls for the next several hours.

As midnight and the dreaded curfew rapidly closed in, two beautiful young Korean women approached our table and introduced themselves as Misu and Insook. They told us they were university students and were interested in meeting Americans.

Of course, we immediately asked them to join us and as soon as they were seated the questions started, "Are you American businessmen?"

"Yes."

"What business?"

"Air freight."

"Can I see your business card?" We gave them our cards.

"Are you married?"

"No."

"How long you stay in Korea?"

"We're not sure."

"What hotel you stay at?" When we told them we were staying on the 14th floor of the Tower, one of the women said, "Oh, the penthouse."

The other woman said, "Can we go see?"

I turned to Larry and he nodded in agreement. I said, "Okay. Let's go."

Once in the room, the women said they loved the view of the city below and went from room to room muttering in Korean. They checked out the well-stocked bar and refrigerator. Larry grabbed one of the girls by the arm and started for the bedroom, but she resisted his advance. She stayed seated on the couch next to her friend and said that she just wanted to talk.

I looked at Larry and said, "See what happens when we take the most beautiful ones."

Larry was pissed as I said, "Let them stay. It's after curfew. We can kick them out in the morning."

With that Larry and Ken both retired to their bedrooms and I crashed out on the mats and pillows on the floor in the living room with my head spinning from 12 vodka tonics. As I slowly opened my eyes in the dimly lighted room with my bladder ready to explode I looked at my watch. It was four a.m.

I started to kick my blanket off for my trip to the bathroom when I noticed a slight movement to my left. I stopped and listened. I heard the faint sounds of movement and papers being shuffled.

I kept perfectly still as I started to make out the form of one of the Korean girls methodically looking through each desk drawer. When she came to the note pad by the phone where we had scratched various phone numbers she took out of her pocket what looked like a small penlight attached to a small dark rectangular object.

She turned the pen light on and I heard the small click of the mechanism. It was a camera and she was snapping pictures. These chicks were KCIA or intelligence operatives. We had been set up like a bunch of college boys.

Chapter 8 Meeting Mieko

After watching the KICA girls rummage through our desk and drawers and silently slip out of the room, I drifted off, waking again at sunrise. While Larry and Ken drank their morning coffee, I filled them in on what had happened the night before. What happened left us not only surprised, but perplexed.

Why would the Korean intelligence people make such an effort to spy on us? Did they really think we had something to hide? Or, were they just paranoid? We agreed it was the latter. Irrational fear.

Monday morning came with the realization that we were starting our third week in Korea frustrated, feeling helpless, with no resolution to our case in sight. Our routine morning meeting with the General started promptly at 0800 hours with his usual recap and summary of our support letters and endorsement. Did this even matter?

The General did have a new development: our case was to be in the hands of the Korean Central Intelligence Agency, the KCIA. They would soon make a final decision on our fate. As my frustration got the best of me, I asked the General, "What the hell does 'soon' mean? We've been here almost three weeks already."

The General smiled and said, "Boy, this is Asia. 'Soon' could mean weeks, months or even years."

I turned and saw Larry's face become as hard as stone. He looked at the General and said, "We don't have months. We need to cut a deal, and, soon. Look, we would be willing to admit we did something wrong, pay a reasonable fine or restitution to whomever, and work closely with the KCIA at the airport. That's the deal; we need some answers this week or were outta here."

The General just nodded, raised his eyebrows, and said, "Okay. Got it." With the meeting ending abruptly we filed out and walked the few short blocks to Bae's office for our routine second meeting of the day.

Bae confirmed the General's story that the KCIA would determine our case. Larry related the same position we had given the General an hour earlier. Bae assured us he would be in contact with his brother at the KCIA and press hard for a quick resolution. Slowly the week dragged on.

I sequestered myself in our hotel room to work on my business plan to open Malaysia and Thailand by the end of the year. Both Ken and Larry were downtown in Seoul's shopping district buying underwear, socks and shirts. Larry figured out it was better to buy these items new and just throw them away when they got dirty because the hotel laundry charged more for cleaning than what they cost new.

At about 6 p.m., the phone rang. Someone at the front desk said that a young Korean woman in the hotel reception area wanted to speak to me. I said, "Put her on."

After a few seconds a young women's soft voice slowly started to speak in careful English. She said. "Mr. John, my name is Mieko. I met you before. May I come up and see you?"

"Met me where?" I replied.

"Oh," she said, "When I come upstairs, I will tell you."

"Okay," I said. "Give me the desk clerk." I knew him quite well. "David," I asked, "Do you know this girl? Is she a pro or what?"

David replied in his high-pitched voice, "No, Mr. John, I don't know her. Never seen her before. But she is nice. Very nice-looking, Mr. John. I know all of the bar girls, whores, and pros. Never seen her before. I don't think she is a working girl."

"Okay, David. Send her up and then you knock on my door in ten minutes just in case this bitch is trying to rob me." In a few minutes I heard the faint knock on my door, opened it, and came face-to-face with a stunning woman. In her mid-twenties, Mieko had short black hair, and fine delicate facial features. She wore a dark business suit with a red blouse and a golden pearl necklace.

"Please come in," I said. She didn't look like a hooker, but I suspected that she was another KCIA chick. I motioned her to sit on the couch. She delicately crossed her legs and looked directly at me as I started my interrogation.

"So! How do you know me? I've never seen you before."

Without any hesitation she replied, "Yes, you have! I met you several weeks ago when you first came to Korea."

I may have danced with her at the Tower disco when I was too drunk to remember so I said, "Okay. I met you at the disco, right?"

She replied, "What? The disco? No, I don't go to the disco. We met at the Bank of America. I am Mr. Gregg Scott's secretary and I greeted you and took you back to the conference room. Do you remember?"

I stared at Mieko more closely. Shit! I had seen so many Korea women, but I started to recall that day. Yes, I remembered. She was still as beautiful as she was then. "Really," I exclaimed, "how in the hell do you know my name and where I'm staying?"

She replied, "Remember? I asked for your business card and it isn't hard to find out where foreign businessmen stay in Korea."

No kidding. I found that out the first night at the Chosen Hotel. I replied, "So why are you here? What do you want from me?"

Mieko sat upright on the couch, folded her hands, and boldly explained in careful English that she was single and was interested in meeting a young foreign businessman. She wanted to go to nice restaurants, the theater, and the many foreign social clubs.

I was completely taken back by this female. Asian women were never this direct unless they were hookers or bar girls. I could hardly believe my ears. "Are you KCIA?"

Without hesitation, she replied, "No!"

"How can I believe you?"

She smiled and said, "Call the General. He knows everything."

"Okay," I said, "Let's go. Do you know some interesting place for dinner?"

Mieko smiled and said, "No problem. I know a very interesting place." With that we grabbed Kimmey and his limo and set off into the dark moonless night.

After a few minutes of conversation in Korean between Mieko and my driver, I said "Okay, Kimmey, where are we going?"

Kimmey looked at me through the rear view mirror with raised eyebrows and exclaimed, 'Shit, boss, she's telling me to take the highway up to the DMZ."

I glanced at Mieko. She nodded and said, "Don't worry. I know where we are going."

After about an hour of winding mountain roads and signs in both English and Korean declaring the approaching restrictive demilitarized zone, we finally pulled off the main road. Within a few minutes, we were in the parking lot of a large beautiful Korean farmhouse that had been turned into a restaurant.

I turned to Kimmey and said, "Do you know anything about this place?"

He looked down at the floor and announced in a concerned tone, "Boss, never been here before, never heard of this place."

"Okay," I said, "We'll go in and have dinner. You go bullshit with the other drivers and get the story."

As soon as we approached the maître de, he smiled at Mieko and the two spoke a few words in Korean. He waved his hand to indicate we should follow him and seated us at a table in the corner of the restaurant. The place was first class: marble walls, chandeliers, candlelit tables, uniformed waiters, and menus in French, English, and Korean.

I looked at Mieko and asked, "Have you been here before? The maître de recognized you."

She replied, "Oh yes, a few times." Immediately she started describing the different items on the menu. Mieko recommended the steak. "It's the best in all Korea," she said.

After she placed our order in Korean, I said, "Tell me about yourself and how you know the General."

Mieko told me she had been brought up in a military family and that her father had known the General for many years. When she graduated from college with a degree in business, the General helped get her a job with Bank of America. She wanted to work for one of the large international companies that offered women more career opportunities than Korean businesses. Her dream was to work for Bank of America at their corporate headquarters in San Francisco.

During dinner I told her about some of my adventures throughout Asia. Within a short time we returned to Kimmey's limo and headed back to Seoul in order to beat the 1 a.m. curfew. After a lengthy conversation in Korean directing Kimmey to her apartment we finally pulled up to the curb in front of Mieko's building.

She turned to me with her beautiful smile and said, "Can we go out again? I have many more places to take you."

"Mieko," I said, "I'll call you." Who was this woman?

She leaned over, kissed my forehead, and said, "I'll be waiting. You know my number at the bank."

Mooncake Man

As we drove back to the Tower Hotel, Kimmey looked into his rear view mirror, shook his head, and exclaimed, "Boss, she trouble. Other drivers said she been there many times and always with a young army Lieutenant. That place mainly for army officers stationed on the DMZ. That's why I don't know anything about it. Shit! Who the hell goes to the DMZ to have dinner? Only army assholes, that's who!"

"You're right, Kimmey. The whole deal is weird." Maybe she was a part-time hooker, but, shit, she never even asked me for money. She was the most beautiful Korean woman I had ever seen. Every man in the restaurant had noticed her. She simply accepted the adoration as if it were expected.

Mieko had to be KCIA or some type of intelligence plant; she was just too good to be true. I couldn't wait to ask the General about her. There had to be more to her story.

Saturday evening finally arrived. At the Tower Hotel disco, Larry and I took our reserved table at the edge of the dance floor just before at eight p.m. At the top of the hour, the strobe lights came on, the band started playing music and jumping, dancers in the cages wiggled their butts, and I ordered three vodka tonics.

Looking around the ballroom, I had an uncomfortable feeling that the disco was all too familiar and I felt a wave of boredom. Then my eyes fell on a sight I had never seen at the disco. I stopped and stared at the dimly lit table with the candlelight bouncing off a young blonde. I had never seen a white woman in Korea. My eyes and mind became glued to her.

What the hell was she doing here? What was her story? I had to find out. As the band played the Beatles song, "She Loves You," I briskly walked up to her table and said, "My name is John. Can I have this dance?"

She smiled and said, "Okay. My name is Sara." Tall, thin, with long blond hair, average looks, a little homely; I guessed she was in her late twenties. Sara wore a loose fitting dress with polka dots, like something from the fifties. She reminded me of the June Cleaver character in the old TV series Leave it to Beaver. She wore very little makeup. The woman was definitely not flashy.

After the dance, we made our way back at her table and she invited me to sit down. Sara introduced me to her girl friend, a young plain-looking Filipina. I told her I been in Korea for several months and she was the first white woman I had ever seen. I asked if she was a tourist.

Sara explained that she and her friend were U.S. Air Force nurses stationed at Osan Air Force Base located about an hour's drive south of Seoul. They had heard about the Tower Hotel and the weekend disco from a friend. They had decided they needed a break from the military and had booked a room for the weekend.

I ordered drinks for everyone and told them a little about myself and why I was in Korea. Turning to Sara, I asked her to tell me about herself and how long she had been in Korea.

Sara told me she had grown up on a farm in Iowa and had gone to a nursing college not far from her home. Upon graduation she decided she wanted some adventure in her life so she joined the Air Force as an officer and a nurse. This was her first time away from the Midwest and outside the USA, she had been in Korea for six months and she was very excited about her job and living in Korea.

Sara asked about my travels and the more I told her, the more questions she had. She appeared fascinated about every aspect of my life. She told me she wanted to travel to every country in Asia. She eagerly drank every drink I ordered. After about five rounds of gin and tonics, Sara slurred her words and her eyes became as large as saucers. The more she drank the more she revealed about her early life.

She grew up in a poor family in rural Iowa. Her parents had very little. She got into nursing school on a scholarship. She got good grades and graduated at the top of her class. She had had several boyfriends but never a close relationship or really fallen in love. As she became drunker she kept saying, she was a lover but had never found anyone who would love her for her true self.

I finally said to Sara, "You've had enough. I know you're drunk because when women get drunk they always cry about how no one loves them." I nodded to Sara's girlfriend and said it was time to take her up to her room because she looked like she was getting sick. We got on either side of Sara, took her arms, and led her to the elevator.

The two women walked into the elevator and as the doors started to close, I told Sara I would call her in the morning. She just nodded. I walked back to the disco. What a break. Sara was a nice friendly girl and she was crazy about me. She was as naïve as hell but she could be very useful to me.

She had access to the military PX and commissary, which were well stocked with American cigarettes and hard liquor. For the past several months I had smoked those nasty Korean cigarettes that tasted like old socks that someone left in their closet for a year.

American booze was very expensive in Korea and some brands like Jack Daniels Black Label were practically non-existent. Yes, she could get all this stuff for me. I would take her to breakfast in the morning, show some interest and she would do anything I wanted. Sara was going to be my little gold mine.

The next morning I called Sara's room and she agreed to meet me for a light breakfast. She appeared promptly at 10 a.m., looking a bit tired and haggard. As I poured her some coffee she told me she seldom drank and apologized for getting so drunk and anything she might have said or done as she vaguely remembered the events of the previous evening. She then looked at me and with a smile and jokingly asked, "Did you take advantage of me in my vulnerable state?"

I laughed and replied, "No Sara, you were too sick to mess with last night." During breakfast Sara started asking questions where she had left off the night before. She boldly asked if I was married and smiled when I said I was not. She asked about my family and where I grew up. I told her I was an Air Force brat and that my family had moved from base to base like a band of gypsies.

She then exclaimed, "Then you must know all about the military."

I nodded and said, "Yes, that's why I am not in the military."

When I told her I would like to visit her on the base, she excitedly grabbed my hand, smiled, and said, "I would love to see you. Anytime! Here is my phone number. Make sure you call me first as you may need a pass to get on the base. But, who knows? Most of time, if you're a white, round-eye, they just wave you in."

As I poured Sara another cup of coffee, her girlfriend appeared and announced that their bus would be picking them up in a few minutes to start their tour of the city and several cultural and religious temples. Sara asked me to if I wanted to join them on the tour, but I declined stating I had other commitments. Since they would be going directly back to their military base after the tour I said my good-byes. I promised Sara that I would call her during the week.

It was Sunday morning and I had better things to do than tour temples. As I started back to my room I decided to take a walk through the beautiful hotel garden overlooking the city. The sun sparkled and flashed off the skyscrapers below. Religion was for weak ignorant people who could not think for themselves and whose lives were so miserable that their only hope was the afterlife.

I remembered sitting in weekly catechism classes, the required religious routine for kids not enrolled in a Catholic school. A fat, steely-eyed, old woman in a black and white habit smacked me on top of the head with a ruler because I failed at memorizing passages about Jesus or some other mystical figure. Nuns. I hated those bitches and their stupid rules.

I was not about to follow the church's rules, or, for that matter, anyone else's. Besides, God had never done anything for me. No one ever gave me shit including my own family. My parents could have helped me financially in college but never did. My old man said, "Son, it builds character to never depend on anyone."

The facts were that my old man was a colonel in the Air Force and could well afford my tuition, and might have paid it if I had followed his ideas. He wanted me to study engineering or science. Instead, I choose a degree in history, a waste of time, in his opinion. Of course, he would not pay for a sissy course. I always felt I never measured up to his expectations.

When I graduated from college without his financial support, he wanted me to go to officer candidate school. Instead, I waited until I got drafted and became an Army private. There was no doubt I was an embarrassment to the old man. While he was still a colonel in the Air Force his only son was a private in the Army. This fact was not shared with his military associates or friends. Perhaps the old man did me a favor. He instilled in me an iron-willed determination to prove him wrong.

I had succeeded by my own wit and intelligence and the ability to take advantage of every opportunity. I got high on the excitement of taking risks with little regard to the consequences. In business and my personal life, I consistently overcame objections through sheer force of will and determination.

I loved sales and the challenge of turning a no into a yes through persuasion. When that didn't work, I used intimation and domination. Yes, I could be harsh and unrelenting, just like my father. One way or another I got what I wanted. God had nothing to do with it.

In the decades yet to come, DHL evolved from a start-up to a world-class multinational known throughout the world. I wasn't yet thirty I had a role in building the company from the ground up.

Chapter 9 Negotiating in Korea

Damn. Another Monday morning in Seoul. Larry and I solemnly filed into the General's office for our routine briefing on any new developments in our case. I was beginning to despise Korea, the constant delay, and the bullshit. Most of all I disliked the waiting, the damn downtime.

As we took our familiar seats in front of the General's desk I looked over to Larry and said, "It's been six weeks now. When are we going to blow this place?"

The General appeared from the door located at the rear of his office. Shit. This guy still thinks he's a real General in the Army. He enters from a side door as if all the troops have assembled and are waiting for his grand entrance.

Beaming from ear to ear, the General announced that the KCIA wanted to resolve the case and a meeting had been arranged at their headquarters for the following afternoon. He told us to make sure we were on time and bring our new partner Bae with us. Larry looked at the General and with a puzzled expression asked, "What's the deal? When can we start up the operation again?"

"That will depend," the General replied, "on your cooperation with the KCIA and Korean Customs." Bae had all the details of what would be required. The General said that the banks had really helped our case, especially Bank of America, which made a strong case directly to the Ministry of Trade and Finance. The General stated, "Okay, gentleman, that's all I've got this morning. Good luck tomorrow."

I looked at the General and with a smile asked, "Are we dismissed now?"

The General laughed and said, "Carry on."

As we started to leave I asked the General if I could see him for a few minutes in private. Nodding to Larry and Ken, I said, "See you guys over at Bae's office."

I took my usual seat in front of the General's desk and asked, "Do you know a girl named Mieko? She works for Gregg Scott, a vice president at Bank of America."

The General tilted his head, raised his eyebrows, and then replied, "Why do you ask?"

"I met her at the bank several weeks ago. I took her out to dinner over the weekend and she mentioned she knew you," I said.

With a surprised expression, the General boomed, "You took her out to dinner? How in the hell did that happen?"

I shot back, "Shit, what's the big deal? Korean women love to go out with American business guys."

The General looked up at the ceiling and with a face as hard as stone said, "You little shit. Yes. I know her and her old man. She is the daughter of a good friend of mine, Colonel Kim Lee. He's retired now.

"Last I heard and this was not that long ago, she was engaged to an ROK army lieutenant. Never met the guy, but from what Kim says, he is a real stud. You had better be careful."

Is Mieko involved with an officer in the Republic of Korea Army? I threw up my hands and replied, "She never told me that. I spent the whole evening with her. Shit, doesn't anyone ever tell the truth in Korea?"

With a stern face and piercing eyes, the General stared directly at me. "Listen here, boy. Stay away from her, at least until your case is resolved. She could mean real trouble for you."

"Okay, General," I replied, "I'm not about to get my ass kicked over some Asian broad. Thanks for the information. I'll let you know what happens tomorrow with the KCIA."

With that I walked out of the General's office and headed for Bae's place for my next meeting.

Why would Mieko lie to me? Is she really engaged to this guy or is this some kind of Asian arranged marriage that she didn't agree to? Or, maybe she is part of the KCIA and just doing her job. I can't believe she is using me. She likes me. I can tell by the way she looks at me. I'll call her later this afternoon, ask her to dinner, and find out what's really going on.

As I entered his office, I found Bae with Larry and Ken, huddled around the conference room table, reading various documents. Larry looked at me and said we needed to discuss the KCIA deal and decide what we really wanted to do.

He explained we would have to agree to three key provisions. First, we had to pay a $100,000 dollar fine for violating Korean import and security regulations. Second, in order to be granted a special license to operate a courier service in Korea, fifty percent of all profits must go to the government. Third, Korean Customs and the KCIA must have unlimited and unsupervised access to all document pouches coming in or leaving the country.

Larry turned to me and asked, "Okay, Fish, What you think?"

Without hesitation I replied, "I think its bullshit." I turned to Bae and asked, "Who do we make the check out to?"

Bae smiled and replied, "They only gave us a bank account number to wire the money. No name or payee information."

"Right," I replied, "that's because it's a payoff to some goddamn general or politician and the KCIA doesn't want us or anyone else to know who it is. I would not give them anymore than 50K."

Still shaking my head I started in on the next provision. The second demand is really highway robbery. They want half? For what? I suggest we give them 25 percent. In return we're granted a special license as the only courier company that can operate in Korea. Who gets the 25 percent? Probably the same guy who gets the100 K fine."

I continued, "Regarding the third provision, this one we need to be careful with. They want unlimited and unsupervised access to all the document pouches. We've never agreed to that anywhere. That means they could take pictures of documents, take out documents, or even put things into the pouches.

"They could plant bugs and tracking devices. Shit, we would have no idea of what was going on. If our customers found out they would drop us in a minute. They expect and we promise a certain degree of confidentially. If we agree to this, we'll be working for the KCIA."

We spent the rest of the afternoon debating the KCIA's demands. Eventually my counter positions were accepted. We would prepare a brief to present the following afternoon at KCIA downtown headquarters. As the day wore on I called Mieko at her bank and asked her to join me for dinner the following evening. I would pick her up at 6 p.m. when the bank closed for the day.

In a dreary rainfall the next day, Larry, Ken, Bae, and I approached a large brown government building in downtown Seoul. As we climbed up the steps we came face to face with a large bronze plague that read, "Republic of Korea Ministry of Security."

Upon entering the building we were confronted by a uniformed and armed guard who spoke to Bae in Korean and then went directly to the telephone. After spending several minutes on the phone, he escorted us to the elevator, rode with us to the 10th floor, and led us into an empty conference room.

As I looked around the vacant room and my colleagues, I considered how vulnerable we were. We could be arrested and sent to some jail and never be heard from again. The Koreans were damn good at making problems disappear forever. But then I remembered that Bae's brother-in-law was with the KCIA and assured myself we would most likely get out of the place alive.

Perhaps we were safe. We would know soon enough if we would get to walk out. After about 10 minutes, four Koreans guys entered the room. One of the men wore a suit and the other three were dressed casually. They took their seats directly across from us.

The middle-aged guy in the suit spoke in Korean to Bae for several minutes; Bae turned to us and introduced the guy as Mr. Park Kim, chief of the KCIA at the airport and his assistants.

For the next 20 minutes, Bae and the KCIA chief conversed in Korean. They spoke back and forth with Bae presenting our counter proposal. Finally, the KCIA chief turned to us and said, in perfect English, "Gentleman, Mr. Bae has explained your position. We will seriously consider your recommendations and we will advise you of our final decision shortly. Thank you and good day."

The KCIA chief got up from the table and exited the room with his three assistants close behind. The uniformed military guard then stepped into the room and directed us to the elevator. Within a few minutes we were escorted to the ground floor and out of the building. The Korean government had a reputation for no-nonsense dealing, and we had just seen it firsthand. I was happy to just be out of there.

It was 5:45 in the afternoon when Kimmey pulled the limo to the curb in front of the Bank of America building. When I hopped in he looked back at me in the rear seat and with his serious concerned look said, "Boss, this Mieko is trouble. I can feel it. Why don't you find someone else? There are hundreds of Korean women in this town who love American businessmen."

I just shook my head and replied, "Kimmey, you may be right, but I'm crazy about her." As I sat in the car waiting for Mieko to appear I asked myself, "Why am I nuts about her? I don't even like Asian women except for immediate sexual gratification. They're shy, stupid, boring, and speak so little English that it's difficult to carry on even the simplest conversation. They're not good looking with hard facial features, skinny bodies with little or no chest, and bony asses."

Then it hit me; I had answered my own question. Mieko had none of those qualities. She was intelligent, well-educated, and interesting to talk to. Her facial features were not hard, neither Korean nor Chinese. She had delicate fine lines and deep set eyes. Along with her name, she seemed more Japanese than Korean.

Her body looked more European than Asian with her well-formed slender legs and a full bust line and a fully formed round ass. She was taller than most Asians, close to five foot nine inches. Mieko was always well-dressed and she wore little makeup except to highlight her stunning eyes. She was smart, well-read, and spoke perfect English. Yes, Mieko was not like any other Asian woman I had met. She was a woman of the world and I wanted her.

Kimmey's booming voice brought me back to reality. He called Mieko's name as she exited the bank. Kimmey open the door of the limo for her and she promptly sat next to me and exclaimed, "Oh, I've missed you. We have another special restaurant to go to tonight." Without any hesitation she then turned to Kimmey and spoke rapidly in Korean giving him directions.

After a short ride, we pulled up to a Japanese restaurant in downtown Seoul. Kimmey dropped us off and headed to a parking area to hang out with other drivers waiting for their clients or bosses.

Once we were seated inside, Mieko asked me about our case. I related the events of the last several days and the details of our counter proposal to the KCIA. Suddenly, Mieko's face took on a look of concern and she asked me, "If you win, will you then leave and go back to Hong Kong?"

I took her hand and replied, "Don't worry, Mieko. I'll be here for a while." Without any response Mieko opened up the wine menu and started talking about the various wines she liked and didn't like. I could hardly believe what I was hearing and asked, "How in the hell do you know about all these wines? Most Korean women have no idea about this stuff."

She smiled and said, "I'm not most Korean women."

"You're right," I replied. "But I need to ask you something else." Mieko looked at me attentively. "I asked the General about you yesterday. He told me that you are engaged to a Republic of Korea Army lieutenant. An ROK officer! Is that true? Is that how you knew about that restaurant on the DMZ?"

Mieko sighed and looked directly at me. "I was engaged to him," she said, "but not anymore."

I replied, "The General said this engagement was very recent. So, what's the story?"

With an agitated expression and squinting eyes, Mieko replied, "The General thinks he knows everything, but he doesn't. I told you I am not engaged to him and I don't want to talk about it anymore. Okay?"

"No, not yet," I replied. "Are you still seeing him?"

I could see anger swelling up in Mieko's flushed face. She lowered her voice and said, "Fine, I'll tell you what happened. I went out with him for about a year before we got engaged. The longer we were together, the worse he treated me. One night when I would not give in to his desires, he raped me.

"I told my father about it and he didn't do anything. Nothing. You know the army code of silence or something. Anyway I'm done with that bastard, I'm not going to be anyone's property and be treated like some whore. I broke off the engagement a few weeks ago and he is still telling everyone that we are engaged."

Then I asked, "So, what did he say when you ended the engagement?"

Mieko started to sob as she said, "He told me my father had already agreed to my marriage to him and that is what is going to happen."

"And what's been going on between you and this guy for the last several weeks?" I asked.

Mieko dried her tears with the white cloth napkin as she replied, "He came to see me at work several times and I told him to leave. He and my father have called me at my apartment and at the bank but I have refused to talk to them. I am going to live my own life. No one is going to force me into this. I don't want to talk about it anymore."

"Okay, beautiful," I replied. "Let's order dinner." The meal was fantastic. The tempura and sushi were fresh and prepared well. Mieko enjoyed commenting on every dish. Neither of us spoke about her personal problems for the remainder of the time at the restaurant.

Soon Kimmey was driving us back to her apartment. As we pulled up to the curb adjacent to her place Mieko turned to me and with smile asked, "Would you like to come in and see my home?"

I quickly replied, "Sure, I would love to."

Kimmey turned to me and shaking his head said, "Boss, I'll wait for you here."

I followed Mieko up the steep winding stairs, thinking, maybe Kimmey was right. This deal could get really complicated. Maybe I should not go into her apartment. Maybe I should tell her I don't want to see her anymore, and just get the hell out of here.

My thoughts were interrupted by a soft voice that said, "Welcome to my home." I looked over and saw this stunning woman and knew I had no defense for her looks or charms as I entered her apartment.

Mieko's home was small with a couch and a small serving table and several chairs in the living room and a bedroom and tiny kitchen. She motioned me to the couch as she went to the kitchen to prepare some tea. As I looked around the apartment I could see it was a reflection of its owner's personality. The few pieces of furniture were good quality; the pictures on the wall were original paintings of landscapes and ocean scenes. There were several photographs of Mieko and what looked like her close family and other relatives.

As Mieko entered the room she saw me looking at photographs and said, "Yes, that's my family. I have two older brothers. One is in the army and the younger one works for Korean Airlines." She then told me more about her family and the many aunts and uncles and what they all did.

I told her about all the places I had lived and how I had moved around so often when I was a kid. When I finished she said, "That's I want to do. I want to travel like you. I want to see the world outside of Korea, the world I have read about."

She came closer to me, put her hands under my chin, and lightly kissed me on my lips. Then she said, "You've been everywhere, I want to go with you when you leave Korea." Before I could respond, she put her arms around me and passionately kissed me.

Electricity shot through my helpless body. Mieko's touch awakened every nerve in my being. The intoxicating smell and feeling of her body next to mine swept me away with passion and desire. She anticipated and accommodated my every fantasy.

The sun's rays hit me directly on my face in the morning as I woke up next to Mieko. As I looked at her, innocently curled up beside me, still sleeping, I realized that she was truly exquisite. The affection I felt was a rare exception to the usual lack of emotion I felt the morning after a sexual encounter.

It was 6 a.m. and I gently shook Mieko and told her she needed to get up and go to work. After a quick cup of coffee and a promise to call her in a couple of days, I walked outside and spotted Kimmey's limo. It was parked in the same spot as the night before.

I looked inside and saw Kimmey sprawled out on the back seat under a blanket. I banged on the window and watched him slowly came to a sitting position and roll down the window. "What in the hell are you doing here? You should have left last night," I said.

Kimmey replied, "Boss, I didn't know you were going to spend the night. I got cold so I put the blanket on and I must have fallen asleep. Besides, I saw some weird shit in this neighborhood last night and I thought I better stick around."

"Yeah, what was that Kimmey?" I asked.

"Well, there was an ROK Army jeep with a couple of guys parked right under her apartment. They sat there most of the night and finally left around 2 a.m."

"Really?" I asked. "Did they get out of the jeep?"

"No," said Kimmey, "They sat there for hours."

"Don't worry about it Kimmey," I said. "It sounds like they were just screwing off or sleeping. Take me back to the hotel. I'm hungry."

As we drove through the morning rush hour in Seoul I considered whether it had been Mieko's ex-fiancé and his army pals hanging around. I didn't notice them when I walked into her apartment complex. Shit, maybe they bugged her place and were listening to us. Man, if that asshole heard us, I bet he was going over the edge. The General was right. I needed to be careful. Korea gave me the creeps.

Chapter 10 Seeing Sara at Osan Air Force Base

slid into the Tower Hotel lobby at 8 a.m. Monday morning joining Larry and Ken for breakfast. We faced another boring week of waiting for the government to decide our case.

Pondering how we would pass the time, I remembered Sara, the Air Force nurse that I had met at the hotel disco. This could be a good time to accept her invitation for a visit and stock up on American cigarettes and liquor from the P.X.

That evening I called Sara and asked if I could visit her for the weekend. She said excitedly, "Of course, I've been waiting for your call. Bring your overnight bag. Call me from the front gate on Friday night at 7 p.m. As the day approached, I enlisted Kimmey to drive me to Osan, the U.S. air force base that was located some 150 miles south of Seoul.

We headed south on the freeway and I was quite surprised at how good the road was. It had eight extremely smooth and wide lanes in each direction with what looked like a large moveable barrier in the middle. While we raced down the highway at some 80 miles an hour, I told Kimmey how surprised I was with the quality of the road and the large number of lanes on each side.

Laughing, Kimmey glanced at me through his rear view mirror and said, "Shit boss, this is not just a freeway; it's a runway for military aircraft. This is our reserve runway system. The middle barrier can be removed and we have over 200 miles of runways, if the North Koreans destroy our air bases we can use these as backups." The South Koreans never ceased to amaze me with their contingency plans and paranoia when it came to the North.

In less than two hours we had covered the 150 miles and turned off the freeway at the sign that said Osan AFB. As we approached the front gate with the U.S. Air Force guards at the entrance, I told Kimmey to pull into the visitor's parking area.

I walked over to the row of 10 phones attached to the side of the guard's building and rang Sara's number. She immediately answered and said, "You're here. I'll pick you up in 10 minutes."

I returned to the limo and told Kimmey he could take off and I would call him at the hotel if I needed him. I grabbed my overnight bag and waited by the phones. In about fifteen minutes I spotted an old beat up purple Toyota approaching the gate from the other side and recognized Sara behind the wheel.

The guard waved her through. Sara made a quick left turn into the parking lot and came to a screeching stop. She stuck her head out the window and said, "Hop in, handsome." I jumped in the front seat. Sara gave me a kiss on the cheek and a punch to my left shoulder. In her Midwestern accent she said, "Boy, we are going to have some fun."

What had I gotten myself into? Seeing Sara was certainly going to be different experience compared to spending time with Mieko. Sara dressed in cutoff jeans and a tank top that accentuated her flat chest and large thighs. I felt out of place wearing my sports jacket and slacks.

The Toyota was a wreck. It was beat up inside and out. The back seat looked as if a wild animal had tried to evade capture. I asked Sara, "Is this your car?" She laughed and replied, "Sort of. You see, I actually own a third of it. Two other nurses own the rest and we share the car."

Sara said, "The cars here have been passed around for years. We bought this one from several nurses who transferred out and when we leave we'll sell it to our replacements. Can you imagine how many drunken nurses have been in that back seat?"

"No," I replied. "I don't even want to think about it."

She made a sharp U-turn and headed back toward the main gate. As we approached the guard, Sara barely slowed down as she stuck her head out the window and yelled, "He's with me." The guard smiled and waved us through.

Sara took me directly to her building which resembled a section of any large apartment complex. A sign on the front announced, "Nurses Quarters--All visitors must sign in at Bldg. 7."

"So what's with the sign?" I asked.

Laughing, Sara said, "Oh that. Don't worry about it. The head nurse lives in this complex and shacks up with the pilots almost every night. No one signs in here."

Sara's apartment, which she did not share with anyone, was situated the ground floor. It was a spacious place with a well-furnished living room, a kitchen, a bedroom, and bathroom. It was clean and private.

As soon as we entered, I placed my overnight bag on the kitchen table. Grabbing the bag, Sara said, "I'll take that. It belongs in here." She placed it on her bed in the bedroom. She told me it was Western night at the officers club and they had great steaks. We could walk there as it was only about a quarter mile away. As we traced the beaten path to the club, I noticed it was lined on both sides by large and all-too-familiar painted white rocks.

The white rocks were nothing new to me. I had seen them on every air force base I had lived on. They always lined some path or walkway. Sometimes they were used to spell out a unit's name on the green lawn in front of the barracks. The U.S. Air Force loved those damn rocks.

All the buildings had numbers, even the toilets at the baseball fields. An Officer's Club at one base looked the same as it did at any another location. Other buildings echoed their global counterparts. Whether it was a P.X., commissary, gym, or school, they looked like recognizable members of the same family. One blueprint was used all over the world.

As we entered the Officer's Club, Sara showed her I.D. to the doorman and as she pointed to me she announced, "He's with me." In the bar adjacent to the large dining room, several young women rushed over to Sara and grabbed her arm as they asked, "Who's the guy? Never seen him before."

Sara smiled and looked back at me as she said, "Oh, this is John. I met him in Seoul a couple of weeks ago. He's a businessman working for a worldwide company." With that, Sara turned abruptly and led me toward the back of the club, a space that featured a large swimming pool and surrounded by a patio checkered with small bar tables and chairs.

As we approached the patio, a couple of young American women waved to Sara and motioned for us to join them. I asked Sara who they were and she told me they were nurses and worked with her at the base hospital. One of the women asked, "Who's your buddy, Sara? Are you going to share him with us? Sit down and we'll buy you a drink."

"Not now, girls. I'm showing him around." She repeated her mantra, "This is John. He's the friend that I went out with a couple of weeks ago in Seoul. He's a businessman working for a large international company." Sara took me to every room in the club, introducing me to the people she knew and she seemed to be friends with everyone.

Within a few minutes of meeting one set of faces, we moved on to the next group. It became apparent to me she wasn't so much showing me around as she was showing me off to her friends and colleagues.

The dinner was a fantastic affair, a Western cowboy theme with all the good stuff: potatoes, beans, large steaks, barbecued chicken, and ice cream. I hadn't eaten so much good American food since I left the states several years before.

After dinner we retired to the bar where everyone knew Sara. She introduced me to both guys and gals. One of the women sitting at the far end of the bar yelled to Sara, "Come on over and bring your friend."

Sara grabbed my arm and introduced me to an attractive young dark haired women who held out her hand and announced in a thick Brooklyn accent, "I'm Janet, Sara's best friend. So you're the guy Sara was telling me about."

I replied, "I guess so. I hope we can still be friends."

"Maybe," she replied with a chuckle. Janet had a contagious smile and told me she and Sara had arrived at the base about the same time and they lived in the same apartment complex. She was also a nurse and one of the part owners of the beat up Toyota that Sara drove.

"Do you work in the same ward at the hospital?" I inquired.

"No, not even close," responded Janet. "I work in the Preventive Medical Ward. That's the nice name for the V.D. clap ward."

"What the hell is that all about?" I asked. Janet explained that Osan AFB operated daily military flights from Korea to Tan Son Nhut AFB in Vietnam and then on to Korat AFB in Thailand and transported both personnel and freight between these points. Soldiers stationed in Korea could go on R & R--Rest and Recreation--after being in the country for six months and most chose to go to Thailand on the military flights.

A major problem at Osan was a continuing epidemic of V.D. for soldiers coming back from Thailand. Bangkok alone was said to have over 100,000 prostitutes. The military dealt with the problem by requiring all G.Is going on R & R to sit through a two hour class on preventing sexually transmitted diseases, STDs, and the use of condoms, before they could depart from Korea.

Once the G.I.s returned, they were subjected to a thorough medical exam and check-up at their home base in Korea. "So how many guys actually get the clap?" I asked.

Janet shook her head as she replied, "Would you believe that after everything we do the infection rate for 1971, just last year, was 10 percent?"

"Well, I replied, "you just give 'em a shot in the ass and that takes care of that, right?"

"It's not that simple," replied Janet. "First, we have to determine the type of infection. We do that by taking a sample of the infection with a long thin needle that is inserted in the penis urethra and then examining it under a microscope."

"Holy shit," I replied, "doesn't that hurt?

"You bet," said Janet, "It hurts like hell. Once the lab identifies the infection we administer a specific antibiotic and the appropriate dosage."

"So," I asked, "once the guy gets the shot how long does it take before the infection goes away?" She said that after a series of shots it usually took about 10 days unless it was diagnosed as an N.S.U.

"What the hell is an N.S.U.?" I inquired.

Janet replied, "N.S.U. stands for Non Specific Urinary infection. This type of infection does not respond to antibiotics. Thailand is the primary infection point for N.S.U.s so that's why we're so concerned with young G.I.s contracting it, coming back to Korea, spreading it around here, or, even worse, taking it to their hometowns in the U.S."

"So, what the hell happens if the antibiotics don't work?" I asked.

Janet shook her head, "Well, the patient will eventually develop secondary infections and most will die. We record the death as heart or liver failure."

"What?" I stammered, "you're telling me that these guy die of the goddamn clap and then you call it something else?"

"That's right." said Janet. "It's military bullshit.

Suddenly Sara grabbed my arm and whispered, "This conversation is boring me. Let's go back to my place." Within fifteen minutes we were back at her apartment. As I sat on the couch, I noticed the large T.V. in corner. I asked if she got any real American shows and she told me it was Armed Forces T.V. which was mostly about what was going on with the American military in Korea and a few delayed sports events. She said she hardly ever watched it.

After making me a double vodka and seven, Sara took my jacket off and sat close to me on the sofa. She said, "I'm so glad you came to see me. I thought you were just bullshitting me back at the hotel. I didn't think you would really come." As she leaned toward me, I put my hand around her head, gently drew her close, and softly kissed her neck.

Sara wrapped her arms around me, pulled me closer, and intensely kissed me on the lips.

She whispered in my ear, "Let's go to the bedroom. We'll be much more comfortable in there." As soon as I sat on the bed, Sara jumped on top of me and started kissing me all over my face and neck.

She said, "I'm so glad you're here to take care of me the whole weekend."

"Gee, Sara," I replied, "I thought I was coming here for dinner and to buy a few things from the P.X."

She immediately stopped kissing and sat up as she said, "We'll get to that later. Now that you've been fed a good dinner, you should have lots of energy and stamina. You're going to need it." On that note, Sara and I commenced to have some good old hard sex. She was a new experience for me. The more sexually intense I became, the more she demanded.

Sara constantly wanted to try new positions and her frequent loud groaning must have been heard throughout the entire building. After about 45 minutes and her several orgasms, I finally succumbed to my inevitable climax. We rested on the bed, exhausted, our sweaty bodies intertwined. I tapped her on the shoulder and asked, "How in the hell do you know so much about sex?"

She laughed and replied, "I used to watch the animals on the farm back in Iowa." I had no doubt that the livestock inspired her imagination. Sara was definitely a change from my usual experience with whores in Asia where I put a couple of coins in the slot and got the same ride every time.

I was tired; it had been a long day and night. I rolled over and said goodnight to Sara and within a few minutes was fast asleep. It was dark, pitch dark. Was I dreaming or was I awake? What was that sensation I felt on my back? Shit, maybe it was some goddamn bug or animal. Then I felt it on my ears, I slowly opened my eyes and in one motion quickly turned over—and came face to face with Sara. "It's about time you woke up," she said, leaning on her arm and smiling.

I looked around the room and glanced at the open window. I proclaimed, "Shit, it's still dark. What the fuck time is it?"

Sara kissed me and with a smirk, she said, "It's 6 a.m. and I'm horny again."

"Holy shit, Sara," I replied. "When was the last time you got laid? In high school?"

"Oh, you're so funny. I just love being with you," she said with a big smile. She sat upright and put her hand under my chin as she said, "Tell you what, stud. You take care of me this morning, then we'll have breakfast, and after that I'll take you to the P.X. How's that for a deal?"

"Okay, Sara," I said, "What choice do I have?"

"None," she said, as she rolled over on top of me. At 10 a.m. Sara and I sat down to breakfast in her little kitchen. I started writing down what I wanted from the P.X. I had it all figured out: 10 cartons of Winston cigarettes, 10 bottles of Smirnoff 100 proof vodka, and a case of Jack Daniels Black Label. I shoved the list across the table to Sara and asked how much it would cost.

She looked at the list and slowly shook her head. I quickly asked, "What's wrong, you can get this stuff, right?"

"Sure," said Sara, "but not all at one time."

"What the hell are you talking about?" I asked.

"Well, it's like this," said Sara. "Officers are only allowed to purchase two bottles of hard liquor and two cartons of cigarettes per day, enlisted people only get half of that. The Air Force feels that if you could buy a lot at one time it would end up in the Korean black market. But don't worry," said Sara with a big smile. "You'll just have to stay here another 10 days. That's all."

"You've got to be kidding," I said. "I'll be dead by then."

I was tired and ready to go back to Seoul when Kimmey's limo pulled into the visitor's lot at the base on Saturday evening. I told Sara that I had to get back to Seoul because of a business emergency. As Kimmey opened the door I placed my overnight bag containing my two bottles of booze and two cartons of cigarettes on the rear seat.

Within a few minutes we were on the huge eight-lane freeway heading back to Seoul. As I melted into the comfortable leather seat of the limo, I closed my eyes and it slowly dawned on me that I really didn't control anything. I was so self-centered and naïve. I was easy prey to Mieko who needed me as her ticket out of Korea and a target for Sara who just wanted me for a weekend tryst.

Chapter 11 Fighting for My Life in an Alley

Shit. Another goddamn Monday morning. I hate Korea. Here we are again, Larry, Ken and I, sitting in the General's office, waiting for his grand entrance at precisely 0800 hours. Maybe, just maybe, God willing, we'll finally get a decision on our case. Even if it goes against us, at least it will be resolved.

Suddenly the rear door to the office opened and the General entered, smiling ear to ear. "Gentlemen," he declared, "It's over! You guys are back in business. They agreed to your offer, except for one item, and I'm sure we can work it out."

"What's that?" Larry asked.

The General replied, "They insist on unsupervised and total access to all documents entering or leaving the country."

I watched Larry as he explained, "That's a key provision. We can't agree to total access."

Turning red, the General leaned over his desk and pushed his contorted face a few inches from Larry's as he declared, "Don't be stupid. The KCIA agreed to the other conditions. They're giving you a special license. You'll be the only game in town, a monopoly, and your partner will be the KCIA. In Korea, it doesn't get better than that."

"Sure," I replied, "But what do we tell our customers? That there will be no confidentially with their documents and correspondence?"

The General's face flushed a deeper crimson and appeared as if it might explode as he boomed, "Confidentially! Hell! If they're bringing in just business documents like they should be, they'll have nothing to worry about. If they're bringing in blueprints of a tunnel under the DMZ to assassinate the President of South Korea like that goddamn Bechtel, then they have a lot to be worried about.

"Listen," the General continued, "The KCIA works closely with our CIA. Don't you know all the secret police of the world work together? That's their biggest secret."

"Well, General," I replied, "How in the hell do you know all this? What our counter proposal was? What the KCIA wanted? Who the hell are you? Whom do you really work for?"

The General sat back in his chair and calmly explained, "Gentleman, let's just say I have an interest in serving the American business community and the security of a long-time ally of the United States."

I turned toward Larry and said, "Looks like we have no choice. Now we have two partners, Bae and the KCIA. One big happy family."

"Fine," said Larry, "but we're not signing any documents on this deal."

The General laughed as he replied, "Don't worry. The KCIA doesn't sign anything."

With that we filed out of the General's place and headed to Bae's office to work out the details of starting up the operation. The first order of business was to pay the fine. Larry told Bae to start the process of wiring the 25K to our unknown recipient. Bae would then work out a plan to get the operation started: hiring ex employees, securing the delivery vans; and re-opening the boarded up distribution center by the airport.

We spent the remainder of the afternoon working out the details and budgets of getting the operation started again. It was late when I finally called Mieko at her apartment to ask her to dinner the following evening at one of my favorite places, the Savoy Restaurant and Bar in downtown Seoul.

As I hung up the phone I realized this would be the last time I would see Mieko. My job in Korea was over. As the limo pulled up to the familiar curb in front of the Bank of America, Kimmey looked at me through the rear view mirror with a serious expression and said, "Are you going to tell her you're leaving, boss?"

I took a deep breath and replied, "I don't know," Kimmey. "I am not sure what I am going to say to her."

"There she is," Kimmey exclaimed. Mieko wore a dark maroon dress that clung to her body outlining every curve, black stockings, and stiletto heels. She had a killer body and knew how to show it. How in the hell was I going to leave her?

Kimmey walked around the car, opened the door for Mieko, and watched as she slid across the seat toward me. She kissed me on the cheek and said, "I've missed you. It's been a week and you didn't call."

"Sorry," I replied, "I've been busy."

I told Kimmey to take us to the Savoy and within a few minutes we had arrived. The doorman quickly approached the car and spoke to my driver. Kimmey opened our doors and said he would be parked across the street if I needed him.

The Savoy was an old fashioned Irish bar and grill. A massive thirty-foot mahogany bar situated to the right of the entrance spanned the length of the restaurant. Tables and chairs were scattered about the bar area which was adjacent to an open area dining room. As we entered the restaurant, we were greeted by the headwaiter and placed at a corner table, 20 feet from the bar.

Mieko quickly grabbed the wine list and eliminated those she didn't like. She finally pointed to her choice, and said, "Let's get this one." She told me how much she missed me and with her radiant smile asked, "How is the case going?"

"Okay," I said. "Same old stuff."

"That's not what I heard," she replied, " I heard you won."

Surprised, I stammered, "Okay, who the hell told you that?"

Mieko paused and with raised eyebrows said, "Do you remember whom in the hell I work for? Your biggest customer, Bank of America, that's who. Greg Scott, my vice president, told me yesterday that you guys won and that the courier service would be starting up in a few days. Why didn't you tell me? It's because you're leaving. Right? Damn it. Tell me the truth!"

"Okay, okay." I repeated. "I'm leaving in a few days but I'll be back."

Her face froze. Mieko glared at me and replied, "Yeah, they all say that."

I put my hand on Mieko"s arm and replied, "I'm not lying. I will come back. I promise. I need to return to Hong Kong for a couple of weeks. And then I'll be back."

Mieko started crying as she said, "You said you would take me with you. Remember that night in my apartment? You promised."

As I glanced around the restaurant I could see we had caught the attention of the other diners and they seemed to be waiting for my reply. "Let's order dinner," I said. "We'll talk about this later."

Mieko wiped the tears from her eyes with the edge of her white linen napkin. As I patted her arm, her expression switched from grief to alarm. Her facial muscles tightened, her eyes grew large, and her color turned ashen white. With her lips barely open, she slowly mouthed the words, "Oh, no. It's him. Oh my God. Not him."

I grabbed her arm and asked, "What is it? What's going on?"

Mieko trembled as she said, "It's him! My ex boyfriend! He's over there, behind you, at the bar, the man in the yellow shirt. He's just staring at us. Oh my God. How did he know we were here? How did he know?"

I spun around and caught sight of Mieko's ex-boyfriend sitting at the bar and smirking at us. The guy was bigger and younger than I expected. He just sat there motionless on the barstool. I stared back at him for several minutes, determined I would not be intimated or show any sign of fear.

Mieko grabbed my arm and frantically said, "Let's go! Let's leave."

"Bullshit," I said, "We were here first." Suddenly the guy got up from the bar stool, turned abruptly, and walked out the front door. Mieko seemed petrified with fear. In a panic, she asked how he knew we were at this restaurant.

I told her that I had spotted two Korean Army men in a jeep early that morning when I left her apartment. I wasn't sure then, but I was now, that her apartment was bugged and those two guys had been listening in all night.

Mieko face turned red as she said, "They heard everything? Do you mean everything? Even when we were making love? My God, John! This shouldn't have happened. You have to take me with you. Don't leave me here. Please!"

"Mieko, calm down," I said. "I need to go to the head. When I get back, let's get out of here. We'll find a nice quiet place and talk about it." I started walking down a dimly lit stairway to the men's toilet. Mieko was getting hysterical. She was wild with worry about that guy. What did she mean, "It shouldn't have happened." Some how I had to get her out of Korea.

I heard a movement to my left as I finished descending the staircase. I was several feet away from the door of the toilet. As I turned I felt a jarring and stabbing pain on my left side. My feet lifted off the floor. Someone I couldn't see slammed me against the exit door.

The door immediately gave way and my body dropped on the cool ground. As a searing pain crept up from my left side to my head, I felt dizzy, dazed and confused. I lay in the alley with warm sticky blood running down my face. What was happening? Was I being robbed? Was this a dream? I blacked out for a moment.

Suddenly I felt another sharp pain on my right side as the assailant kicked my ribs. I strained my eyes in the dim light through the bloody film over my eyes trying to see who was trying to rob or kill me. Curled-up and motionless, I saw a big guy circling my lifeless body. He shouted something in Korean and kicked me every few seconds. I hoped he would just take my wallet and leave. But he didn't go away; he kept yelling and jabbing his foot into my side.

Finally, the alley grew silent. I groaned and tried getting up. As I slowly crawled to my knees, I peered at my assailant who stood motionless a few feet away. I froze. It was the man in the yellow shirt. Oh my God. It was Mieko's boyfriend.

This guy wasn't going to rob me. He was going to kill me. As I carefully rose to my feet, he said something in Korean. Then I saw it. The knife. The blade sparkled in the moonlight. As he steadily advanced toward me, I glanced to the right and left. I had no way out. He blocked my only escape route.

This crazy Korean was going to kill me because I screwed his girlfriend. Shit! I never thought it would end this way in some dirty back alley in Seoul, Korea.

Shouting in Korean, he charged toward me. I saw the shining knife coming toward my right side. As I threw my right arm up to block his downward motion I felt the burning pain of the blade entering my flesh just below the elbow. I staggered backward several steps, stopped, and paused for a microsecond. Then, with one swift move, I kicked him squarely in the balls. He collapsed, his fall broken by one knee hitting the ground before the other. He lay there groaning deeply and muttering in Korean.

When I tried to kick him in the head, he ducked, rose to his feet, cursed, and yelled. The guy was tough. I knew now that it was going to be him or me; one of us was not going to walk away from the fight.

As I waited for his next charge, my mind took control. I was transported in time and heard the husky voice of my Army drill instructor, yelling at me during my hand-to-hand combat training. "Hey, butthead! It's either you or him. Kill him. Kill him. You've got to do it now boy. Do it." My D.I.'s voice kept yelling in my mind. "Do it."

The Korean charged toward me wielding the knife. Seeing the blade coming down toward my chest, I quickly turned sideways and with all the strength in my being, drove my elbow directly into his face. He screamed in pain, stumbled back a few feet, and with the knife dangling from his fingertips, collapsed to his knees. His face was covered in blood.

When he tried to get up, I grabbed the knife and plunged it deep into his chest. He let out a deep groan and still staring at me, fell face down into the alley. I gazed down at the lifeless figure; this thing that threatened my very existence was dead. I had killed him and I had no remorse. Fear gripped me. Had anyone seen this?

Looking around, I couldn't see anyone. The alley had no lights. It was almost dark and I had to get out of there. As I emerged from the passageway, I spied Kimmey's limo a short block away. I walked briskly, almost running to my escape and salvation. I saw Kimmey sleeping in the front seat as I opened the rear door and slid into the back seat. My driver turned around and exclaimed, "Jesus! Boss! What happened to you? You're a mess."

"Don't worry about that now. Let's get the hell outta here. I'll explain later." Kimmey turned the key in the ignition. The engine rumbled to life. What a break. No one saw me; no one will know I was involved. The cops will just find a dead guy in the alley with a knife in his chest. Then it hit me. The knife! Holy shit! I left the knife in him. What an idiot, my prints are all over that damn thing. The goddamn U.S. ARMY has my prints. They will know it was me. I have to get that knife.

"Kimmey," I yelled, "Keep the car running. I'll be right back."

Blood ran down my face and my ribs burned with pain as I ran back to the alley. My assailant had not moved. I turned him over and pulled the knife out of his chest. He was still breathing and emitted a low gurgling sound. He was still alive. I folded the knife and put it in my suit pocket and hobbled back to Kimmey's limo. Once inside the limo I keeled over in pain and whispered, "Take me back to the hotel."

Kimmey stared into his mirror. "Boss, you look terrible. I'm taking you to the hospital."

"No!" I screamed. "No goddamn way! That S.O.B. I killed back there was a lieutenant in the ROK, those Korean bastards will lock me up forever for this. Damn it! Take me to the hotel. I'll stay in the limo. You go get Larry."

"Right, boss," said Kimmey. "I told you she was trouble," he reminded me.

As Larry slid into the back seat, he surveyed my wounds and exclaimed, "Jesus! You are all fucked up. What happened?"

I explained the entire episode to Larry and when I ended, I told him, "I'm not going to turn myself in. I'm not taking any chances whether the Koreans will treat me fairly. Shit, I may never even get a trial."

During the drive to the hotel I formulated my escape plan. Kimmey would drive me to Osan Air Force Base and I would get Sara to hide me until this thing blew over. Even if the Koreans figured out that I was involved, they would never look for me on a U.S. Air Force Base. Shit. I was a civilian.

I shared my plan with Larry and ordered him to go up to my room, pack my one suitcase, and get my shaving kit. I wanted several towels, sheets, and my first aid kit. Within 15 minutes, Larry returned with my requested items. I told him I would call in a couple of days.

Kimmey started up the black limo and in a few minutes we were barreling down the huge eight-lane freeway. I got busy in the back seat trying to patch up my battered body, changed clothes, and took an inventory of how badly I was injured.

My ribs hurt like hell, both sides were black and blue, and it hurt every time I took a deep breath. The part of my right arm just below the elbow was still bleeding profusely. I squeezed an entire tube of antibiotic ointment in the wound and wrapped it tightly with a strip of the hotel sheets.

I pulled myself up to the front of the limo and surveyed my wounds in the mirror. My right eye was nearly swollen shut. Bleeding lacerations peppered my torn-up face. I pulled apart another section of white sheet, poured some shaving alcohol on the fabric, and patted the wounds to clean them.

I lay back in the rear seat and applied my shaving septic pencil to each cut. God it hurt like hell. The limo raced down the dark freeway in the middle of the night. What the hell had just happened? What was going to become of me? Where was I going to end up?

Chapter 12 Escaping from Korea

*J*ust before midnight my black limo turned into the visitor's parking lot outside the front gate at Osan Air Force Base. Sitting in the back seat, I hoped Sara was home and not somewhere partying and drinking at this hour. As I looked out the side window, I saw young Air Force guys returning to the base after a night on the town.

One taxi after another dropped off G.I.s at the entrance to the front gate. They scrambled out and staggered along the narrow sidewalk leading to the entrance of the base. The Air Police Guard was stationed on the sidewalk at the entrance to the base.

As each soldier approached and started to pull out his military I.D. card, the guards simply looked at his face to make sure he was an American, then casually waved him thorough, not even looking at his identification. Should I just walk in with the next group of drunken G.I.s and get waved through? If I got stopped I could show my U.S. Army Reserve I.D. card, the one I had not turned in after my discharge.

The more I thought about it the more I realized what a risk it might be. My ID card was red, which meant reservist. Active duty military I.D. cards were green. Besides, I had a suitcase. No, I could not draw any attention to myself. The fewer people that knew I was on this base the better.

I followed the routine to contact Sara. I walked to one of the phones that hung on the side of the guard shack. I dialed and it rang, rang and rang, it least 20 times. Shit, she wasn't home. I walked back to the limo.

I hoped she wasn't spending the weekend in Seoul again. I got back in the limo and said to Kimmey, "We need to kill some time. We can drive around the town next to the base and return in an hour." I would try again. I didn't want to arouse any suspicions by having the limo parked by the guard shack for the next hour.

The small Korean town adjoining the base was like all the other military towns in the world. I knew them well because I grew up as an Air Force brat and moved with my family from one base to another like a band of homeless gypsies.

Typically, the towns got rougher and seedier the closer you got to the base. This place was no different. Each side of the street leading to the main gate was lined with a string of small bars, massage parlors, tattoo shops, whorehouses, cheap by-the-hour hotels, small stores selling liquor, and the usual assortment of pimps, pickpockets, whores, and con artists selling everything from watches to drugs. The whole scene reminded me of when I was a twelve-year-old kid. I walked down streets just like this one on my way home from Military Dependent School in Japan.

My house was located just outside the base. In the late afternoon, with books in one hand and an empty lunch pail in the other, I peered into the dimly lit bars and windows of the whorehouses.

Like a kid in a candy store, I spied on the ladies getting ready to service the wave of G.I.'s that arrived at the end of each workday. The ladies fascinated me. They were beautiful, wore wildly colored short dresses, and smoked cigarettes. I noticed they talked and waved their hands in expressions that seemed crazy yet alluring.

Within a short time, the women who saw me everyday with my books and empty lunch pail, started making fun of me. They called me itchi white boyson, little white kid. Finally one day, I walked up to a group of women standing in the doorway and yelled in English, "What do you whores want from me?"

Silence followed. After a few minutes, an older women with a stern hard face stepped out of the group. In perfect English she said, "Okay, kid, tell you what. We will give you some money and you can buy us what we want from the P.X. We will let you keep the change. Is it a deal?"

"How much do I get?" I replied.

"Don't worry said the old lady, we will make it worth your time."

For the next several months the ladies gave me lists of items to buy: perfumes, nylons, cigarettes, and chocolates. I bought the items at the

P.X. after school and delivered them on my way home. The military called this black marketing. I called it my first job.

The old madam said I did such a good job that for my thirteenth birthday she was giving me an all day sex education class with her two youngest whores. It lasted only fifteen minutes. Sadly, shortly thereafter, my first job ended with a visit by the military police to my home.

After about an hour of driving around the town we returned to the guard shack and I approached the row of phones. If she didn't answer this time I was really screwed. After the third ring, Sara answered. I told her I was at the front gate and to pick me up. I would explain everything later.

Sara said she would be there soon so I returned to the limo and waited. Within ten minutes her beat up old Toyota turned into the visitor's lot. As soon as I slid into the passenger seat I could see the annoyed look on Sara's face. She said, "Why didn't you call me and tell me your were coming? I might not have even been home."

Suddenly she turned the interior lights on and said, "Shit, what happened to you? You're all beat up."

"Sara," I replied, "Don't worry. I think I'm okay. Some asshole Korean guy jumped me in an alley and tried to rob me. I've got some cuts on my face and my ribs are sore, but I don't think anything is broken."

"Did you go to the cops?" questioned Sara.

"No," I said, "What the hell would they do anyway? After that experience in the alley, I just needed to get away from Seoul and I thought of you. I know I should have called, but I took the chance you would be home. I missed you."

Sara smiled and said, "Okay, sweetheart. Go and get your stuff. I'll wait here."

As I slid into the back seat of the limo, Kimmey was leaning over the seat with a concerned look on his face. "Don't worry, Kimmey. I'll be okay. If the cops track you down, tell them you dropped me off at the Central Train Station in Seoul and you have no idea where I was going."

"Okay," said Kimmey as he extended his hand for a farewell handshake. I saw the tears in his eyes as he grasped my hand and held it for a few seconds. With that I tossed my suitcase in the backseat of Sara's car. She abruptly made a U-turn and, without slowing down, she stuck her arm out the window and waved at the guard proclaiming, "He's with me." I had made it inside the base.

Within a few minutes we were at Sara's apartment. While she parked in the carport, I couldn't help but wonder how long I could stay before I wore out my welcome. As soon as we entered her place she ordered me to remove all my clothes so she could thoroughly examine my wounds and determine how badly I was hurt.

Being a surgical nurse, Sara meticulously looked at my body from head to toe. She told me to breathe deeply and exhale slowly as she pressed on various spots on my ribs and back. "Does it hurt?" she asked.

"Hell, yes!" I snapped.

Sara took the bandages off my arm and examined the deep knife wound. "It could already be infected," she said. She opened her hallway closet and brought out a huge case, an Air Force Medical Survival Kit. It contained numerous medications and first aid instruments. She then gave me several pain pills and antibiotic capsules. As Sara washed and treated my lacerations, I closed my eyes and slowly drifted off to sleep.

The next morning I awoke will a dull throbbing on both sides of my ribs. When I tried to sit up, I felt the rush of a stabbing intense pain that convinced me to abandon the effort. I gently lay back on the pillow.

Sara heard me from the kitchen and sat down in the chair next to my makeshift bed on the couch. She explained that my ribs were badly bruised but she didn't think they were broken. Of course, she explained, the only way to know for sure was to have an x-ray.

I told her that was out of the question and asked her not to tell anyone I was staying with her. "Why not?" she asked, "Are you in some kind of trouble?"

"Sara," I explained, "the guy that robbed me? Well, we had a fight in the alley. I stabbed him with his own knife. I don't know how bad he's hurt. Until my guys in Seoul figure out what's going on, it's best for everyone that no one knows I'm here. Now, how long is it going to take until I can walk around without my ribs hurting so damn much?"

Sara raised her eyebrows, tilted her head, and replied, "Oh, about two to three weeks if they're not broken."

"Oh, great," I exclaimed, "I don't have that much time."

"Neither do I," replied Sara. Then she explained how I needed to rest and take the pain pills so I could sleep. For the next several days it seemed like I was in some type of dream, coming in and out of consciousness only long enough to awake and take more medication.

The next thing I knew it was Monday morning and Sara was gently shaking my arm and telling me she had to go to work at the base hospital. She left several pain pills and soup on the table next to my bed as I weakly said good-bye. I dozed off after she left and woke up in the late afternoon.

An hour passed before I decided to call Larry at the hotel room to find out what was going on and whether anyone was looking for me. Dialing the number, I wondered if the guy had died. He was still breathing when I yanked the knife out of him.

After a couple of rings Larry answered. Recognizing my voice, he said, "Can't talk to you now. Call me in an hour at this number." He then gave me the number and hung up.

His hotel room phone must have been bugged or maybe there was someone in the room and he couldn't talk. An hour later I called the number and Larry promptly answered. He immediately asked about my condition. I brought him up to date on my injuries and explained, "I'm staying with Sara on the base."

"Good move," replied Larry. "The cops were here Sunday morning looking for you. They sent your description to every airport, bus, and train depot in the country."

"Shit," I replied, "What's going on?"

"Well," explained Larry, you were right; the Koreans are out to screw us on this deal. The guy that you stabbed was Mieko's fiancé and an ROK lieutenant. He's in the ICU ward at the hospital and it looks like he's going to make it.

"He told the cops that you had ambushed him. He said he was going downstairs to the toilet and you pushed him out into the alley and stabbed him. He said you wanted to kill him because you were jealous that Mieko was going to marry him. The cops believed him because he didn't have a knife or any kind of a weapon on him when he was found lying face down in the alley."

"How in the hell do you know all this, Larry?"

"The General." Larry replied. "He knows everything." Larry explained that the General had called him to a meeting and filled him in on the condition of Mieko's boyfriend, the statements he had made to the cops, and how they were looking for me.

Larry said the General was pissed off at me, that he had told me to stay away from Mieko. He was upset that he had publicly supported the courier service, used the chamber's influence, and then, when we finally won, I pulled this shit. He said if he could find me he would ring my little neck.

"Larry," I replied, "you have to tell him what really happened; get Mieko to tell him what was really going on with her boyfriend. Tell the General the best thing for everyone is for me to get out of the country. The publicity of a trial would not be good for him or his precious American Chamber of Commerce. Tell the General that I have a plan but I will need his help. I know he is well connected to the U.S. Military and Korean Intelligence. Hell, I bet he's on the CIA's payroll.

"Ask the General to get his buddies at U.S. Army headquarters in Seoul to cut me R&R (Rest and Recreation) orders on one of the flights out of Osan AFB to Thailand. Sara told me there are daily flights to Korat Air Force Base just north of Bangkok. Tell the General that I still have my military I.D. card, it's the red Ready Reserve Card but it will be a valid I.D. as long as I have orders. Tell the General I will never come back to Korea. Never. I promise."

"Okay," replied Larry. "Call me tomorrow. Same time, same number." With that I took a couple more pain pills from the table and fell fast asleep.

The room was dark when I felt my arm being shaken. I opened my eyes and saw Sara staring down at me in her crisp white nurses uniform. "How are you doing sweetheart? I brought you some dinner from the club and some more pain pills. These are Vicoden. They should really knock the shit out of you."

As Sara started to open the bag and put the containers of food on my bedside table she slowly shook her head and said, "I know you're in some kind of serious trouble. You can't stay here forever. What's your plan?"

"Look Sara," I replied. "I'm working on it right now. I'll be out of here in 48 hours, I promise."

"Okay, sweetheart," she replied. "You're so beat-up we can't even sex."

"Sorry," I said. "I'll try not to get in your way." The next day I slept most of the morning and then waited for the rest of the afternoon until the agreed-upon time to call Larry. Within a couple of rings Larry answered and immediately started telling me about his meeting with the General that had taken place just a few hours before.

The General had conducted his own investigation of the alley fight. He had talked to Mieko and confirmed my story that her boyfriend had been stalking us. The last time she saw me was when I had excused myself to use the restroom.

Unfortunately, the General went on to say there could still be a trial. The Korean Army was pressing charges of attempted murder. There would be a lot of publicity. It wasn't every day that an American businessman tried to kill a Korean Army officer. Larry added that the General wanted the military serial number from my I.D. card. I was to call him at his office at exactly four p.m. the following day.

It was with sweaty hands and crossed fingers that I called the General at his office at the appointed time. After three rings the deep, gruff voice of the General roared, "Hello."

"This is John," I replied. "Calling as instructed."

"Well," said the General, "you sure have got yourself in some deep shit. Did you plan this or are you just stupid?"

"Sorry, General," I replied, "I had no idea I was dealing with a crazed boyfriend."

"Why not?" replied the General. "I told you not to see that girl, Mieko."

"Yes, I replied, "I should have listened to you."

"Okay, stupid," retorted the General. "I know what happened. That asshole waited for you to go to the bathroom and then he jumped you. The problem is that the Korean Army legal people believe him. I couldn't persuade them to drop the case. They want a trial and that would not be good for the American Chamber or me. If it weren't for that I would let them have your ass. So I'm going to get your butt out of Korea.

"Army intelligence in Seoul will cut you orders for Thailand. We'll have your driver deliver them to you within the next 24 hours. By the way, I ran your serial number. You still have two years left on your Army Reserve commitment. In fact, you are supposed to be reporting back to that Reserve unit in California next month. What the hell are you going to do about that?"

"Oh, right," I replied, "I'm trying to get an extension on that reporting date.

"Bullshit!" roared the General. "You're just a fuckup. Okay, tell you what. I'll get you out of Korea and out of that Reserve unit. According to the Army your country of residence is Singapore. Is that right?"

"Yes," I replied. "My apartment address is 43 Lewis Road, Singapore. However, I haven't been there for a couple of months. My neighbor picks up my mail."

"Okay, here the deal. As soon as you get to Thailand I want you to call Al Steber. His phone number will be with your military orders. Al runs an import/export trading company and will help you get settled in and assist in starting up the courier company. Al has a lot of contacts."

"General," I replied in an agitated voice, "perhaps you don't understand. I appreciate your help, but I have my own contacts and plans for starting the courier service in Thailand."

"No boy," replied the General, "You're the one that doesn't understand. You work for me now."

Chapter 13 An Evening at Sophie's Massage Parlor

*T*he steady drone of the turboprop engines of the U.S. Air Force C-130 slowly dissipated as the huge cargo plane began circling and descending for its final approach into Korat Air Force Base, Thailand. I had made it. I had escaped from Korea and I knew I would never go back.

Official orders were gold; if they said to kill the Pope the goddamn Army would give you a jeep and drive you there. Getting out had been a piece of cake. I had military orders that said I was heading for R & R in Thailand and was not required to be in uniform. I just hung around the Osan Air Force Base passenger terminal and got on the first departing flight for Thailand.

But I wasn't used to this type of travel. I rode in a military plane with fold-down canvas seats on each side of the fuselage and tons of cargo strapped to pallets running down the middle of the entire aircraft. There was no noise insulation. As I rested my head against the aircraft's thin aluminum skin, the engine noise and vibrations numbed the brain.

Closing my eyes, I could hardly believe what had happened to me. I felt like a candle in the wind, completely at the mercy of events and circumstances in which I could not predict or influence the outcome. I had no control over anything.

My best intentions and actions had nearly cost me my life and freedom. Somehow, someway I would never again be that vulnerable. Korea would be just a memory of a dumb kid doing stupid things.

I had only one regret, that I might not ever see Mieko again. I had real feelings for her and believed that she trusted and cared about me. I guess we never get to choose the people we love. It just happens.

As for Sara, she brought out the worst in me. We both used each other for our own selfish needs. I didn't even give her a kiss good-bye. I just left her a little thank you note on the kitchen table. I was sure she would not miss me or my problems.

Suddenly the aircraft turned abruptly and the flaps and landing gear made grinding noises preparing for our landing into Korat Air Force Base. Looking out the small porthole windows at the lush green countryside of Thailand with its tiny canals intersecting a few scattered farmhouses, I wondered what lay ahead of me in this strange country I had never visited.

As the aircraft landed and started its slow taxi to its parking place on the tarmac, I searched my pockets for my passport. It suddenly hit me. I didn't need a passport. Active duty military personnel only carried an I.D. card and orders. Passports were prohibited items as they could be used by G.I.s to go AWOL and leave the country.

There would be no immigration or Customs. I would simply walk off the airplane. As soon as the aircraft parked and the engines were turned off, the huge back doors of the plane opened up. Almost immediately I felt the rush of intense heat and humidity washing over me. It felt like a huge rogue wave that smacked my body from head to toe and left me breathless and disoriented.

How in the hell did people live here? As soon as I stepped off the plane onto the tarmac, the ground crew directed me to a small air-conditioned terminal building about fifty yards away. By the time I entered the building with my suitcase in hand I was covered in sweat and totally dehydrated.

A sergeant standing in the main terminal gave out packets that contained information on base facilities, bus and taxi fares, and various approved and recommended hotels in Bangkok. As I spied the numerous telephones on the wall I debated if I should call Al as the General instructed, or just take a taxi into Bangkok.

As I reached into my packet of orders for Al's number I knew if I didn't call him either he or one of the General's people would track me down. I might as well get it over with and see what the guy wanted. I placed the call from a payphone and after a couple of rings, a deep voice answered.

Al told me he was expecting my call. He would pick me up in an hour at the visitor's parking lot next to the main gate. He would be in an old tan Toyota station wagon with shaded windows. After figuring out the base transit schedule, I seated myself under the overhang of the bus stop in the visitor's parking lot. It was hot and I was still sweating, even in the shade.

After about 45 minutes, I spotted an old tan Toyota station wagon slowly turning into the visitor's parking lot, stopping within a few feet of my rest area. The rear window slid down, a huge white arm stretched out, and a voice said, "I'm Al. Welcome to Thailand. You'll love it here."

"Thanks Al," I replied. "If I don't sweat to death first."

"You'll get used to it," laughed Al. "Everyone feels that way when he first gets here."

As I threw my bag in the back of the station wagon and slid into the rear seat I came face-to-face with a smiling Al Stebe, a man in his mid 40's, dressed in shorts and Hawaiian shirt. Tanned and clean-shaven with a crew cut, Al's body looked like he worked out in the gym everyday. The guy had not one ounce of fat. He looked like a recruiting poster for the U.S. Marine Corp. Al muttered something to his driver in Thai; he immediately made a U-turn, and within a few minutes we were on the main highway to Bangkok, about an hour away. With the air-conditioning in the car beating a steady drone, Al told me the General had called him the day before and filled him in on my situation in Korea.

"Don't worry," said Al. "that's all behind you now. The Koreans won't pursue extradition. They have been told this is a security matter. It has all been swept under the rug. It never happened. Isn't that right?"

"Yes, it never happened," I quickly replied.

"Great," beamed Al. "Nothing like a fresh start. I booked you at the Montien Hotel; it's just down the street from one of Bangkok's little red light districts, called Patpong. From what I hear about you, you'll love it there. All the expats hang out there, especially Americans. Patpong has the best bars, nightlife and the prettiest massage girls in Bangkok; it's like Disneyland for horny American hound dogs.

After about an hour of high-speed maneuvering through a gauntlet of overweight beat-up trucks on the main highway we came to a complete stop as we entered the city limits of Bangkok. The traffic was a nightmare; there were cars, motorcycles, buses, trucks, three-wheeled pedicabs, and pedestrians all jammed into narrow roads, honking, and no one going anywhere. It was hot, humid and the brown haze of smog and smell of exhaust hung everywhere in the calm air.

I turned to Al and said, "This really sucks. Is it always like this?"

"Yeah," he replied, "and this isn't even rush hour. We need to do something about this traffic. Of course, we say that every year."

After about an hour and half we finally inched our way to the Montien Hotel. As soon as the car stopped we were greeted by the uniformed doorman and led into the reception area. The place was small, modeled after a Parisian first class hotel, with architecture and furnishing very similar to what you would find in Europe.

After checking in Al led me to the hotel bar with its long teakwood tables and indoor garden. He ordered a Coke and I asked for my usual, double vodka seven. As the drinks were placed on the small teakwood table. Al started talking about how he could help me start up the courier service in Thailand. I wasn't paying attention and after a few minutes I rudely interrupted him with the question, "Can I make a long distance call from my room to Korea?"

"Yeah, sure," said Al, "the operator will place the call and then call you back when a line is open, usually in 10-15 minutes. Who do you want to call in Korea?"

"Oh, just someone," I replied.

Al looked at me and with a serious face asked, "Is it the girl named Mieko?"

"Yeah," I replied. "how did you know that?"

Al replied, "The General told me about her. Look, boy, you better have another drink. She won't be there and she will never be there."

"What in the hell are you talking about?" I yelled. "I can reach her at the bank this afternoon and if I miss her there I'll call her at her apartment. Now that I'm out of Korea they can't trace the call."

"Look boy," Al insisted, "she won't be there. She's a KCIA agent; her job was to find out what you guys were really up to in Korea. There is no Mieko, you bonehead, that was her cover." She doesn't exist anymore. Go ahead and try. Call her, but she's gone boy. Time to move on."

As I looked at Al I could hardly understand what he was saying. And as it slowly sunk in it was like a dagger had been thrust into my heart. I felt like there was no air in the room and my mind and all my senses had been suspended in time. Mieko, my beautiful Mieko, the woman I had trusted and confided in, the woman I had made meaningful love to, the restaurants, the good times, I just couldn't believe she had been working me the whole time.

"What the hell," I stammered, "did the general set me up? Was he behind the whole deal? Hell, I even went to him to verify that Mieko worked for the bank and was not a KCIA agent. Besides, it doesn't make any sense, if the General did set me up why would he tell me to stay away from her?"

Al smiled, put his drink on the table and said, "Because he knew if he told you that you would continue to see her, he told me you were a hard head."

"Look Kid, what did you expect would happen? You guys came out of nowhere, some little courier service named DHL after three guys no one ever heard of, hell for a while we thought you guys were part of us. Then by sheer chance a Korean Customs officer found a blueprint of a tunnel under the DMZ. The KCIA, CIA and all the intelligence guys went nuts."

"Okay then," I replied, "why didn't they arrest us at the airport?"

"Because," said Al, "they wanted to see who your contacts were, what were you up to, you know, like following dope dealers."

"Yeah, you're right. The first letter that Ken got from his girlfriend in Tokyo had a razor slit on the envelope. They had removed the letter, read the contents, then put it back in the envelope."

"That's right," laughed Al, "they do that to their own people as well."

"Anyhow," continued Al, "the KCIA then decided to send the chicks into the Tower Hotel and you caught them in the act going through your desk. So then they got pissed and decided to send in one of their pros, it was your Mieko. Problem was she had a jealous boyfriend who went nuts when he found out you had sex with his girlfriend.

"He was an ROK intelligence guy but he was not supposed to have access to the case or even know anything about it. He had several buddies who were assigned to the case and got access to the wire taps on Mieko's apartment and heard every detail of your sexual escapade and a week later where you were going to take her to dinner. So he decided he would show up at the restaurant and rough you up a bit."

As Al started to continue, I interrupted and said, "So when Mieko saw him in the restaurant, she was really scared, I thought so, she couldn't have faked the fear I saw in her eyes. But what did she mean when she said, 'It shouldn't have happened.' Was that the wiretap?"

"Must have been," said Al. "Sounds like the KCIA was not supposed to bug her place, at least not the bedroom. I would never trust Koreans. The boyfriend is a nut case, he lost it. When he saw you head for the bathroom in the basement he ambushed you, but he didn't count on you almost killing him. The KCIA took care of him, they're pissed he screwed up the case, that's why they are willing to forget the whole deal, provided of course you never set foot in Korea again."

"Al, I have one more question. If Mieko was KCIA, why was she always asking me to get her out of the country?"

Al laughed, "Hell boy, she was trying to find out if you had any foreign embassy or consulate contacts that could get her a passport, that would have showed you had some real connections, say coming up with a Libyan passport or some other weird shit would have definitely freaked out the KCIA."

"So Al," I interjected. "are we clean? Have we passed your loyalty test?"

"Yeah," replied Al, "we checked out everyone of you guys, even got Interpol involved. We had a little concern that your Hong Kong manager had some ties to the commies on the mainland but it turned out to be nothing serious. Yeah, you guys are clean. You're too stupid to be anything else. I'll tell you something else kid, if it makes any difference now, the pro, Mieko, she really liked you boy."

"I'll tell you what Al," I exclaimed, "some how, some way, I don't know when, I will see her again."

Al threw back his head and laughed, "Boy, the most beautiful women in the world are in Thailand. I know. I married one. You'll forget her in 48 hours."

"Okay, okay," Al, I responded, "so what do you and the General want from me now? You guys never doing anything for free."

"Well," said Al, "let's not make this complicated. Once you have the courier service in operation and if we need some information or access to the document pouches of someone we are interested in then I'm sure you can arrange it."

"Oh," I replied, "like the deal we made with the General."

"Yeah," said Al, "the same thing."

"Okay," I said, "it looks like we have no choice, but there are two conditions. One, only Larry and I are your contacts, we are the only people you can talk to about this. Two, I don't want you or your guys snooping around my operation, you come to me first."

"Don't worry," said Al, "as far as your concerned I'm just a small trading company trying to make a meager living in crazy Thailand, you won't hear from me again unless I or the General want something."

With that Al stood up and with his infectious smile held out his hand and pronounced, "Welcome to Thailand partner." He finished his Coke, turned abruptly, and walked out the barroom door.

As I sat back in my chair and finished off my last double vodka tonic I thought to myself, "These people! All of them are bastards. I can't trust any of them. Never again will I be conned or used like I was in Korea, I am going to survive out here by being the biggest, baddest SOB of them all."

As I slowly open my eyes a bright ray of sunlight streamed in from the large bay window and hit me squarely in the face. I just lay in the bed staring at the partially opened French curtains and wondering what my life was going to be like in this place called Thailand.

The previous day had been a long one, the flight from Korea and my meeting with Al had left me physically and mentally exhausted, as soon as I had unpacked my suitcase I fell asleep. I glanced at the clock on the dresser; it was almost 10 a.m. I had slept some 14 hours.

As I slowly rose from the bed there was a faint knock on the door and when I opened it standing before me was a young skinny Thai boy dressed in a crisp white uniform with gold buttons and smiling from ear to ear as he said, "Sir, my name is Billy, your floor boy at your service. Just tell me what you want, I can get you anything, can I get your breakfast sir?"

"No thanks," I replied. "Did you say you could get me anything?"

"Yes sir, replied the boy," my job is to make sure all the guest on my floor are properly taken care of. Please call me anytime. I have a small room at the end of the hall.

"Thanks," I replied, "but I plan on having breakfast downstairs." With that Billy saluted and promptly closed the door.

As I started to get dressed I realized my first order of business was to call Po in Hong Kong and get some money. Even though I had several company credit cards most transactions in Asia were still strictly cash and besides I needed to get the names and contact numbers of our prospective business partners the company had been corresponding with for the last six months in anticipation of opening up the courier service in Bangkok.

I placed the call with the hotel operator and in about fifteen minutes as I was about to shave the phone rang and I heard the familiar voice of Po who started the conversation by pronouncing he was glad I was still alive. I told Po I needed him to deposit $25,000 in my Hong Kong Shanghai bank account. Without hesitation he said it would be done by the end of the day.

As I started to talk about the plan to open Bangkok, Po interrupted me and asked, "Guess who I ran into the other day at a chamber function?"

"Have no idea," I replied.

"Shit," said Po. "did you forget already? I saw Jenny. Remember Jenny? She asked about you."

My mind went blank. Jenny. Yes, I remembered. It seemed like a million years ago, another world, so much had happened in such a few short months. Po reported that she had broken up with her fiancé and had given him her number for me to call her. Po then rattled off the number and ended by saying, "Are you going to call her?"

"I don't know, Po," I replied. As I started to think about it I realized that this woman Jenny and I, we lived in different worlds, it was as if I didn't know her anymore. At first I couldn't even remember what she looked like.

Po brought me back from my thoughts as he started to talk about the three best business prospects for the next thirty minutes and we ended the call by agreeing I would call once a week with a progress report.

As I returned to my shaving I thought about the three prospects and decided I would try and contact them over the weekend and set up interviews starting on Monday. These guys had no idea what they could be in for. The courier service operated on the fringes of the law. The transportation of any written correspondence in most parts of the world was the sole monopoly of the postal services; most called it the private express act, which forbid the private carriage of letters.

We got around that by simply declaring that we did not carry letters, that any correspondence we carried were "company documents" and consisted of items such as canceled checks, credit card receipts, ship's manifest, and bills of lading. The Hong Kong government had taken issue with our interpretation and had shut us down, only to have Hong Kong businesses rally to our support and change the law.

Bangkok would be no piece of cake, but the service was desperately needed by the banks and shipping companies who had been pestering us for the last several months to open it up. We could get documents delivered overnight from Hong Kong and within 24 hours to and from the U.S. The best the Thai Post Office could do would be three to four days from Hong Kong and a week or more from the U.S. if the documents got there at all.

The Thai postmen had a habit of peeling off the stamps and selling them on the black market. Just like we had done in several Asia countries before, our plan of action was simple. First we would run actual couriers on the airplanes and our guys on the ground would convince Customs to meet them in immigration and recover the big green bags containing the document pouches.

We would clear Customs in the baggage area and then load the bags directly on to the curbside vans and then depart to Bangkok City. The individual pouches would be separated by address in the back of the van on the way to the first delivery.

Our first customers would be the U.S. banks and shipping companies. The first two were always Bank of America and Sealand. After that the word would spread fast and all the other banks and foreign companies would call us to start the service, A conservative estimate of profitability was 300 to 500 percent.

The next and very important part of the start-up was to get as many large Thai banks and government agencies to use the service. We would give them huge discounts to use us as these customers were our best defense against the postal authorities who at some point would always try to shut us down.

In the Hong Kong case when the Customs and postal authorities seized our shipments, the first pouches they pulled out of the shipping bags were there own Ministry of Public Works who were using the courier service to ship blueprints of the new Hong Kong airport to and from an architectural firm in the U.S.

The person who would be our partner in Thailand had to have a legal company that could operate a ground transportation service. But most important they had to be a renegade like the rest of us, a bit crazy, and willing to take some risks, we wouldn't ask permission to do things, we would do it and then deal with the aftermath and consequences later.

Sane, normal people wouldn't touch this, I needed another character, and I couldn't wait to meet my three business prospects.

As I finished shaving it was almost noon, too late for breakfast, so I decided to check out the pool and have lunch at the poolside grill. As I got off the elevator and stepped out into the sun I felt the rush of hot air like the door of blast furnace had opened. It was May and one of the hottest months of the Thai dry season.

I found a table underneath a huge umbrella that created a cool shaded area and as I settled back in the chair I noticed a short fat bald white guy in a pure white suit and tie approaching me with a beaming smile. He held out his hand and in a squeaky high pitched voice with a thick French accent said, "Welcome, Mr. Fischer. I am Pierre Defronti, the manager and concierge of this fine hotel. I understand you will be with us for a few weeks. If there is anything I can do, anything you need, please let me know."

"Thank you," I replied, "is it always this hot? I was thinking of taking a walk through the Patpong District this afternoon."

Pierre shook his head and muttered, "No, no my friend. This is the dry, hot season. Only mad dogs and Englishmen go out in this heat. I suggest you relax by the pool today. Toward evening it will cool off and that's when Patpong starts to come alive, especially on the weekends."

"Thanks, Pierre." I replied. "Tell me about Patpong. Are there any good restaurants and nightclubs? Or is it just a bunch a crappy bars and whorehouses?"

"Oh no," exclaimed Pierre, as he threw up his hands, "you can find anything you want in Patpong. It has some sleazy bars but also some very nice nightclubs with good entertainment and some really good restaurants."

"Okay, Pierre, give me some recommendations. I want to eat dinner around seven or eight, then check out a nightclub with some good entertainment and then have a nice relaxing massage with a beautiful Thai girl. How about it?"

"Okay," said Pierre, "for dinner go to Beppi's. It's a very nice German Swiss restaurant. I know the owner Beppi Foster. The place is straight down Patpong about eight blocks. Then hit the Horny Toad Bar and Grill. It has good live rock bands every Friday and Saturday nights. Lots of tourist and Americans hang out there."

Pierre smiled and said, "You will like those places?"

"Well" I replied, "what about the massage place?"

"Oh, Mr. Fischer," Pierre said in a low apologetic voice, "the hotel cannot recommend these types of establishments." He stammered, "I have heard that if a man wanted a classy and sophisticated experience and were willing to pay a little more, he would stop by Sophie's. It's just down the street from Beppi's."

With a smile and a wink, Pierre patted me on the back and said, "You'll love Patpong. I have lived here for eight years and I still love it." He turned away and headed for the elevator.

As I sat back and took a long gulp of my cold Amrit beer I thought, "I can't wait to experience my first night in Sodom and Gomorrah. It was about 8 p.m. and it was just starting to get dark as I walked out of the hotel into the cool evening air. The hotel doorman in his crisp white uniform spotted me and introduced himself as Steven and asked me if I wanted a cab.

"No, thanks, Steven," I replied. "but, perhaps you can tell me where I could get a good massage tonight."

"Oh, no problem, sir. The best place in all Bangkok is just down the street. It's called Roma's. Just give them my card and they will take good care of you."

"Thanks Steven," I said, placing his card in pocket. I thought, "Whenever there was a scam or kickback at a hotel, the doorman was always in on it."

As I started to leave the hotel's circular drive and enter the main street I could see several guys on each side of the entrance. These had to be the local hustlers that could be found all over Asia at the hotels where foreigners stayed. They were especially aggressive with Americans and Japanese men and would try and sell you everything from changing money, to fake watches, drugs, and any type of sex imaginable.

As I stepped into the street the first guy on my left approached me and in a low voice whispered, "Sir, want to see live sex show, two girls, one guy, beautiful young girls? Sir, only 1500 baht, fifty dollars."

"No thanks," I replied. Then the guy on my right came over to me and in a low voice said,

"Sir, you like to have sex with young girl, very young girl, or you want young boy, I have boys and girls."

"No thanks," I replied.

"Okay, okay," replied the guy, "I have lady boy. You want lady boy? Come with me I show you, not far from here."

By now I had three guys around as I suddenly stopped, turned around, and said, "Fuck off, I don't anything from you guys tonight, leave me alone."

With that they all turned around and headed back to the hotel entrance to wait for their next victim. I never really took offense at these guys. They were just trying to make a living like everyone else in this town but going anywhere could be a risk and result in a strong-arm robbery. I always had that in the back of mind when I went out on the town in Asia, my wallet, passport and watch was always hidden somewhere in my hotel room. I only took enough money for the evening and if I got rolled or my pockets were picked that's all I would lose.

The truth was sex in Thailand was an important part of the economy, even the government admitted there were over two million people employed in the sex trade. The Europeans came in by the planeload and the American G.I.s, especially those that were not married came by the hundreds for their R & R leaves from Vietnam.

The Thais accommodated everyone, there was nothing that was too weird or kinky, there was no stigma or discrimination with gays and most Thais believe that sex with anyone should be a pleasurable experience, like a good meal or a day a the beach, a refreshing change from the uptight morals of Western cultures.

As I walked down the crowed streets of Patpong, the hustlers and bar barkers were everywhere, just like in Hong Kong trying to get men to buy a drink or a girl for the night. I finally spotted Beppi's restaurant and as I walked in the door the coolness of the air conditioning was a welcome relief. The place was nice, clean, and decorated with Swiss and German paintings. The meal was excellent and as I sipped my after dinner coffee I looked up at the clock and was surprised to see it was after 10 p.m. and time for my next adventure.

A few blocks from the restaurant I spotted a large lit up golden Eiffel Tower, with the word, "Sophie's" underneath, right where Pierre said it would be. As I approached the place I could see the front of the building had no windows and was made of some type of large brown stone and had a circular drive where taxis and cars could dislodge their passengers directly into the huge front doors.

Leading up to the entrance was a large red carpet and as I approached, the huge doors magically opened and a smiling heavyset Thai in a white suit and red tie proudly greeted me. "Welcome Sir, my name is Frankie. Welcome to Sophie's. We have the most beautiful girls in all of Thailand.

Please come take a look." Frankie gently put his hand on my shoulder and led me through a second door, stopped, held out his hands, and said, "Look, aren't they all beautiful? My little kittens."

I was speechless and just stood there stunned, not moving and staring. In front of me was a huge window, 25 or 30 feet in length and at least 15 feet high. Behind the window were three platforms, each one elevated a few feet higher than the one below, and covered with a thick red carpet. On the platforms, seated very close together were young Thai women, each wearing identical low cut maroon evening dresses. A large white disk with a number on it pinned to each one's garment on her left shoulder. Every row had about 15 women, a total of 45.

The women were all beautiful and as I continued to stand motionless I heard the low whisper of Frankie in my ear saying, "Which one would you like? They will all please you. Or maybe you want two; I will give you a good deal on two."

"Frankie," I replied, "how long do I get?"

He laughed and said, "An hour, but you young guys can't last that long with my girls."

"Yeah, sure," I said, "that will be the day. I can wear any of them out." I like women with a big ass and big tits. They're all sitting down, wearing the same dresses, and I can't really see them."

"Oh, no problem," said Frankie. He turned around in the dimly lit room, shouted something in Thai to a fellow that was standing at a podium with a microphone, who then barked something in Thai to the girls on the stage. Immediately two girls stood up, smiled stuck out their chests, then turned around, pulled up their dresses, bent over and touched their toes.

"See," proclaimed Frankie, "they have nice tits and big asses. I will give you both numbers 33 and 14 for 4000 baht."

"Bullshit," I replied, "that's $132.00 U.S. and I have never paid over a hundred in my life. Tell you what, I don't how good these girls really are, I'll give you 3000 baht for number 14 or I'll go down to Roma's, the place my doorman at the Montien recommended."

"Okay," said Frankie as he yelled something to the guy at the podium who yelled something into the microphone. Number 14 got up and headed for a side exit door. After I gave Frankie the money out of nowhere stepped a young Thai fellow with an armful of towels that grabbed my arm and led me down a hallway lined with rooms on each side and after depositing the towels and me in one of the rooms quietly bowed and left.

This place was not the usual whorehouse; the room was large and was divided into two almost equal sections. On the far side opposite the door the area was completely covered with light blue tile. A foam mat with holes in it to drain the water was in a shallow tub and directly overhead was a showerhead with a hose and spraying attachment. The entire tub area was lined with various oils, shampoos, and lotions. The other half of the dimly lit room had a thick red carpet covering the floor with a double bed and huge mirrors lining the walls and ceiling, a large ceiling fan was positioned in the center of the room and made a noticeable swishing sound every few seconds.

Suddenly the door opened and in stepped Number 14 who announced that her name was Sonja and she would take care of me. She was young, beautiful, wore little makeup, had fine facial features, and a short cut hairstyle. As I started to say something in English she walked over to me and put her finger on my mouth and said, "Speak little English. I take care of you," and she proceeded to take off all the clothing that covered my body and then gently and thoughtfully placed my trousers and shirt on a hanger. In several quick motions she took off her dress, panties, and bra, stood back and looked me over from head to toe and announced, "Big Boy," and put her thumbs up.

She then led me over to the shallow tub and sat me down on the edge, grabbed my penis at the base and then squeezed tightly as she rotated it up and down and with a serious look bent over and examined the tip, after a few seconds announced, "Good," and another thumbs up. This girl may be young but she was all business when it came to a V.D. exam.

Smiling, Sonja then led me over to the partially submerged foam mat and motioned me to lie on my stomach as she turned on the shower attachment and poured liquid soap all over my body.

With a soft sponge she gently washed me everywhere continually pouring the oily liquid on my back and legs and spending considerable time thoroughly washing and cleaning between my legs. The warm water, lotions and massage strokes with the sponge totally relaxed me as I drifted off to mindless oblivion.

I had lost track of time when I felt Sonja tap me on my shoulder and motioned for me to turn over on my back. Smiling, she commenced to thoroughly clean my front as she had done my back and as I started to get aroused she poured even more liquid on me and began to stroke faster, and then she climbed on top of me and with the warm water and soapy liquid between us slid rapidly up and down my body only stopping momentarily to kiss me as her face came close to mine.

I closed my eyes. God this was good and I'm going to do this every night. Sonja kept sliding on top of me for the next ten minutes then stood up and motioned for me to stand up as she turned on the shower and thoroughly rinsed us both off. She than took me over to the bed, placed me on my back, and thoroughly devoured me for the next five minutes and when she stopped, sat up in the bed, and pointing with her thumbs up, proclaimed "Big Boy." Reaching over to a small cabinet by the bed she carefully unfolded a condom and completely covered my erection as she climbed on me and began a slow pelvic thrusting motion and then systemically increased the intensity.

I was helpless; she owned my body and soul. I had no control over anything as the wave of climatic pleasure overwhelmed me and drained every ounce of strength and energy from my body. As I lay exhausted on the bed, I looked over at the small clock next to me. Shit! Frankie was right. I hadn't even lasted an hour.

Chapter 14 Stan's the Man

*T*he loud ring of the travel alarm woke me from a deep sleep at the Montien Hotel. Monday morning had arrived. Before getting up, I lay motionless in bed for a few minutes. I couldn't help but mentally replay my first weekend in Bangkok. "Fantastic," I thought to myself.

Pierre had it right. His recommendation of dinner at Beppi's followed by a massage at Sophie's had been the highlight of my weekend. The next evening I ate at a Japanese restaurant and then tried out the massage parlor called Roma's, the place recommended by Steven, the hotel doorman. Both the food and sex were disappointing and overpriced. The girls at Roma's weren't nearly as good looking as the one's at Sophie's. Once you paid, the aim was getting you out the door as fast as possible.

On Sunday I rested. Sitting by the hotel pool, I contacted three prospective business partners and set up meetings starting on Monday.

At exactly 12 noon on Monday, my first prospective partner, Richard Brewster, walked into the hotel bar and introduced himself. Richard was in his early 40's, good-looking, tall, with blond wavy hair. He wore a white shirt, a sport coat and dress trousers.

Richard said he had lived in Thailand for the last ten years, married a local Thai girl, and built up a successful moving and storage business that was jointly owned by himself and his wife. He said he handled mostly American companies that were relocating their executives into and out of Thailand.

I spent the next twenty minutes explaining the courier service and how successful we had been throughout Asia. When I finished, Richard sat back in his chair, put his hand on his chin, and announced, "In order for us to do any business in Thailand, I want a minimum of fifty percent ownership."

Taken back by his comment, I replied, "Really? Perhaps you misunderstood my company's previous correspondence. I am not here to offer any ownership. What we want is a legal company who can operate a delivery service for our courier business. We will offer a service contract that will pay you very well for each pickup and delivery in Bangkok and the surrounding areas."

After a few minutes of silence, Richard leaned forward in his chair and said, "If I don't get part of the action, then it's no deal."

"Okay," I replied, "then it's no deal." I stood, extended my hand and said, "Richard, thank you for your time."

He looked surprised. As we shook hands, he asked, "Don't you want to negotiate this?"

"It's not negotiable," I replied. "Good day." That's one arrogant S.O.B. I thought as I watched Richard leave the room. I can't stand people like him.

After lunch at the hotel my next prospect showed up forty minutes late and introduced himself as Frank Middleton. After apologizing for being late and blaming it on the infamous Bangkok traffic Frank went on to say he was the local manager for Flying Tiger Cargo Airlines and had been in the country for a little over four years. Frank was an American in his early 40's, tall and thin with long wavy brown hair, dressed in jeans, and an open collar sports shirt.

Frank said his time with the Flying Tigers would make him uniquely qualified to run the courier service in Thailand. He indicated that he could obtain ramp passes and access to all the carriers. Frank had recently married a local woman and wanted to stay in Thailand for many years and start his own business.

I explained that we were interested in signing a service contract for delivery services, but we would not directly invest in any equipment or facilities. Frank said he could subcontract out the deliveries and would have no problem in acquiring warehouse space close by the airport. He told me he was very excited to have this opportunity and would look forward to building a successful business in Thailand as he planned to make it his permanent home so he could pursue his mission.

"Mission?" I asked. "What are you talking about?"

Frank leaned over the small teakwood table and in a low voice whispered, "I do God's work."

"Oh," I replied. "What is that?"

"Well," said Frank, "just look around you. This town is Sodom and Gomorrah. These people are sinners. They have no morals whatsoever."

"Oh," I replied, "I thought they were Buddhist."

"Yes, you're right," screamed Frank. "They are anti Christ. My mission is to turn these ignorant, helpless people into children of Christ our savior."

As I stood up I held out my hand and announced, "Frank, this is not going to work."

Frank stood there, dumbfounded. He begged, "Can't we talk about it?"

"No Frank," I replied. "I can't stand religious fanatics much less work with them. Besides, from what I've seen, the Thais are wonderful people. Good-bye Frank."

As I watched Frank leave I ordered another double vodka tonic and thought to myself, "Two down and one left. If the four p.m. guy is no good, I'll have to dig out my own prospects." It was five p.m. when my last appointment showed up and introduced himself as Stan Giddings. He apologized for being late.

Everything about Stan told me he must be an interesting character. He was in his mid 50's and overweight with his belly hanging over his belt. Sweat beaded on his balding head and trickled down into his two-day old beard. He wore a wrinkled shirt with the last three buttons undone and pants that looked like they could stand up by themselves.

Stan immediately signaled to the bartender for an Amrit beer. He pulled out a Camel cigarette from the food-stained pocket on his shirt and with one motion lit the cigarette with his Zippo lighter. He promptly announced, "Nice to meet you. I expected an older guy."

"Well, thanks, Stan," I replied. "I'm sorry to disappoint you. Maybe I should just come back in ten years."

"No offense intended," smiled Stan. "It's just that you don't see many business guys in Asia in their 20's."

"I've noticed that. And all you old fuckers are married to young, good-looking Thai women. So, what's the deal? Are they that hard up?"

"Hell," laughed Stan. "It's a good deal for both of us. Where else are we going to find a young, good-looking piece of ass like that and ones willing to marry us? Besides, most of us started businesses in Thailand and as foreigners we're not allow to own a Thai company. So we put it in the old lady's name, keep a tight lid on the books, and live happily ever after."

"What do the women get out of the deal?" I asked.

"They do all right," replied Stan. "Most of us keep our U.S. citizenship. Thailand recognizes duals so the women become U.S. citizens. Most of these gals didn't have shit when we met them. Now they have big houses, cars, and servants. The whole deal. They love it."

Stan spoke at length about how he had been in the country for the last fifteen years. He had married a local Thai and had two teenage kids. He had built up a successful freight forwarding business that would complement the courier service. He had contracts with the U.S. State Department to move airfreight to U.S. embassies and consulates throughout Southeast Asia.

Stan's company, Giddings Associates, had a number of trucks and vans and could deliver documents throughout the Bangkok area. Stan had done some checking into the courier company and found out how successful we had been in such a short time. He definitely wanted to work with us in Thailand. I asked Stan if he had any other business interest in Thailand and he assured me he didn't. His wife, however, was the manager and part owner of a restaurant.

I explained to Stan that we had been successful elsewhere in Asia and we were opening up Bangkok at the request of several key customers. As in other countries we expected Customs officials to be suspicious at first. They had no concept of documents having any real value and could not understand the care and urgency in which we operated our business.

We would have to go out of our way to convince the airline personnel as well as Customs and the airport police that we were legit, not smuggling anything or pulling some crap on them. Our transit operation in Hong Kong would thoroughly check every pouch carried on the first flights into Bangkok.

As Stan ordered his second beer, I looked at him and asked, "Are you willing to deal with that?"

Stan took a long gulp and then a hit off his cigarette, "No problem, as long as it doesn't risk my current business."

Looking at Stan I thought to myself, this guy is a slob, but I like him. He's a no bullshit kind of guy and besides he has people and vehicles to do the job. "Okay, Stan," I replied. In that case I'll write up a monthly service agreement. If things don't work out, we can each go our own way."

Stan held out his hand and said, "Agreed. Let's meet at my wife's place tomorrow at noon and go over all the details."

"Where's that?" I replied. "Oh," said Stan, "down the street, here in Patpong, the Horny Toad Bar and Grill."

It was almost 12 noon the next day when I stepped out of the hotel into the blazing sun. The blast of hot air smacked me square in the face, almost stopping me in my tracks. This was Thailand in the dry season; soon the monsoon would arrive and drench everything for months.

After walking several blocks and sweating from head to toe I spotted the Horny Toad Bar and Grill. You couldn't miss it. Above the entrance the top of the building held a huge green toad sitting on a lily pad with a monstrous red glowing tongue that stretched out several feet from its open mouth.

As soon as I opened the double teak doors, I felt the refreshing rush of cool air sweeping over my entire body. The place was nice; on the left side of the entrance way was a teakwood bar about twenty feet long with bar stools neatly lined up. Behind the bar was a huge mirror with bottles of premium liquor sorted by brand.

Directly across from the bar were several rows of tables with three or four chairs each and lining the walls on both sides and in the dimly lit rear of the room were circular booths with tables surrounded by overstuffed red leather couches. Walking toward the bar I heard my name called and looking around, I spotted Stan standing up and waving from one of the booths.

As soon as I sat down Stan raised two fingers to the young female Thai bartender who just nodded and then immediately brought over two cold Amrit beers. "By the way," said Stan, "I should warn you. These aren't Buds; they're 25% alcohol."

"Don't worry, Stan," I replied, "I can drink you old fuckers under the table."

Stan laughed as he said, "We'll see about that." We got right to work plotting out the possible morning delivery and pickup routes with my list of committed customers. We discussed flight arrival times and the airport operations. When we finally agreed on the fees per stop and a per hour compensation for the airport operations, I filled in the numbers on the agreement and gave it to Stan for his signature.

While Stan read the final agreement I looked around the place and realized it had suddenly filled up with customers. The bar was almost full of old white guys. Other customers had moved to the tables where they were ordering food off the menu.

Stan looked over at me and proclaimed, "Best damn burgers in Thailand. Right here--real American beef, not the local crap."

"Yeah, they must be good," I replied. This place really got crowded fast. Is it always like this?"

"We're this busy everyday at lunch during the week." said Stan. "Those guys at the bar, they're all Americans working around here. We call them the nooner bunch. They all know each other, talk about sports back home, American baseball, football, lots of bullshit."

"Stan, this place is a gold mine. Why are you working at all?" I asked.

He answered, "My wife and I are part owners of the place. We have a silent partner. She manages the place and I stay out of the business. She even makes me run a tab that has to be paid in full every Friday by noon or I get cut-off." His wife came in everyday during the week around two p.m. and worked until early evening to prepare for the evening crowd.

Stan signed both copies of the agreement, gave me a copy, and then help up two fingers for the young Thai bartender. As she nodded I looked at my beer; it was still half full. I looked at Stan's; it was empty. Shit. This guy was a pro. Me and my big mouth. This guy could drink me under the table.

As Stan grabbed the newly arrived beers, he stood and motioned for the bartender to ring the huge bell. He bellowed, "Everyone, I have an announcement to make. I want you all to meet my new partner." Motioning for me to stand up, he said, "This is John Fischer. We have just started the first ever courier service in Thailand. I want you all to use us."

Everyone clapped until a guy standing at the bar shouted back, "That's Great Stan, but what the hell is a courier service?"

"Don't worry about it," replied Stan. "Have a few more drinks and we'll explain it to you later." Shaking his head, Stan said, "There's always a smart ass. Let me give you the lowdown on these guys. The guy with all the hair wearing the white shirt and tie at the far end of the bar, that's

Harold, the nerd. He works for IBM just a couple of blocks away. He's been here a couple of years, knows everything about data processing.

"When he first came here from IBM's headquarters in upstate New York, he was a fish out of water. Now he loves it here. He has a great pad overlooking the river and lives with two beautiful Thai women.

The fat bald guy sitting next to Harold eating the hamburger is Wayne. He's the local branch manager of Sealand, the container shipping line and soon to be one of our first customers. I checked out your courier service with Wayne. He verified that you guys were doing a great job handling their shipping documents in Tokyo and Hong Kong.

The big guy with the dark hair and handlebar moustache standing up and drinking the beer, that's Rocky. He's a pilot with Air America, the cargo airlines that runs freight throughout Southeast Asia; I use these guys to move my embassy shipments from Bangkok to Cambodia, Laos and Burma.

"Rocky only shows up on the days he's not flying, after a few beers he works himself into a depression talking about how he misses his wife and kids in the states. The only thing that snaps him out of it is a trip across the street to Sophie's massage parlor; he always comes back a new man.

"The tall thin guy with the black hair is Jerry. He looks like a wop and that's because he is an Italian-American. His last name is Garibaldi. Jerry is the local manager of Del Monte Foods; his company runs the pineapple and sugar field up north. Jerry's a great guy, on the board of the American Chamber of Thailand. He knows everyone.

"The other tall thin guy, the one talking to Jerry, that's Beppi Foster. He owns the Swiss-German restaurant down the street. Beppi came here about ten years ago to be the executive chief at the Bangkok Hilton. When his employment contract ran out he decided to open his own place. He comes here everyday at noon before he starts getting ready for his evening dinner crowd.

"The big fat bald guy wearing the sunglasses trying to make time with my bartender is Murray. He owns the Triple 7 girlie bar down the street; he's an ex-Army Sergeant that used to run the main NCO club in Saigon. Army said he skimmed money off the club's slot machines. Murray decided it was time to leave Saigon so he married a local and bought the club with what he called a family inheritance.

The nooners, Stan explained, usually had a few beers, ate lunch, and returned to work by two p.m. A few dropped by after work for a quick drink and were headed home by six p.m. By early evening when the bars and massage parlors started getting busy, an entirely different crowd appeared, one made up of American G.I.'s on R & R from Vietnam, Air Force guys stationed at bases throughout Thailand, and tourists from Europe and other parts of the world. The Horny Toad did a great bar business and had rock and roll bands playing on the weekends.

As the crowd thinned out, Stan grabbed my arm and said he wanted me to meet Apri, his right hand girl. Apri was not only the noontime bartender, but also the day manager until Stan's wife showed up in the afternoon. As we slid onto the bar stools I could see Apri was a beautiful woman. She had fine features, beautiful eyes, wore little makeup, and had long black hair that fell to the middle of her back.

Apri wore a loose fitting long white dress and you could see the outline of her attractive body through the thin lace material. I guessed her to be in her late 20's, but with Asian women it has hard to tell, they always looked younger than they really were until they reached the age of 40 when they looked like 60 overnight.

When Stan introduced me, she broke into a wide smile, held out her tiny hand, and in perfect English said, "I'm so happy to meet you." She grasped my hand briefly and then put her hand to her mouth and started to giggle as she turned to Stan and rattled off four or five quick comments in Thai.

Stan started laughing and said, "Apri says you're too young to be a businessman in Thailand. She says you have no wedding ring and wants to know if you are married or have a Thai girlfriend."

"No on both counts," I replied.

"Oh boy," said Stan. "you are really going to like Thailand."

"Okay, Stan," I said, "what's the deal with these Thai women?"

"I thought they were supposed to be shy and unassuming. Even the girls at the hotel wanted to know everything about me. Where I'm from, where I work, how long I will stay in Thailand. Don't get me wrong. I love the attention, but why the hell do they ask so many questions?"

Stan slapped me on the back and held up his two fingers for more beer as he said,

"You're a fine catch my friend for a respectable single young Thai woman. This is how it works in around here: Thai women that go with G.I.'s are looked upon as whores, the same as bar and massage girls.

"But don't get waitresses and hotel workers mixed up with bar girls, they're not prostitutes. Take Apri over there, you call her a bar girl and she'll kicked you right in the nuts."

Stan explained that there were many high class and well-educated Thai women in Bangkok that were only interested in businessmen who could provide them with a comfortable life, nice house, expensive car, and all the good stuff. "Hell," said Stan, "women are the same all over the world. What makes you so different is that you're not an old fucker like the rest of us."

"That's for sure," I replied.

Looking at Stan I saw him talking to me but I couldn't hear him. I moved closer. He continued talking and as I strained to understand what he was saying I began to feel dizzy. Suddenly darkness swept over me and everything went blank.

The next thing I remembered was the sensation of something cold slowly moving across my forehead and cheeks. I recognized Stan kneeling over me. "Hey kid," he said, "Wake up. Are you okay?" He wiped my forehead with a damp bar towel.

"I don't know. Where am I?" I said.

"Shit," said Stan. "You passed out, slid right off the bar stool. Bam, you hit the floor like cold salami. Good thing you missed the footrest. Hell, it's my fault. I shouldn't have ordered you all those beers, but you told me you could drink us all under the table. What the hell was I suppose to do?"

"Okay, Stan, you're the man," I replied. "I've got a big mouth. Now where's the head? I think I need to puke." After twenty minutes in the head and several more cold compresses I decided it would not be a good time to meet Stan's wife who was coming on shift. I excused myself and like a dog with its tail between its legs slithered back to my hotel room.

The next morning I woke with a splitting headache and a body that ached from head to toe. I couldn't believe this was just a beer hangover. After several cups of coffee, toast and five aspirin I decided to call Po and Larry in Hong Kong and give them an update of the last few days.

When I told them I had hired Stan they both objected saying that I had made a bad decision. They felt Frank, the guy at Flying Tiger Airlines, should run the operation.

I responded, "Frank is a religious freak and I don't give a damn how capable you think he is. I'm not going to work with an asshole."

After several seconds of silence, Larry replied, "Stan is not the guy."

I raised my voice to an angry pitch. "If you don't like my decision then get your asses down here and take over. The reason you're not here is that you're a couple of chickenshits, just like in Indonesia. No one wanted to help me start that place, either.

"You knew damn well you might wind up in jail or maybe get shot in the head by some corrupt Army General who wanted more of a cut. If I take the risk, I make the choice, and my choice is Stan. So fuck off.

"We should be ready to start next week. And one more thing," I said, "put another 25K in my bank account. I'll call you in a couple of days."

"Okay," replied Po.

"Okay," echoed Larry.

Hong Kong Reunion March 2011 –The author with Po Chung

25th DHL Reunion-Sept. 1994. The founders
seated and the early employees.
*Left to Right Standing: Mr. Kim, Robert Ozaki, Rod Feliciano,
Paul Chan, Bruce Walker, Po Chung, John Fischer
Seated: Adrian Dalsey, Larry Hillblom, Marge Dalsey, Robert Lynn*

DHL-the founders Sept. 1994. All three would be dead within a year.

Reunion Breakfast. The author John Fischer and
Adrian Dalsey in the background.

Reunion 1994, the author with Larry Hillblom. He
was killed in a plane crash seven months later.

One of the first DHL ID's

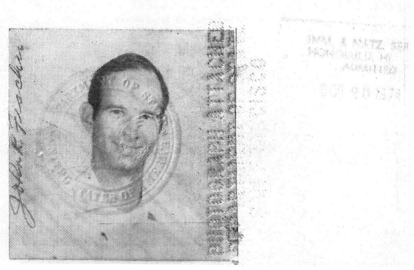

My passport photo. I was 26 but looked 16,
that's why they called me "The Kid".

Chapter 15 Start-up in Thailand

*O*n Monday morning, the first rays of sunlight lit up the curtains of my new accommodations. I had made myself comfortable at the Montien Hotel by getting a small suite on the top floor for a just a few baht more than a regular room, about $25.00 per day. I convinced Pierre, the hotel manager, to rent me the suite on a monthly basis. It was just the right size, a separate bedroom, a living room and a small kitchen. My new home.

The Montien's location was perfect, halfway between the airport and my customers in the city. It was just down the street from Stan's place, and, best of all, I had the entire Patpong District nearby with its multitude of bars, massage parlors, and restaurants to keep me entertained.

At twelve noon Stan met me at the hotel coffee shop to go over the game plan to start the courier service by the end of the week. I reiterated our plan for the Hong Kong operation to screen all the pouches and make sure only company documents were sent. Stan interrupted me and with a serious look on his face asked, "Do you think we should get a legal opinion?"

"Legal opinion for what?" I asked.

"You know," said Stan, "to see if we could be in violation of any postal or custom regulations."

"Stan," I replied, "you need to calm down. I've been down this road before. I'm not paying big bucks to some lawyer and have him tell me what I can't do. As I told you before, we only handle company documents, not letters. We have to make sure everyone, and especially our employees make that distinction. We need to start the service and deal with the situations as they come up. I started Indonesia last year; it is strictly third world like Thailand; we can use a similar game plan.

Stan settled back into his rattan chair and ordered his first beer of the day. I continued explaining my plan. The first step would be to meet with our most important customers, Bank of America and Sealand.

These two customers had requested we start the service into Thailand and both had been very supportive in every one of our start-up operations. They would give us instant credibility with the Thai government and would vouch for us when Thai Customs questioned why we were in possession of their documents.

Both of these customers shipped what we called 'hard documents' in the pouches. There was nothing that could be considered a letter or personal correspondence. The Bank of America documents consisted of canceled checks, accounting ledgers, credit and legal contracts. Sealand had stacks of ships' manifests, bills of lading, cargo insurance certificates, and load and stowage diagrams.

Next we needed to meet with the Thai American Chamber of Commerce. I had already met Jerry, the Del Monte manager and friend of Stan who was on the Board of Directors. The chamber had been a key supporter of our operations throughout Asia and had connections with the Thai Government as well as the U.S. Military, American CIA, and the DEA that was trying to operate undercover in Thailand.

The operational plan would be to initially use an actual courier from Hong Kong to arrive in Bangkok on the early morning flight, clear Customs, and deliver those pouches by noon and pick up the outgoing pouches for the same courier to depart for Hong Kong in the evening.

The courier pouches containing the documents were color coded by city, Bangkok being maroon, and had the company's name printed on the white handles. These pouches were placed in larger green canvas bags, tagged as the courier's baggage, and placed in the belly of the aircraft.

Upon arrival at the destination airport, the courier would recover the large green bags from the passenger baggage carousel, clear Customs, and declare all items as company documents with no commercial value. If Customs wanted to inspect the bags, the pouches could be pulled out and the contents examined. Once cleared through Customs, the courier took the bags to our delivery vans waiting at curbside. The van drivers delivered the pouches to the customers.

We anticipated that after the first week, the number of pouches would greatly increase as more of our regular customers began using the service from the U.S. and Asia. Our ground crews would approach Customs and ask permission to enter the restricted area to assist the courier in recovering the multitude of large green bags that were mixed in with suitcases and causing other passengers difficulty in finding their possessions.

The plan worked. Day after day, the same two guys from our ground crew gained access to the baggage and Customs areas. They grabbed the bags, cleared the shipments through Customs, and took them directly outside to the waiting vans. Within a week the courier became obsolete and we eliminated him completely.

Our agreement with the airline was to buy a round trip ticket and pay the standard excess flat baggage fee of $7.00 per bag. Before the days of real airline security, we bought daily round trip excursion fare tickets, paid the required excess baggage fee, and did not put a courier on the plane. The airlines loved it because they could sell the same seat twice.

The ground operations worked well and were efficient as long as we had an ample supply of white envelopes containing a few baht to keep everyone in the baggage area motivated. We never called it bribery; that was a word use by Westerners.

We simply took care of people that took care of us, a reciprocity that was centuries old in Asia. In Malaysia it was called "Raswah," in Indonesia it was "Wang Sagoh," and in Thailand it was "Sinbone." For Americans living in Thailand it was still plain old 'grease'.

In the third world, Asian public servants like police, Customs officials, and others, all received low pay. If they were ambitious, they could supplement their salaries by taking advantage of revenue opportunities.

When Indonesia was under Dutch colonial rule they would hire locals as tax collectors at very low pay with the understanding they could make up the difference by overcharging taxes or by collecting additional bookkeeping fees. These countries were a nightmare of inefficiencies and red tape due to bloated bureaucracy. The typical government practice was hiring five people to do one person's job in an attempt to reduce the rampant unemployment rates. Long lines and hours of waiting in hot, humid government buildings for any public service was considered normal and accepted by the locals.

The main reason we ran couriers on the aircraft or handled the pouches as passenger baggage was to avoid the long lines and inefficiencies of clearing the shipments as general airfreight cargo. The normal time to clear the shipment if it was not dutiable was a minimum of one day if you were lucky. Usually it took two days and that was after getting fourteen different Customs authorizations stamps--chops--on the Airway bill.

The commitment to deliver the documents within hours after the aircraft landed required working the passenger system to our advantage. We seldom, if ever, paid anyone to actually circumvent the law. However, we greased the hell out of their existing procedures.

While passengers had to line up and wait for Customs inspections; we got our own Customs guy to inspect our shipments. When curbside parking at the passenger loading areas got backed up or had time limits, we always got our own area for as long as we wanted. When the big green bags were loaded on departing aircraft in the passenger compartment, ours always went in last so they could be the first off.

In some of our locations, when we were late getting to the airport with shipments, aircraft were held on the ground. Several times with Pan Am on the West Coast, we had the jet brought back to the gate after it had departed and was moving toward the runway.

There was a real art to greasing or taking care of people, it should be a required class at business colleges and MBA programs. It could be called "Introduction to Bribery 101," and be followed by Bribery 102, 103, and so on until you covered all the countries or regions of the world.

To me, it seemed simple as first. But it quickly got complicated and out of control to the extent that we had to hire a "bookkeeper" to keep everything organized and functioning on a daily basis for the payment of 20 or 30 people. The issues were endless. Who did you take care of? What was their job? Did they really control what they said they did? Did they have a manager or supervisor? Did we need to take care of him, too? How much more did we need to give to the manager than the worker? What happened if the guys rotated their shifts, got sick, or went on vacation? How did we keep the amounts straight? We sure as hell couldn't put the amounts and the names on the envelopes.

What would happen if we gave the wrong envelope to someone, or the wrong amount to someone? Hell, what if couldn't just hand out envelopes, especially in a monitored restricted area? How we would take care of those people?

Fortunately for me, Stan's number one operations guy, Pera, was a master at taking care of people. He had been doing it for years in the airport cargo areas. Pera's solution to the envelope problem was the same as I had seen in Jakarta a year earlier. Everyone in Asia loved newspapers, whether it was sports, betting on the races, or just reading the gossip column. Newspapers were commonplace at the airport as a way to deal with waiting in long lines and Customs delays.

A folded newspaper could contain hundreds of baht notes to take care of an entire work crew or could be left at a prearranged spot so there was no evidence of a handoff. The biggest problem was human greed; it was only a matter of time before it reared its ugly head.

Once the business started increasing people wanted more money. Most of the time we could negotiate on a case by case basis. But sooner or later we'd get a troublemaker. One of them was the captain of Customs at the Jakarta airport. He wanted some ridiculous amount of money under the threat of seizing our shipments and holding them for ransom. In most cases when this happened, we relied on our connections with some very influential government and commercial accounts. We could make some calls and our established contacts would convince the Customs or airport people to rethink their position and accept our offer.

But this guy was a real hardhead. Every time we tried to negotiate with him he doubled the price. I even told him that most of the documents coming into Jakarta were for Pertamina, the powerful government-owned Oil Company of Indonesia.

Every day we carried in millions of dollars of checks from American oil companies based in Houston for payment of offshore oil concessions. Nothing fazed this Customs guy; he insisted we would not get the documents until he got paid in full.

I discussed the situation with Heri, my operations manager, and we decided that he should call our contact at Pertamina and advise them of our predicament. After explaining the situation, we were told to remain at the airport Customs area and the matter would be resolved shortly.

After about twenty minutes of waiting next to the Customs inspectors building, I heard the thunderous sound of heavy trucks approaching and as the dust cleared I recognized two large brown Army trucks with troops sitting in the open back bed. As the trucks roared to a stop, an officer got out of the cab, and shouted something in Indonesian. Immediately 40 well armed PTK military police fell into formation.

The officer approached me and Heri and starting talking angrily and rapidly to Heri, after a few seconds Heri pointed to the Customs building and the officer walked back to his troops. "What the hell was that about?" I asked Heri.

"The Army Major wants me to point out the Captain of Customs who ordered our shipments held," said Heri.

The Major then barked an order to his forty armed soldiers and motioned for us to follow him into the Customs building. As we entered the building marked, "Restricted Area-No Entry" in both English and Indonesian, the Major barked another order and his soldiers slung their weapons off their shoulders.

The place was filled with office people, clerks, and Customs people who immediately froze; it became so quiet all we heard were the two air conditioners in the rear of the building humming away. The Major turned to my man Heri and shouted something in Indonesian. Heri just stood there and with a frightened expression on his face slowly pointed his finger at a closed office door in the corner.

Shouting angrily, the Major pointed to several armed soldiers next to him and they immediately walked up to the closed door and in one coordinated movement kicked the door off its hinges. The Major then drew his revolver and walked in. After a few minutes of shouting, Heri and I edged closer to the open door now hanging by one hinge and saw the Army Major standing over the Customs Captain who was crouching on his knees. The Major's pistol rested squarely between the crying eyes of the unfortunate soul.

I turned quickly to Heri and asked, "What the hell is going on?"

"The Army Major," Heri replied, "is telling the Captain that he had no authorization to seize Pertamina documents, this was an illegal seizure and now he would be executed.

The Customs guy starting crying hysterically, putting his hands to head, moving his torso up and down and mumbling and crying at the same time.

"Heri," I asked, "what's he saying?"

"He's begging for his life," Heri replied. "He's telling the Major he is a true believer of Allah. He has a wife and children. He will never make this mistake again."

The Army Major just stood expressionless; with the pistol still held to the man's forehead he slowly pulled the hammer back.

Heri then whispered in my ear, "We're going to find out if he's a true believer now. I think the Major's going to do it. Stand back. There's going to be blood everywhere."

Oh my God, this guy is going to kill him right in front of me.

Silence, not a sound then--- CLICK--the metallic sound of the hammer hitting an empty chamber. The Customs guy screamed and hit the floor face first; the Major turned and motioned for his soldiers to return to the trucks. Standing over the collapsed motionless figure lying at his feet, he quickly said something in Indonesian and left the room "What the hell did he say Heri?" I asked.

"He told him that Allah saved him this time, but it will never happen again."

After that, Customs always asked for permission to open the green bags. We always denied the request.

Stan finished his beer and looked at his watch and said we needed to leave in a few minutes to make our appointment to see the local manager of Bank of America. It was starting to rain signaling the start of the rainy season as Stan's car and driver pulled up to the curb. As Stan and I settled into the back seat of his five year old Toyota and prepared for an hour's drive in congested traffic I figured that this was a good time to ask Stan some questions without the interruptions of the bar crowd and constant noise.

"Stan?" I asked, "Give me an honest answer if you can. Who really runs this town? In Jakarta it was the Generals and the wealthy Chinese.

"Same here," replied Stan. "take Patpong. A wealthy Chinese family owns most of the land and buildings. You pay their price and there's no competition. The Generals, they take a cut of all the action. If you hold back or try to screw them, they'll kill you or burn you down. Everyone that operates in Patpong has partners, silent partners.

"Gee, Stan, is there anything the Generals don't get a cut of? Are they into everything?" I asked.

"Just about everything, except for one thing," replied Stan. "Child prostitution. The General's despise it. Like most Thais, they love their families, especially the children.

If they catch you running a place like that in Patpong, they'll kill you."

"That's bullshit Stan," I replied. "I get propositioned everyday by street hustlers trying to sell me young kids, seven and eight-year-olds, for sex, although now that they've figured out I that live at the hotel they leave me alone."

"Yeah," said Stan. "but they won't do it in Patpong. They'll take you to some underground little hole in the wall someplace in Bangkok or some village on the outskirts of the city. If the cops catch them, they will bust their asses. They hate it. This is not Cambodia, where no one gives a fuck."

"Stan," I asked, "Doesn't this shit get to you sometimes, the child prostitution, drugs, and the poverty? Why do you put up with it?"

Stan looked at me and with his face turning red exclaimed, "Why are you asking me this shit? *You're* the one who goes to the massage parlors every night. From what I hear, *you* are one of Sophie's best customers."

I didn't answer Stan. Instead, I looked out through the side window that was fogging up. The drenching rain made thunderous sounds hitting the hood of the car. *He's right; I'm just as much a part of this shit as the whores and the rest of them.*

"Okay, Stan," I replied, "I know. I'm an asshole like the rest of them, but how in the hell does stuff like child prostitution happen? How can someone sell their kids?"

"Its poverty," said Stan, "I mean real poverty, not like in the states. Thailand is not just Bangkok, Chiang Mai, and the beach resorts. It's mostly poor subsistence farmers trying to feed their families off a few small strips of rice paddies. They have lots of kids, not just because there is no birth control, but so the kids can help them in the fields.

A few bad years, a drought or flood, and they can no longer support the children. So they sell off a few. It's pure survival of the fittest. Darwin's theory gone mad."

"And who buys them?" I asked.

"Mainly brokers and procurers. Most of it is controlled by the Chinese gangs. They go up to the villages buy the kids for a set amount and then sell them to all the brothels and massage parlors throughout Thailand. The older, best-looking girls end up in the tourist areas like Patpong because that's where the money is."

"Stan," I asked, "Are these people like indentured slaves the rest of their life? Say the girls at Sophie's. Are they someone's property?"

"Maybe," replied Stan. "The way it works is that the procurers sell girls to brothels for set amounts. Then the brothel takes the girls' earnings to pay off the amount of her contract. The owners provide living quarters, food, and medical attention.

"Most of the girls continue to work in the sex industry after they paid off their contract because the money is good. Most of them have no skills for other employment," Stan said.

"What happens if the girls get the clap?"

They agree in their contract to always wear a condom, if they catch a disease they can no longer work. In Patpong the American military business is where the real money is and if a G.I. gets infected and it's traced back to your place, the military police would declare the establishment off limits. Your profitable business would disappear overnight."

"Hell, condoms don't prevent everything." I repeated, "What happens if a girl does get the clap?"

Stan replied, "The owners have no obligations to her. She broke the rules."

"Jesus, Stan," I replied. "This sounds like Mississippi before the civil war."

Stan's muscles tensed up. His face got red and he angrily replied, "Look, kid, YOU fuckers from the States that live in your comfortable suburban house with your two fucking cars and your two fucking kids. Yes sir. You can afford to judge us because none of you have ever walked in these poor people's shoe.

"Every day for them is 24 hours of survival. Christ, do you think they really want to sell their kids? They do it so the rest will survive. You American fuckers have no concept of what I'm even talking about do you? Boy, you better learn something quickly out here.

This is the way it is. You're not going to change it. Either accept it or go back home."

I didn't say anything more to Stan as we slowly crawled our way through the traffic and the flooded streets. After about twenty minutes we pulled up to the curb outside the Bank of America headquarters building. We made our way up to the eighteenth floor where we were met by a security guard who directed us to the manager's office. Upon entering the door with a Vice President nameplate, we were greeted by a beautiful young Thai girl. She introduced herself as Winnie, the private secretary to Mr. Richard Sorensen, the bank manager.

After asking for our business cards she directed us to an adjoining conference room and said that the bank manager was on the telephone but would be with us shortly. As I sat there waiting with Stan I thought of the last time I was in a Bank of America and had given my business card to a secretary.

It was Mieko, my beautiful Mieko. I wondered where she was, what she was doing and if she ever thought about me. I did try to call her at the Bank in Korea the second day I was in Thailand. Al had said, "She won't be there kid," and he was right. The lady at the bank speaking in broken English said, "Mieko doesn't work her anymore." I couldn't believe I was still thinking about her after what she did to me.

Mieko played me like the fool that I was. I trusted and confided in her. She pretended to love me but she was lying the whole time. How could anyone be that cold and calculating? How could I have been so blind not to see it? I needed to forget about her and never again be so stupid and vulnerable.

The booming voice of the bank manager startled me out of my thoughts. As I looked up and saw the smiling face of an American who introduced himself as Richard Sorenson the vice president in charge of Bank of America in Thailand.

Richard was in his early 50's, a big guy with a receding hair line. He wore the standard banker's charcoal grey suit, white shirt, and dark tie. Richard had received notice from the bank's regional headquarters in Hong Kong that we would be starting the courier service in Thailand. He was pleased knowing it would have a positive impact on the bank's daily operations.

I told him Richard that would be starting in a few days and would appreciate his confirming our relationship should Customs or airport authorities contact him about our services. Richard raised his eyebrows and asked, "Why would Customs call me? You guys are legal, right?"

"Yes," I replied, "but sometimes Customs doesn't understand what we do and the type of documents we carry. If they call you about us, just verify what we do for you. That's all."

With that we left the bank and got into Stan's car for our next appointment with the Thai American Chamber of Commerce. After an hour of the normal slow traffic we found ourselves in front of the young director of the Chamber, Allan Hudson. As I started to explain our service and our start-up in Thailand, Allan suddenly held up his hand

and declared, "Say no more. I know who you guys are. A couple of weeks ago we had our annual Regional Chamber meeting in Hong Kong.

"Your company's name came up in a conversation with Dan Green, the retired general who runs the American Chamber in Korea. There was also a guy named George Chen from the Hong Kong Chamber who seemed to know a lot about you. You guys made quite a name for yourself in Korea and Hong Kong.

"I guess we're next here in Thailand. I think you'll find the Thais are much more accommodating than the Koreans if you treat them with respect and know how to take care of them. Stan, he's been here a few years. I'm sure he will give you the proper guidance." The Chamber director looked at his watch and declared he was late for a meeting. He shook our hands and left the room.

The following morning the sun was just starting to come up as I waited in my hotel lobby for Stan and his driver to pick me up and meet our first courier flight arriving at 7:45 a.m. on Cathy Pacific Airlines from Hong Kong. After forty-five minutes of driving we parked just outside the arrival hall at the international terminal and waited for Stan's operations manager Pera, and the courier to appear with our large green bags containing the documents.

After about an hour of waiting, Pera suddenly appeared and signaled for Stan and me to come to the customs area. Stan looked at me and angrily exclaimed, "Shit! We got stopped at the first Goddamn shipment."

"Relax, Stan," I replied. "Let's go inside and find out what's going on."

Entering the immigration and customs arrival areas, we saw Pera talking with two customs officials and pointing to a stack of bank checks protruding out of several pouches that has been opened. Stan leaned over and whispered in my ear, "Kid, I've lived in this country for fifteen years and never had any problems with customs. I meet you a couple of weeks ago and I'm already in deep shit."

"Don't worry, Stan," I said. Turning to Pera, I handed him my company I.D. badge and a letter from Bank of America World Headquarters in San Francisco that authorized the courier service to handle their documents worldwide and the phone number of the vice president of the local Bank of America.

Pera handed my documents to the customs officials and after several minutes of conversing in Thai looked over to me and Stan and said everything was fine. The pouches would be released. As Stan and I walked back to the car, I explained to him this situation was expected, after all no one had ever done this before in Thailand. It would get easier from now on.

And it did ease up. My routine became the same almost every day. I got up at 6 a.m. Stan's driver picked me up at the hotel. I met the incoming flight from Hong Kong at 7:30 a.m. and with Pera's crew of three men cleared customs by 8 a.m. We sorted the pouches by company and address, loaded the vans, started deliveries by 8:30, and finished all the routes by noon.

After calling on some customers and trying to acquire new ones, I would be back at Stan's bar and grill in Patpong for lunch and have several beers with the nooner crowd.

At 3 p.m. I met with Pera and his three drivers to organize the afternoon pickup schedule. We were back at the airport at 5 p.m. to sort and manifest the outgoing shipments for the 7 p.m. flight to Hong Kong.

By 8 p.m. I was back in Patpong having dinner at Beppi's and wondering if I was still in the mood for a visit to Sophie's.

Saturday night was my crazy night, the one night I could really get ripped and sleep late. the next day. I always checked out the live Band playing at the Horney Toad, Stan's place. that played until well past midnight. There was always Americans there, usually G.I.s with their Thai girlfriends, but sometimes there were European women tourist, Australians and American nurses stationed in Thailand. I had to check out the white women, their big asses and boobs drew me like a fly to honey. I knew all the bartenders at the Toad and my usual routine was to sit at the bar, order my standard double vodka and seven and ask the bartender if there were any good looking white women in the place. Without hesitation he would point them out and give me his rating from 1 to 10, most of the time I rated them lower than the bartender but after numerous double shots and dancing with whoever was available they all became 10's.

The schedule was the same except for Sunday, the only day all the businesses were closed and my only day off. Sunday mornings were always an adventure, I would lie in my big double bed at my hotel with a splitting headache quietly listening to hear the sound of someone next to me, if there was no movement or sound I felt instant relief, I had not brought anyone home with me.

But most of the time, there was breathing, movement. I then started to think, to try and remember, I *couldn't* remember, *Shit I was so ripped I couldn't remember anything, I was in a blackout, I heard that's what happens to alcoholics, but shit, I was too young to be one of those.*

Finally the inevitable would happen. I'd look over to the person lying next to me and feel thankful it was a woman. As she smiled I would think, *Oh, My God.*

One rainy Saturday evening at about midnight I sat down on my favorite bar stool at the Toad, Tony the bartender immediately came over with my double shot and excitely whispered, "Boss, we have a real "10" tonight, young, good looking blonde with big tits and ass. Boss, this is no bullshit. Look, over there, the table to the far right of the band, she's with two beautiful Thai women."

"Yeah, I see her, Tony." Have you ever seen her before?"

"No," replied Tony, "but I only started working the weekends about a month ago."

I couldn't keep my eyes off her as I said to the bartender, "I bet she's a tourist, maybe an Australian; I have to check her out." As the music started I took a few deep breaths and trying to appear sober walked up to the table with the three women and as I approached the blond turned her head and smiled, God she *was* beautiful. She looked like a young Hollywood movie star.

I just looked at her, standing in front of her table. I barely remember asking her to dance. She must have accepted because the next thing I remembered we were dancing to one of the Rolling Stone's songs. As I led her back to her table I asked her if I could buy her a drink.

She shook her head and said that it was getting late and she and her friends were about to leave. I sat down at her table and ignoring her Thai girlfriends asked, "What's your name?"

She replied with a southern accent, "My name is Vina. What's yours?"

I could barely get the words out fast enough as I replied, "I'm John. So you're an American from the south. Where? Alabama? Mississippi?"

"Louisiana," she dryly replied.

"What are you doing here?" Are you a tourist?" I asked.

"No," replied Vina. "I live here. I work for an import/export company in Bangkok."

"Really," I replied. "How come I've never seen you here before?"

With an annoyed smile she replied, "'Probably because we run around with a different crowd. We have to go now. Nice meeting you."

"Vina, please. Give me your phone number. I want to see you again," I said.

"I don't think so," she replied.

"Then here," I said. "Here is my business card. Call me."

"No. I don't do that. Excuse us. We have to leave." With that dismissal, she abruptly turned, grabbed the hands of her two Thai girl friends walked out the door.

I ran over to the bouncer, Billy, and said, "Follow them and see if they get into a private car. Get the license number."

After about ten minutes the bouncer came back and said, "Sorry boss. No private car. They got into a taxi."

"Shit, Billy. Have you ever seen that blonde before?" I asked.

"Sure," replied Billy. "she's been here a couple of times, always comes in late, after midnight."

"Does she always come in with the same two beautiful Thai women?" I asked.

"Right, Boss, except, those Thai women, there *not* women, there're men," he said.

It was Sunday morning as I slowly turned over and glanced at the clock on the bed stand that said 11 am. The throbbing dull pain in my mind from the previous night's drinking gave way to wandering questions of the beautiful blonde girl named Vina.

She *was* gorgeous: tall, about five foot ten inches, natural blond hair, a fine featured face with little makeup, her body was well proportioned with a nice round Western ass and a full bust line. She wore a simple once piece tan dress, not showy but tight enough to exhibit her undeniable sex appeal.

What was her story? I had to find out. What was she doing with two transvestites? I was so enamored with her I that I hadn't really checked out her friends, except noticing that they were beautiful. I still couldn't believe they were men.

How was she working for a local Thai trading company? If she was a U.S. citizen how could she get a work visa? It was hard enough to get one of those if you worked for a large multinational, and that was after you paid everyone off.

A gorgeous chick like that? Coming into Patpong on a regular basis? Someone must know something about her, I'll ask Stan about her tomorrow, or even Al, he said he runs a trading company.

As my mind continued to grapple with the endless possibilities of the girl named Vina the phone next to the bed rang. As I slowly picked it up I heard the deep gruff voice of Adrian, the company owner pronouncing my name.

I hesitated before answering as I started to think to myself, *Adrian only calls me when he wants me to do something no one else will do.* After a few minutes of praise for my starting the operation in Thailand, he abruptly announced, "We're opening up Saigon, all the American Banks and American Express have been begging me to start the service, when can you get up there?"

"Wait Adrian," I stammered. "That's Vietnam. That place is in the middle of a war. Neither side is winning and the entire country is unstable as hell. Those banks could pull out at any minute. Besides, we don't even have an agent there."

"No problem," replied Adrian. "I've taken care of that. A company that has been our customer for years called P.A.E. --Pacific Architects and Engineers-- is a military subcontractor at Tan Sun Nut Airbase just outside Saigon. They have agreed to be our agent for the entire country.

P.A.E. has its own fleet of vehicles and a warehouse at the airport. This is a great opportunity for us. Get up there by next week at the latest. If you need any money, call Po. And let Larry know what's going on. Good luck."

The phone clicked. All that remained was silence as I placed the receiver back in its cradle. This was an absolute disaster. It's now December 1972. We have been fighting this war since 1965 and nothing has changed.

In January 1968 the communist Tet offensive overran the entire country and it became clear to everyone that the U.S. was not winning this war as the American politicians and Generals had insisted. President Nixon declared a new policy called "Vietnamization" in which U.S. troops would be systemically pulled out and the war would be increasingly fought by the ARVN, the Army of South Vietnam. The question of whether ARVN troops could stand up on their own without the support of U.S. troops was debatable.

Mooncake Man

Only a couple of days before I had read in the English version of the Bangkok newspapers that President Nixon had ordered the bombing of Hanoi in North Vietnam by U.S. B-52 bombers to force the communist back to the Paris Peace Table.

This would be a new experience, starting a courier service in the middle of a stupid war. It was ironic. I managed to avoid the place when I was in the Army. Now I will see it firsthand after all.

Chapter 16 Vietnam During the U.S. Troop Withdrawal

ooking out the window of the departure lounge at the Bangkok airport, I admired the pearl white Air Vietnam 727 passenger jet that would take me to Saigon. A huge jade green dragon head graced the tail; the creature's body stretched the length of the fuselage on both sides. What a gorgeous plane.

As I settled into my seat for the ninety minute flight to Saigon, I thought about Vina, the blonde I had met and danced with only a few days before. I had asked around Patpong and while a few people had seen her, no one really knew much about her. Even Stan wasn't much help.

In desperation I had called Al, the undercover CIA guy and friend of the General who met me when I first arrived in Thailand. Al and Vina were in the same business, export trading, perhaps he knew her. As the plane started to be pushed back on the tarmac to the taxiway, I remembered the conversation I had with Al the day before.

Al had told me he had met Vina several times at trade shows and that she worked for one of the richest men in all of Asia, an older Chinese guy named Wintoon. The man was in his seventies and controlled all the teakwood exports in Thailand.

"Al," I replied, "don't bullshit me. Does she work for you and the General? Is there any connection at all?"

"Jesus, John," Al replied, "after Korea you don't trust anyone, do you? Look, I only met her about six months ago; she just came out of nowhere. The story I heard is that she got into some kind of trouble in the states and the old man took her in. So why are you so interested in her?"

"Damn it, Al, you didn't answer my question." I repeated, "Does she work for you or any of your intelligence buddies?"

"No," shouted Al, "like I said, I only met her six months ago. Why are you so worked up about her?"

"Well, Al, I danced with her a couple of nights ago in Patpong. She's a knockout, but she was with two transvestites. I couldn't believe that shit."

"What are you getting so freaked out about?" laughed Al. "This is Thailand. Transvestites are common as hell. A lot of men and women go both ways here. You should try it. They say it's the best of both worlds."

"Al," I replied, "you've been here too long. You're getting weird. Do you have the company address where she works? When I get back from Vietnam I'm going to buy some teakwood."

"Vietnam?" shrieked Al. "You didn't tell me you were going to Vietnam. Shit, the General and I have a lot of friends there."

"Yeah," I replied. "I bet you do. This is a short trip. I'll call you next week."

The Air Vietnam jet turned to line up on the runway. I must have been crazy to call Al. Guys like him never do anything for free. I can hardly wait to get his bill.

The engines of the jet roared to life and the plane headed almost straight up. The flight path would be directly over Cambodia and then into Vietnam. I had heard most of the pilots flying for Air Vietnam were Americans. I always felt safer with round eyes flying airplanes in Asia. I probably should have checked as I boarded, but it was too late now.

After about 30 minutes of flying, the pilot announced in a recognizable American accent that we were at an altitude of 35,000 feet and just entering Cambodian airspace. I looked out the window and all I could see was an endless sea of bright green jungle with periodic plumes of smoke rising from the slash and burn practice of clearing of the land for agriculture.

This had to be one of the most isolated and inhospitable places on earth. If a plane crashed down there and passengers survived, no one would ever find them. After about thirty more minutes the pilot announced we had just crossed into South Vietnam and that we should arrive in Saigon in about twenty-five minutes and on time.

The pilot said that passengers should not be alarmed but due to the possibility of an enemy missile launch we would continue to fly at a high altitude until the last ten minutes of the flight at which time the aircraft would be put into a steep dive and level out just as we approached the runway of Saigon's Tan Son Nhut International Airport.

Shit. Is the guy kidding? Telling me not to be alarmed but we could be shot down by a missile?

Feeling helpless, I looked out the window and down to the earth below. I didn't know Vietnam had so many little small lakes and so few trees. I kept looking at the endless miles of this geography. Yes, then it dawned on me. Shit, these weren't lakes. They were bomb craters filled up with water from the monsoons. There were no trees or jungle because the herbicide Agent Orange had killed anything that grew. God, we have really screwed up this country.

The pilot announced that all passengers should have their seat belts properly secured. The airplane went into a steep dive, an almost 70 percent downward descent that strained my body against the seat belt and seemed to shake every bolt in the aircraft. After about five minutes in this position the plane leveled off.

I felt as if my stomach had been torn out of my body as we skimmed just a few feet above houses which had the bright yellow flag with red stripes of the South Vietnamese National flag painted on the roofs, symbols that loudly proclaimed, "Don't bomb me."

It seemed to happen almost at the same instant as the wheels hit the ground with a thud and the engines roared into reverse thrust, a few seconds later the squeaky high-pitched voice of the stewardess announced, "Welcome to the Republic of South Vietnam."

As the aircraft taxied to the passenger terminal at the far end of the airfield it became apparent that this was a military air base. As far as I could see in any direction there were rows of elevated camouflage rebuttments each with its own small hanger with a U.S. Air Force Fighter jet parked in each one.

The huge mounds of earth surrounding the aircraft were designed to protect it from Viet Cong rockets that periodically rained down on the base. As our passenger jet make it final turn to the terminal we passed an odd assortment of old aircraft dating back to WWII which at first I thought was some kind of aircraft museum but with closer inspection noticed these aircraft ranging from a WWII B-26 bomber to a C-47 Cargo plane had been outfitted with rockets and cannons for ground support missions. Each aircraft had the U.S white star insignia with the Vietnamese red and yellow stripes on each side of the fuselage, maybe this was to show who was really paying for this war.

The Air Vietnam 727 passenger jet stopped in front of the terminal building and the rear door was lowered. Almost instantly I felt the rush of hot humid air mixed with the smell of jet fuel. The weather smacked me squarely in the face like a giant wave. Hell, I didn't know the stench and heat in Vietnam would be worse than Thailand.

As we exited the plane, the ground crew led us to the immigration and Customs area, which is unlike any other airport in Asia and somehow looked nearly deserted. Maybe it was because everyone was trying to leave. The immigration officer seemed bored and uninterested as he thumbed through my passport looking for my Visa. Once he spotted it he quickly administered the official stamp and motioned me to proceed to the baggage area.

With my bag in hand I approached the Customs examination area and the officer just waved me through. No one seemed to give a shit, which was fine with me. As I exited the Customs area and strode into the main terminal, the usual crowds I expected were nonexistent. Only a few people hung around.

I spotted my name on a huge sign held by a young Vietnamese guy dressed in street clothes. As I approached him he confirmed my identity and introduced himself as Trang who would take me to his company. P.A.E. would serve as our agent in Vietnam and was located on the air base just a few miles away. Trang took my bag and I followed him to an olive drab 1965 Chevy with the words in dark black letters, "U.S. Army" on the door and parked under a sign that said. "No Parking or Stopping."

"Is this your car, I asked. He nodded affirmatively.

"Why is it an Army car?"

Trang smiled and proudly expanded his chest as he said, "Everything we drive says U.S. Army. We run this base: the water, sewage, roads, and everything else. P.A.E. runs it all. Now I take you to Mr. Roy. He is the big boss and is waiting for you."

As I slid into the back seat, I heard yelling and screaming coming from the opposite side of the road. Young women vied for the attention of men in passing cars. They wore short dresses, high heels, and low cut tops, and waved at me to come over to them. When I looked at them across the pavement, several gals pulled their dresses over their heads, exposing themselves from their legs to their necks.

As Trang started the car I asked, "What the hell is that all about, all those women, flashing their naked bodies? Is this some kind of weird welcome to Vietnam?"

Trang peered into the driver's mirror on the windshield and laughed as he said,

"Never thought of it that way. Those women are hookers. With all the U.S. troops leaving, many bar girls are unemployed. Some say almost 100,000 prostitutes have no work in Saigon. They come out to the airport and any other place where they can meet foreigners. The airport police do not allow them in the passenger terminals so they stay on the opposite side of the street and try and get customers."

As the car pulled out into the traffic, I looked at all the young women. Good God. We not only destroyed their country, we turned their women into whores. How tragic that we Americans who have funded this war don't realize that Asian people simply want to live their lives in peace.

Most of the people here could care less about democracy or politics, much less the domino theory—the notion professed by the Americans that the communists will take all of Southeast Asia unless stopped by force in Vietnam. Like all wars the real tragedies are the children, the women, and the weak that cannot defend themselves. But hell, I'm not above any of this. The only reason I'm here is to profit from their unfortunate circumstances.

In a few minutes we had arrived at the P.A.E. headquarters. The place looked like all the other buildings with its bright aluminum skin surrounded by a multiple of humming air conditioners. Inside, Trang led me past several rows of desks where local Vietnamese typed and sorted papers until we reached a corner office with a door marked, "Roy Matthews, Transportation Manager."

As soon as Trang knocked on the door, a deep voice boomed, "Enter."

I opened the door and Roy quickly rose from his desk, stretched out his hand, and greeted me in a Texas drawl, "Welcome to the Nam. There is never a dull moment here."

Roy was a big guy, at least six foot-five and about 250 pounds with brown crew cut hair. He wore blue jeans, cowboy boots, and a bright red

Hawaiian shirt. Roy described his conversation with my boss, Adrian, and said he felt our companies would be a good match all around.

"We'll see about that," I replied. "What about Customs? How difficult will it be to clear the documents coming in from Hong Kong?"

"Hell," laughed Roy, "that's a piece of cake. We clear Customs every single day and we bring in all sorts of stuff, mainly hardware, pipes, all kinds of crap. Boy, as far as Vietnamese Customs is concerned, we are the U.S. Army."

Roy looked at his watch and said he needed to be someplace in ten minutes. He explained that I had been booked into the Continental Palace Hotel in downtown Saigon and Trang would take me there.

We departed the air base for the twenty-minute ride to the hotel, which was located in Saigon's high rent district on its most famous street, Tu Do. As we drove the main highway into Saigon, I marveled at the number of old beat up Renault taxis that constantly changed lanes to avoid the many motorcycles and pedicabs that traveled the boulevard that looked like a street in Paris. In the middle of the street was an island of green grass and colorful flowers that separated the incoming and outgoing lanes, on each side of the street was a single row of tall trees with a park bench every twenty yards or so.

This was unusual, not something I had ever seen in other countries in Asia. Instantly, I remembered that this was part of Indochina, a colony of France for some seventy years, until the 1950's when the French got kicked out in the Vietnamese War of Liberation. I wondered what fate the Americans would have in this country that seemed to be constantly at war.

As we drove up to the hotel I noticed it had been modeled after a French hotel. The interior was outfitted luxuriously with marble floors, a huge cut glass chandelier, teakwood floors, and walnut walls. After checking in I tossed my bag in my spacious, well-appointed room, I took the elevator downstairs and stepped outside onto Tu Do.

I hadn't eaten since early in the morning before my flight and hoped to find a restaurant on the main thoroughfare. Within a few blocks I spotted a pizza place that boldly advertised "American Pizza." Once inside the decor reminded me of a stateside Round Table with its bulky wooden tables and bench seats. It was three p.m. and there were only a few other customers in the place. I ordered a pizza and a beer and sat by the windows. The breeze generated by the swirling overhead fans provided only slight relief from the heat. As I looked at the open window

I noticed what looked like a thick wire mesh, the kind I used to see attached to the backstop at baseball fields when I was a kid.

When the waiter delivered my pizza he asked me in broken English if I wanted anything else. I nodded no and asked, "What's in the window? Is it wire? Why is it there?"

"Oh, yes sir," stammered the waiter. "Yes. Wire. Last week VC throw hand grenades in here. We put wire to stop them."

Shit. Is this how it is here? You go out for pizza and someone you don't even know tries to kill you? Maybe that's why it's called a war zone.

It was exactly seven p.m. as the sun started sinking and the oppressive heat began to diminish. I waited for Roy in the hotel bar's open veranda adjacent to busy Tu Do Street. A few minutes after seven Roy appeared and immediately ordered two gin and tonics. Yes, it looked like this guy and I would get along.

Roy told me he had been in Vietnam for two years working for P.A.E. and that he had one more year left on his contract. He said he had saved almost all his paychecks and planned to return home in West Texas and buy a small cattle ranch.

I told Roy about the window at the pizza place just down the street and asked, "Is this place really dangerous?"

"It can be," replied Roy. "It's all about being in the wrong place at the wrong time. The Viet Cong are terrorists. With the U.S. troop withdrawal underway, they've stepped up their activities. Just last week they rolled about 10 hand grenades into a crowded movie house in the Cholon area, the Chinese district of Saigon. They killed a bunch of women and children. It was bad, real bad. Yeah, just one more year, the U.S. is pulling out more troops daily. It's just a matter of time before the entire country, or what's left of it, falls to the communists."

"It's unbelievable," I replied. "I saw some of the destruction on the flight from Bangkok this morning. The pilot announced we had just crossed into Vietnam from Cambodia and when I looked down all I saw was miles of bomb craters and barren ground. The trees and jungle were gone. It looked like a moonscape."

"Oh, yeah," replied Roy, "that was part of America's secret war. We bombed the shit out of that area. We even went into Cambodia with U.S. troops and then denied it later. We were trying to stop VC infiltrators. We leveled the place and then used Agent Orange, a chemical that kills anything that grows. That's not all, that Agent Orange stuff, well, when the monsoons comes it washes into the rivers and streams that flow into the Mekong Delta where it kills all the shrimp. Before the war Vietnam exported shrimp. No more."

And the trees that are left after the saturation bombing that happens every day in this country, there's so much shrapnel in them from exploding bombs that they cannot be harvested. The chain saw blades hit the metal and disintegrate or explode sometimes killing the operators. The teak wood industry in this country has been devastated; Thailand is now the region's largest exporter.

As Roy downed the last of his first drink and reached for the second, he shook his head and said, "Yeah, Kid, I want to get my money and get the hell out of here before it falls to the commies, and I want to forget this place forever."

The next morning I had breakfast in the hotel's cobblestone sidewalk café and waited for Roy to arrive. We planned to call on our clients at the American banks. I would introduce him and his company as our agent in Vietnam. I had contacted all the banks prior to leaving Bangkok and at the urging of their corporate offices they had agreed to use the courier service as soon as it was operational. Our service would save days or in some cases weeks in the processing of checks, credit card receipts and commercial letters of credit.

Roy and his driver Trang in their olive drab 65 Chevy arrived at 8:30 and after a short drive we arrived in the financial section of Saigon where all the large commercial banks were headquartered. It was nice to be in an air conditioned car even for short distances as the humidity and the heat even in the early morning made walking in my light colored suit an ordeal that quickly resulted in a wrinkled and sweat-stained appearance. Almost all the foreign businessmen in Asia had drivers as the congested traffic, brutal climate, and lack of parking in the major cities made it a practical necessity.

At exactly nine a.m., we arrived for our appointment at Bank of America's Vietnam Headquarters to meet the manager. After being led into a conference room, we were greeted by Donald Lewis, a vice president. He looked like a typical middle-aged bank manager wearing a dark suit, white shirt, striped silk tie, and glasses.

I introduced Roy and explained that P.A.E. would be our contracted agent who would deliver and collect the daily bank documents that would be transported through the courier service hub at Hong Kong and then on to the bank's headquarters in San Francisco.

The vice president listened intently and when I finished he looked at me with raised eyebrows and said, "It's great you're finally here, but aren't you a little late? The boom times are over in this country. The U.S. is withdrawing more troops every day. The building and expansion plans of all the foreign corporations have stopped.

"No one knows what's going to happen here. Unless the South Vietnamese Army can quickly show they can defeat the communists without the support of U.S. troops, this country will go into a tailspin. The banks are already losing money; our biggest customers are the U.S. military and their subcontractors."

We heard the same story at the other American banks we saw that day. The executives at Chase, Citibank, and American Express all had doubts and concerns whether the country could survive without a large presence of American armed forces. It was late afternoon when we drove back to the hotel.

I looked at Roy sitting next to me in the back seat of the 65 Chevy and asked, "What about P.A.E., your company? When will it pull out?"

Roy smiled and laughed as he said, "We'll be the last ones out of Dodge. Our contract is with the Department of Defense, not just the U.S. Army. As long as the U.S. gives assistance to this country, we will be here.

"But the banks and the foreign corporations, that's another story. As soon as the U.S. announced the troop withdrawal about six weeks ago, all the investment stopped. The Hilton was supposed to break ground just down the street from your hotel and that stopped dead in its tracks.

"The banks are especially vulnerable. The value of the piaster, the local currency, is falling like a rock against the U.S. dollar. A month ago it was 300 piaster to the dollar, now it's over 700. If things get any worse there will be a run on the banks. The rumor is that the American banks could pull out of the country at any time."

Jesus. It's just like I told my boss, Adrian. This place is screwed up.

As we approached the hotel Roy invited me to his house the following Saturday evening for what he called a "real Texas barbecue." His driver would pick me up at the hotel at 6 p.m. He also suggested since the following day was Saturday that I take in the huge street market on Mong street just a short distance from the hotel. The staff could give me directions, he suggested.

Mooncake Man

On Saturday morning, I had a late breakfast and lounged by the pool on the hotel roof in the ever present heat and humidity. After getting written directions in Vietnamese from the desk clerk, I took a pedicab to the street market in the afternoon. The market was huge, at least four city blocks in each direction that had been blocked off to any motorized vehicles or motorcycles.

As I walked into the market and its crowded narrow streets I could see that it had been organized into sections, the first being produce where every conceivable type of fruit and vegetable were displayed. Adjacent to that was a live animal area where fowl, pigs, monkeys, and dogs could be selected by the customer and butchered on the spot.

Next came a huge display of fish and shell fish, some still alive and others neatly stacked in rows on ice, food stalls were everywhere, from full course meals to sweet snacks. The smells overwhelmed, a mixture of every possible odor assaulted my senses all at the same time. As I walked along, a thick cloud of heat and humidity made my clothes feel like they were permanently pasted to my body.

As I continued to wander through the endless narrow streets of the market, I came upon a section that sold military clothes. As I looked closer at the items I could see there were stacks of real U.S. Army boots, socks, shirts, jackets, pants and rows of stacked K-rations, first aid kits, and even bayonets.

Seeing weapons sold so openly in the market surprised me as they were undoubtedly stolen from the U.S. Army. As I look closer at the bayonet a young Vietnamese guy introduced himself in English as Steven said, "You like the bayonet? Brand new. I give it to you for five bucks, U.S. money---you have U.S. money?"

"Yes," I replied, "Do you have the rifle that goes with this?"

The young Vietnamese stopped smiling and gave me a serious look as he said, "You Army Cop?"

"No," I said.

The Vietnamese shot back, "I don't believe you."

"Okay," I replied. "Here's my passport. I'm staying at the Continental Hotel on Tu Du Street. I'm a businessman. G.I.s don't have passports."

"Okay, okay," said the young Vietnamese guy that called himself Steven. "Come into the back. I show you all kinds of guns."

I followed him into an adjoining room at the back of the shop. From underneath a table he pulled out every type of weapons used by the U.S.

Army in Vietnam from the standard issue M-16 rifles, 45 caliber pistols, hand grenades, M-30 machine guns, to M-60 grenade launchers.

"Which one you want to buy?" asked the young storekeeper. "I give you good price. I have the ammunition, too."

"Not today," I replied. "I'll be back tomorrow." I abruptly made my exit from the small room and out into the narrow streets of the market. As I entered the jewelry and watch section of the market I thought to myself if a small shopkeeper in an open market has these types of American weapons just think what the communists must have. God, this country is really corrupt.

As I glanced at the eager shopkeepers all thrusting fake Rolex watches at me, I heard men and women yelling and screaming behind me. I turned and saw two Vietnamese policemen grabbing a young skinny teenage boy by both arms. The boy was shaking his head and screaming in Vietnamese at the top of his lungs as the policeman were tearing at the pockets of his pants and emerging with various articles of jewelry and watches.

Several women and men were hitting the boy with their fits and yelling at the cops who then started yelling at the angry shopkeepers. It looked like any minute the place was going to erupt into a mob scene.

One of the cops grabbed his pistol from his holster and in one swift motion raised the barrel to the boy's temple and pulled the trigger. In a split second there was a thunderous explosion and a flash of bright yellow and red as the opposite side of the boy's head disintegrated into a thousand splinters of skin, bone, blood, and brains that left a grotesque imprint on the opposite wall of the narrow street.

The men and women in the crowd grew silent as they looked down at the lifeless body of the young boy with blood pouring from his demolished head. Then they slowly turned away and walked back to their market stalls. It was like a movie flash, like a speeding train had passed me in a millisecond with its horn blasting so loud I could not hear or think of anything. My mind was blank.

I felt a hand on my shoulder. I looked over and it was Steven, the young shopkeeper who had tried to sell me the guns. He said, "You okay mister? Your clothes are a mess."

I looked down at my pants and shoes, Oh, my God, there was blood and pieces of flesh and brains on my shoes. I felt faint and staggered to the side of the narrow street where I collapsed to the foul ground and threw up my breakfast. After a few minutes Steven the shopkeeper helped me to my feet and wiped me off with a wet towel as I asked him, "What the hell happened? Why did they kill that boy?"

Steven just shook his head and said, "The boy was a thief. He had been caught here before stealing, the shopkeepers and the cops told him if they caught him stealing again they would shoot him. The cops didn't really want to shoot him but the merchants got really pissed, so the cop shot him."

"My God," I replied. "No jail? No trial?"

"No." replied Steven. "We don't have time for that here, and that's one less thief in this market.

It was exactly 6 p.m. as I slid into the back seat of the 65 brown Chevy with Trang, Roy's driver, at the wheel. As we drove through the dimly lit and congested streets toward Roy's house located on the outskirts of the city I tried to forget about what had happened at the market by drowning myself in vodka tonics at the hotel bar and arguing with the floor boy who insisted he could clean my bloody clothes. I finally told him sternly to throw the clothes away. I never wanted to be reminded of that tragic event again.

Roy's house was a large two-story residence, surrounded by beautiful landscaping, with a long circular driveway which was lined with cars and their idle drivers. The backyard was spacious and had a huge patio where several bars and barbecue were strategically placed among the scattered tables that stretched on to the grass lawn. There were people everywhere with a mixture of Westerners, Vietnamese, and Indians drinking and talking in little scattered groups.

As I ordered a vodka tonic at the bar, Roy greeted me and introduced me to several of his company's managers and various U.S. embassy employees. As I waited at the bar for my second drink a Vietnamese guy introduced himself as Jerry Tu and said he was a Captain in the ARVN and a close friend of Roy.

He seemed very interested in the courier service so I told him how we moved documents throughout Asia servicing major corporations. I asked him how he knew Roy. Jerry told me he had met Roy about a year ago when he was first assigned to the airport security detail and they had become close friends and then he asked me about the customers in Saigon.

I told him about the meetings that Roy and I had the previous day with the banks and how they were not optimistic about the future of

Vietnam. "I know," replied Jerry, shaking his head, "a lot of companies are getting worried because of the U.S. troop withdrawal."

"You're an officer in the South Vietnamese Army, the ARVN. What do you think?" I asked.

Jerry took a drink, looked around the room as if to make sure no one heard him, and said, "Everyone is scared as hell. The U.S. had over half a million troops here. Now we have fewer than 50,000 and we're pulling out more by the day. If you were in my place, wouldn't you be scared?" he asked.

"Yes, I probably would," I replied.

Jerry took another drink as he said, "The VC guerillas have spies everywhere. They know exactly how many U.S. troops are in the country and how many are leaving every day."

I asked, "Can the ARVN hold its own against the VC? or not? Shit, from what I've seen, the U.S. is leaving enough equipment behind."

"Yes, we can hold out against the VC" said Jerry. "But it won't be just the guerillas. When the time comes, the NVA, the North Vietnamese Army will come over the DMZ and obliterate the ARVN, the South Vietnamese Army. This country is corrupt. It will be every man for himself."

"What will happen to you?" I replied. "You're a Captain in the ARVN, right?"

Jerry look down and shook his head as he said, "If I survive the battles, they will kill me. They will not take me prisoner."

"I can't believe they'll kill every officer in the ARVN. I'm sure they'll take some prisoners."

"Maybe," replied Jerry, "but not me. I was born in the north, before the French defeat at Bien Dien Phu and chose to immigrate south before the country spilt. My family and two brothers still live in the north and are officers in the NVA."

"Really?" I replied. "Are you saying that if you were captured by your brothers they would kill you?"

"Yes," replied Jerry, "to them I am a traitor to my country. I have fought against them and like every Vietnamese in this room that works for an American we will all be killed if we lose this war. Yes, we are scared. You Americans started this war, escalated it, and now you're abandoning us."

I just looked at Jerry, tilted my head, and pointed to the waiter serving food at my table, walked away. He is right. The Americans started this war when they landed the Marines at Da Nang Air Base in 1965. Now, eight years later, we finally realize that this war is unwinnable.

On Monday morning and the start of another hot and humid week, I waited for Trang to take me to meet Roy. We would supervise the first incoming courier shipment from Hong Kong. As Roy and I waited outside the Customs area, I was pleasantly surprised to see his guys emerge from the baggage area with the big green bags containing bank documents. The bags cleared Customs and were placed inside the van for delivery within forty minutes of the flight's arrival.

Roy turned to me and smiled as he said, "See, I told you. It's a piece of cake."

"I'm impressed. Just remember that any grease is at your expense," I said.

Roy smiled as he told me it was time to go back to his office and firm up all the details and sign a contract. It was nice to get back to Roy's air-conditioned office. I looked forward to completing the our agreement and leaving for Bangkok as soon as possible.

As Roy and I were reviewing the contract details his secretary came into the office. She said that Trang was on the phone and urgently needed to speak with him. Roy picked up the phone and after a few minutes his face turned ashen white as he said to Trang, "Are you sure? What did the sign say? Okay, check on the rest of the banks and call me."

Roy hung up the phone, sat down at his desk and said, "You're not going to believe this but our first delivery to Bank of America is not going to happen. The place is padlocked. All the Vietnamese employees are locked out and there is a sign on the door that says the bank has ceased operations and any deposits can be claimed at a local Vietnamese bank."

The phone rang again and Roy hurriedly picked it up. After a minute, he turned to me and said, "Those bastards! They're all pulling out. City Bank and Chase are padlocked. The American Express office is open but only for credit card transactions. I need to find out what's going on. I'll have Trang take you back to the hotel."

It was late afternoon when Roy called and told me the story of how the three American banks had chartered a World Airways DC-10. In the middle of the night they transferred all their U.S. currency and assets to the aircraft along with their families and left Vietnam for San Francisco.

"Gee Roy, let me get this straight. These American bankers chartered a huge jet and after the close of business on Saturday afternoon, loaded all their U.S currency on board. They gathered up their old ladies and children and fled the country, all before the start of business on Monday? And nobody knows shit until they read the sign on the padlocked doors?"

Roy said, "Pretty goddamn slick. They must have paid off every son-of-a-bitch in this country above the rank of sergeant."

"Well, Roy," I replied. "There's no use in me hanging around. I'll be leaving for Bangkok this evening. If business comes back, you know how to reach me."

The sun was setting as I buckled my seat belt in the beautiful pearl white aircraft with the bright green dragon. The 727 taxied to the runway, the engines roared, and in no time we were lifted skyward. As the jet turned south toward Bangkok I looked down at Saigon and the surrounding countryside. I felt tremendous relief that I was leaving and wondered what would be the fate of Vietnam and its people.

Chapter 17 Launching
Yvonne's Massage Parlor

God, it's great to be back in Thailand. The plane's engines slowly hummed to a stop at the Bangkok airport passenger terminal. I felt exhausted, tired and sick of business; I wanted to forget about everything.

The pleasures of Sophie's massage parlor filled my imagination. As soon as I got off the plane and into the city, I planned to drop off my bags at the hotel, drink myself to oblivion at the Horny Toad, and spend the rest of evening at Sophie's.

I passed through immigration and Customs quickly because few planes were landing that Monday afternoon. I jumped into one of the old beat up taxis that waited at the curb. The highway from Don Muang Airport to Bangkok was as dangerous as being in Vietnam with the little taxi traveling at its maximum speed and constantly swerving, braking, and weaving between overloaded ancient trucks.

We reached the city in less than an hour. I pointed the driver in the direction of my hotel. When he turned onto Patpong Street, the sight completely stunned me. Sophie's, the classiest massage parlor in all of Bangkok had burned to the ground. Missing from view was the large golden neon Eiffel Tower. All that remained was a big black pile of debris and a yellow rope surrounding the place where the building once stood.

As the taxi drove onto the curved cobblestone drive of the Montien Hotel, Steven the doorman, quickly recognized me and flashed his familiar smile. As I handed him a 100 baht note, I told him to take the bags to my room.

Entering the Montien, I spotted Pierre, the manager, and motioned for him to come over. As he approached, I asked, "So what happened at Sophie's? When did it burn down?"

Pierre sadly shook his head and said, "It happened about a week ago. I think it was the day after you left on your trip. It occurred in the early morning hours. All the girls and customers got out, thank goodness."

"So how did it happen? Who did it?" I asked.

Pierre raised his eyebrows and wiggled his nose as he said, "Don't know how it started, but, you know Patpong. There are a lot of stories out there, from a jealous boyfriend to one of the Generals not getting his fair share of the pie."

"Shit," I replied, "I planned on going there tonight."

Pierre laughed as he said, "Don't worry about that, the pretty ones went over to Roma's, Sophie's rival, just down the street. I bet they're doing a hell of a business. I heard that they raised the prices. Maybe they burned Sophie's down, you never know in this town."

It was late afternoon when I finally walked into the Horny Toad and found it almost empty. I slid onto the bar stool and ordered three vodka tonics from Apri, the daytime bartender. She said, "Welcome back. How was Vietnam?"

"Depressing, really depressing," I responded. "I'm glad to be back home."

Apri winked her cute smile and turned around to the bottle shelf to find my 100 proof Smirnoff. I couldn't help but look at her little butt. She was not a bad-looking woman. I guessed she was in her late 30s, but it was hard to tell with Thai women. They just didn't seem to age until their 40s.

For some reason she looked better than usual in her paper thin dress that showed every curve in her body. As she set the three drinks in front of me she said Stan had told her that if I showed up today to call him because he needed to discuss some urgent business.

"Screw the business," I replied. "I'm tired of business. I'm tired of having fuckers calling me and telling me that things are urgent. I'm going to get good and ripped and then screw my brains out with as many women as I can get my hands on."

Apri just looked at me. She put her tiny hands to her chin and said, "I've known you for over six months now. You're a young, rich guy, and you could get any Thai girl in Bangkok. Instead you get drunk all the time and go to the whorehouses. Don't you ever get tired of that? Don't you want to find a nice girl who will love you and care for you and help you raise a family?"

I stared at her and held up three fingers for my triple vodka refills, and said, "Jesus, Apri, why in the hell would I want to do that? I love women. I crave all kinds of women. I would never be happy with the same woman every single night for the rest of my life. I'd get bored sexually after a couple of nights."

"But," said Apri, "there's more to being with a woman than having sex. Haven't you ever cared about someone deeply? Have you ever really loved a woman?"

"Look, Apri," I angrily shot back, "women are all the same to me. As soon as I get feelings for a woman, she becomes possessive, demanding, and tries to control my life. Sure, I know about women. They lie when it's convenient and have no remorse. They use me for their own purposes and when they're done they throw me away like a piece of shit.

"I don't want women to care about me. I only need them for sex. To me, it's just a business transaction. I pay for their services and I don't care to know anything more about them."

Apri waited a moment and said, "I am sorry for you, that you feel that way about people."

"Fuck you, Apri," I said, "don't preach to me, from what I heard you used to work in the houses and used drugs." What has gotten into me? Why I am taking out my anger on Apri?

"Yes, you are right, but I finally found my Buddha. I changed my life. I hope you do, too, because if you don't, you will have a very lonely and unhappy life," she replied in a gentle voice.

"Don't worry about me, sweetheart. Give me a refill in a paper cup. I'm going to get laid," I answered.

What? What the hell is that sound? Oh, it's the phone. My head, my fucking head, my back hurts, too. Who the hell is calling me?

I didn't want to leave the warm bed in the dark room, but I had to know the time. As I glanced at the clock on the nightstand, I noticed that I was in my own bedroom. I was relieved. The clock said 10:30, but was it day or night? I felt groggy, hazy, as if my mind was operating in slow motion and not attached to my body.

I looked at the closed blinds and saw the splinters of bright light beaming into the room and realized it must be 10:30 in the morning.

The phone finally stopped ringing. I lay perfectly still, held my breath for several seconds, and listened for any sound in the room, any human sound. Nothing, thank god. I hadn't brought anyone home with me.

What the hell had happened last night? I must have really tied one on to feel this shitty. I just stayed reclined and tried to remember. I had arrived at the Bangkok airport, stopped at the Toad on Patpong, drank vodka, and talked with Apri the day bartender. I got a little loaded there and went to Sophie's.

No, it wasn't Sophie's. That place was burned down. But where did I meet Frankie? He used to be the hustler at Sophie's. Oh, now I remember, Frankie was at Roma's massage parlor and brought some of his best girls with him. I don't remember anything after talking to him in front of the huge windows with the girls sitting in rows staring at customers.

Oh hell, where was my wallet? I had about 500 bucks in it left over from my Vietnam trip.

I crawled out of bed and spotted the wallet on my dresser. Thank God I still had it. I opened it and found it was completely empty of cash. The credit cards were still there. Without Western names, passports, or other identification, the local thieves probably had a hard time using stolen credit cards.

Slipping back into bed, I wondered how the hell I got back to my hotel. Did someone take me? Shit, I didn't remember anything. As I rested on the bed with the pillow covering my face I told myself I would never leave the bed again.

I don't want to be in this world anymore. I want to be left alone. I don't know what happened to me and I don't care anymore. Maybe I am an alcoholic and I have to do this. Maybe I don't have a choice.

The sound of the ringing phone jerked me out of my self-pity. After a few rings I picked it up and Stan bellowed, "Where the fuck have you been? I've been trying to reach you for two days. We need to talk about business, the new revenues and taxes. If we don't do something very soon, the government will take it all.

"Meet me at the Horny Toad at noon. I'll buy you a greasy hamburger. It will go great with your hangover. I heard you really tied one on last night."

"Shit," I replied, "I don't even know what I did last night. How the hell do you know what happened?"

Stan laughed as he said, "I've got spies all over Patpong. I'll fill you in on all the sordid details over lunch."

"Oh, I can hardly wait," I replied.

It was almost noon as I started to walk the three blocks from my hotel to Stan's place. I was sure that Stan couldn't wait to tell the nooner crowd about my behavior. With each step I tried to remember all of the events of the night before, but only bits and pieces emerged from my latest alcoholic blackout.

As I entered the Horny Toad and I was welcomed back by the usual cast of characters at the bar. I heard Stan's voice coming from one of the corner booths and I immediately joined him. He held up two fingers to Apri the bartender and then tuned to me with a big smile on his face as he said, "Okay, kid, are you ready for the hair of the dog that bit you last night? You look like you got hit square in the face by one of those crazy pedicabs."

"What the hell are you talking about Stan? Are you asking if I want a beer, just smelling it makes me want to puke," I said.

I looked up from the table and Apri was standing there with Stan's two beers as she said, "I will get you some warm coconut milk. It will help your stomach."

Apri placed the two beers on the table and as I watched her walk back toward the bar I remembered what a bitch she had been the day before. The more she preached at me and told me how to live my life the more I drank triple shots of 100 proof vodka. No wonder I got screwed up so fast.

"Well," said Stan, "do you want to know what a real asshole you where last night? Do you remember anything?"

"Not much," I said, "except Apri being a real bitch to me yesterday."

"Really?" said Stan with exasperation. "It was Apri who took care of you last night. After you got good and drunk here on an entire fifth of vodka, you staggered over to Roma's. They threw your ass out and then you went over to the 007 Club and drank some more. You got into a fight with some Australian tourist.

"After they threw you out at the 007, you came back over here and tried to drink some more. Apri refused to serve you and you got all pissed and took a swing a Tony the bouncer and he threw your sorry ass out into the street.

"Apri found you passed out in the gutter, loaded you in a cab, and accompanied you to your hotel. She and the doorman dragged you back to your room and put you in bed.

Let me give you some advice kid, if you want to be a big shot and mouth off and start fights in Patpong, you're going to end up in some alley with a knife in your back.

"Shit, you little fucker! You're only 26 and if you keep this up you won't make it to 27.

Apri saved your little ass last night, you owe her your life," Stan said.

I could only look down at the floor as I said, "You're right Stan. I was a jerk. It won't happen again."

As I looked up and saw Apri placing the warm coconut milk on the table I said, "Thank you for taking care of me last night." She smiled, said nothing, and turned away.

"Now," said Stan, "let's get to the money."

We had both agreed at the start of the service some six months earlier that all billing for the courier service to the large multinational banks and shipping companies would be done at their corporate offices in the states. The charges for pickup and delivery services performed by Stan's Thai company would be paid by a wire transfer from my Hong Kong courier company.

Thai government regulations did not allow a foreign corporation to operate a service company in Thailand; only a local Thai company owned 100 percent by a Thai national could legally operate such a company in the country. In Stan's case, his company was owned by his Thai wife.

As the courier operation in Thailand became successful we started to handle local Thai banks and trading companies. Billing for these services was done by Stan's company and the revenue was deposited in his company's local bank account. Within three months we were billing enough revenue that no wire transfer of funds from Hong Kong was needed to pay Stan's operating cost and we started to develop a surplus.

By the end of the fifth month we had an operating surplus of $20,000. And every month it was increasing threefold. Stan said that if we did not invest the money back into the business or into some other venture, the Thai government would take at least half for taxes.

"So, Stan, what's the problem?" I asked. "Buy a few new trucks."

He threw up his hands and said, "We don't need any trucks. We don't need anything. This surplus isn't going away; it's going to get bigger every month. I have a better idea, a business where we can make some real money, where we can double or triple our investment in less than a year.

"The only catch is that we have to move quickly. This business has hardly any competition right now. It's a very limited opportunity. I'll cut you in for 25 percent."

I threw up my hands as I said to Stan, "Okay, okay. Is it legal?"

"Hell, yes," said Stan.

"Okay, damn it. Do I have to guess? What is it?" I asked.

Stan's face beamed like a light bulb from ear to ear as he proclaimed, "We're going into the massage parlor business. Sophie's burned down. Roma's got no real competition. Shit, they doubled their prices and the place is still packed with G.Is. I've already checked. We can buy the building two doors down from the Toad. We can be up in running in two weeks."

"Are you kidding, Stan? You want to go into the whore business? Hell, I only go to them, I don't know anything about running them," I said.

"Neither do I," said Stan. "But Wei does, and don't ask me any details. We'll put the money up, be on the management board, oversee the books, and see that we make a good profit."

"Okay, Stan, what the hell? I guess it's better than the government taking the money. So it will be you, me and Wei right? So, why do I only get 25 percent? Why not 33 percent?"

"Oh, you're a smart ass, kid. That's because we have another partner, a silent partner, the same partner I have at the Toad," said Stan.

"So, does he put in any money?" I asked.

"No," said Stan, "he's just a partner. Don't ask me for names. Trust me, it has to be this way." Stan looked at his watch and said he was running late and would meet with me the following day at noon to discuss the details.

The nooner crowd had left and the place was almost empty. As I started to leave I saw Apri seated alone in the far corner booth eating her lunch. I sat down opposite her and said, "Thank you for taking care of me last night. I know I said some ugly things. It was the booze talking, not the real me. I apologize."

Apri smiled and told me that I shouldn't drink so much. "Next time I might not be around to take care of you. Patpong can be a dangerous place at night, especially if you get drunk."

"You're right," I said. "I need to stop drinking like that."

"And the whorehouses? Apri asked. "What about the whorehouses ?"

"Shit, Apri, that's just good exercise. There's nothing wrong with that," I said.

Apri finished her lunch, patted her lips with the cloth napkin, folded it, and gently placed it beside her plate. She looked up at me and said, "Do you think I'm pretty? Do you think I'm good looking?"

"Not bad for an older woman," I replied.

Smiling, she said, "I'm 38 and I am beautiful. You really don't know the difference of being with a beautiful Thai women and a whore, do you? You don't even know what I'm talking about."

She looked at me with her piercing brown eyes and pulled a small piece of paper and a pen from her hip pocket and started writing something in Thai characters. When she finished she looked at me with a big smile and said, "Tomorrow is my day off. Give this to the taxi driver at your hotel at five p.m. He will take you to my place. I will make you a nice Thai dinner and afterwards you will know the difference."

It was exactly 5 p.m. the next day when Steven, the hotel doorman, opened up the rear door of a taxi and gave the driver my wadded up note with Apri's address. As the taxi turned into the traffic I thought to myself, why did she invite me to her place for dinner? I can't believe she has any romantic interest in me. She knows I drink like a fish and love the whorehouses.

Why did I agree to see her? Maybe it's because I feel guilty about how I treated her the night I got drunk and then found out it was she who took care of me. Besides she has an interesting past. Since I'm going into the whore business I'm curious about her life, how much money she made, and why she quit.

As the taxi continued to swerve in and out of traffic and make turns down one way streets I remembered the meeting I had with Stan just a few hours earlier. He was all excited about the new place. He had negotiated a good price for the empty building just a few doors down. He was busy calculating the cost of refurbishing the site and making it into a first class massage parlor. Stan had wanted to call the place, 'Sophie's Too,' but the previous owners wanted a ton of money for the name so he suggested all the partners come up with a new name by the end of the week.

After thirty minutes of tires pounding up and down and the car swerving around rocks, potholes, and huge cracks in the road, the driver abruptly pulled over to the curb and pointed to a large apartment building. After paying the driver the fare that was negotiated by Steven the doorman, I stepped on to the sidewalk and was immediately met by a smiling Apri who told how pleased she was that I had come to her house.

Apri wore a traditional narrow light blue skirt with a colorful blue and yellow silk blouse. She grabbed my hand and led me up the three flights of stairs to her apartment and then ordered me to remove my shoes. As she opened the door I could see the place was small but very clean and well kept. The entryway had a tiny kitchen to one side and a bedroom on the other side.

The short hallway led to a quaint living room and dining area that had a Japanese style table with a floor of tatami mats. Directly overhead was a huge ceiling fan that produced a cooling swath of air and a swishing sound as it continued its endless rotation.

Several feet from the dining area was a little patio that overlooked the street below. Apri seated me at the Japanese table and within a few minutes retuned with a pot of hot tea and as she poured the tea she smiled and said, "This is a special tea; it will calm you. It is very good for you. I'm sorry but I do not serve any alcohol in my house."

"Really," I replied, "but you serve it at the bar."

"Yes, but that's work and this is my home," said Apri. She told me she would prepare my favorite dish, jumbo shrimp and curry over rice.

"How the hell did you know that?" I asked.

"I'm the bartender," said Apri, "I know everything. That, for instance, you, Stan and Wei, are opening up a massage parlor just a few doors down."

"Okay, if you know everything, who is Stan's silent partner in the Toad? Hell, he's the guy that owns the same percentage as I do in the new place and doesn't even have to put up any money," I said.

Apri laughed as she said, "What makes you so sure it's a guy? Maybe it's a woman?"

"Look," she said, "this is the way it is in Patpong. Everyone that does any business here has a silent partner. It could be one of the rich Chinese families, the biggest one is run by a woman or it could be one of the

Army generals. They own part of your business and you pay protection money on top of that. If you try and cheat them, the business ends up like Sophie's, burned to the ground."

"So you didn't answer my question. Who is Stan's silent partner?" I repeated.

"I don't know for sure, but I think it's one of the army generals. He comes in every few months with his two mistresses. Stan always knows when he's coming and kisses his ass from one end of the place to another," said Apri.

Suddenly there was a knock at the door and Apri jumped up and said, "That must be Nicha returning from the market with the fresh shrimp." After a few minutes in the kitchen Apri returned holding the hand of a young girl who was dressed in a skirt and blouse similar to her own. "Let me introduce you to Nicha," said Apri. Nicha was very young, in her late teens or early twenties, short, flat-chested, with a beautiful face that had no signs of makeup.

"Nice to meet you," I said.

Nicha smiled and held out her tiny hand toward me. In perfect English she said, "It's a pleasure to meet you." As we all sat down at the table ,Apri poured tea in the cups. She looked at me and said, "Have you ever seen Nicha before?"

"No," I replied, "Why would I?"

Nicha giggled and Apri smiled as she said, "Well, she has seen you before. The last time was when you got drunk and I had to take you back to your hotel room."

"Shit," I said, "I hardly remember anything about that night. Exactly where did she see me?"

Nicha smiled ear to ear as she said, "The last time I saw you was when the bouncer threw you and an a big Australian guy out the side door for fighting."

"Oh," I said, "you saw me at my worst. Was that the 007 Club? Do you work there?"

"Yes," she replied, "I'm a bar girl there and I hate the place. The managers are mean and they cheat me all the time."

Apri turned to me and with a stern look, and said, "I took care of you and now I need you to do something for me. I want you to hire Nicha at your new place, the massage parlor. She is beautiful and a hard worker. She will make you money."

"Jesus, Apri, I'm just a partner in this. I don't do the hiring. Wei does that," I hedged.

"Yes, I know, but Wei hates me. If it wasn't for Stan, she would have fired me years ago. You're a part owner. Please tell Stan you want to hire Nicha and that you knew her from Sophie's and she's good. Don't tell anyone she is my cousin and lives with me."

"Okay, okay. I will try Apri. At least now I know why you invited me here," I replied.

"Yes," said a smiling Apri, "and after dinner Nicha will demonstrate her massage skills."

The dinner was delicious; the prawns were huge and fresh and steamed along with the rice and topped with hot curry sauce.

As we finished eating and Nicha poured tea into my glass, I asked Apri to tell me about her life and how she ended up working for Stan. She turned and looked at Nicha and then at me as she said, "Nicha knows my story. That's why I want her to get out of the bars. They're worse than the whorehouses. There is too much alcohol and drugs.

"I was born in a small village in the northern part of Thailand close to the Burmese border. My family worked as poor tenant farmers growing rice. Every year was a struggle to survive. I came from a family of three brothers and three sisters. After a flood wiped out the crops one year, my father sold me and my two sisters to a Chinese procurer who then resold us to various whorehouses in Bangkok."

Apri said she was fourteen at the time and never saw her sisters again, even to this day. She wonders if they are still alive. She was told she would be required to work at least two years to pay back the money given to her family. She said it was the darkest time of her life; she had no family, no friends, and was not allowed to leave the house unless escorted by one of the pimps.

Every day she saw as many men as she was told and after several years she ran away and tried to get a regular job in Bangkok but found it was very difficult as she had no education and no skills. She didn't want to go back to her family so she became a bar girl and worked from one bar to another and found the money was much more than she could have ever made in a straight job.

After a few years of working in many different bars she became an alcoholic and then became addicted to heroin and tried to commit suicide. One morning she woke up in the hospital with a monk chanting over her badly bruised and emaciated body. At this point in her story, she turned to me and asked, "Do you want to know what he was saying?"

I nodded and Apri said, "He was giving me the final farewell; in your country they call it the last rites. He told me I was dying, that I was a drug addict. I was only twenty-four and I was dying. I knew then my only hope was to find a belief in a higher power, any power that would give me the strength to overcome my self-will and addictions. This gift was given to me and I stopped destroying myself. Slowly my health and sanity returned. I was very fortunate, and I am very grateful for my life today."

"I'm glad you changed your life, Apri, but your niece has been doing the same thing, working as a bar girl," I said.

"That's right," Apri shot back, "and that's exactly why we need to get her out of there."

"Okay, okay, I'll see what I can do," I promised.

As we finished dinner Apri gathered up all the dishes and went into the kitchen. Nicha went to the closet and returned with a silk robe and told me to take a shower and put it on. When I finished my shower Apri had disappeared and Nicha was waiting for me in the living room dressed in only a loose fitting towel and seating next to a series of pillows she had placed on the floor.

She instructed me to take off the robe and lie on my stomach and almost immediately I felt the soft skin of her body against my back and the sweetness of her kiss on my neck as she slowly started to rub my shoulders. I closed my eyes, hearing only the occasional whisper of her breathing and the endless swishing sound of the ceiling fan. My mind started to slowly drift away and I was filled with anticipation of Nicha and the evening ahead.

Who the hell is calling me at this time of the morning, it's not even eight o'clock? I rolled over and pulled the pillow over my head and finally after ten rings the phone stopped making noise. I might as well get up as I had promised Stan I would meet him at his office at ten to discuss his business plan for our new venture. I also needed to talk to him about hiring Apri's cousin at the massage parlor. Ever since I had spent the evening at her home with Nicha present the week before, Apri had been bugging me every day at the Toad.

God, the phone had started ringing again. After the fourth ring I picked it up and heard the energetic voice of Al saying, "Hey kid, wanted to catch you before left for the day. Thought you were going to call me when you got back from Nam. I need a favor."

"What is it Al?" I replied.

Al said, "I'm interested in one of your clients, The Asia Foundation. The organization used the courier service daily from San Francisco to Bangkok and several other Asian locations.

"Why the hell would you be interested in them Al? They are some kind of educational foundation that deals with college exchange students," I said.

"That's not your concern," shot Al, "and we have a deal, remember? I need access to their document pouch, maybe 20 or 30 minutes at the most, that's all."

"Okay, but remember, this is just between us. The next shipment arrives at nine tonight. Come by the hotel and pick me up at seven. We'll go to the airport together and I'll get you the pouch," I said.

"But first you need to do something for me. Get the me address where the blonde works. You know, the girl named Vina that I asked you about and who works for the wealthy Chinese guy who exports the teakwood?"

"Okay, okay," replied Al, "my driver and I will pick you up at your hotel at seven."

As I started to shave I thought about Al. He looked like a CIA guy. He was built like a body builder. He didn't have a piece of fat on his six foot frame. He had a tanned face, blond hair, and wore shades all the time.

Maybe Al was an example of CIA reverse psychology. If you looked like a spy, you couldn't be a spy. God, it had only been nine months but it seemed like years that Al met me at Korat Air Force Base on that hot and sticky day I arrived from Korea, confused and scared as hell. Al and the General took care of me. I owed him.

After grabbing a cup of coffee to go from the hotel café I walked next door to the Chinese bakery for my favorite treat, fresh baked mooncakes and then took a cab to Stan's office on Wireless Road just a few miles from Patpong.

Stan had just arrived a few minutes earlier and was spreading out various sheets of paper and rattling off numbers as he looked at me and said, "Looks like the total investment will be close to 100K. Your share will be a third or 33K. Sign here," he said, "this is the partners' agreement. You put in a third of the investment, and you get a third of the profits, payable every quarter. Now let's go over all the expense items."

"Shit, Stan, I don't give a damn about the numbers. If you say it's workable, its fine with me. But as a part owner I want to hire one of the girls, someone I know will do a good job for us. Who do I need to talk to, Wei?"

"Yes and no," replied Stan. "Wei is in charge of all the employees, but we've hired Frankie from Roma's to help handle the girls. Before he worked at Roma's, he was the hustler at Sophie's, so he knows a lot of them already."

"Hell Stan, how much is he going to cost us? I'll bet he's not cheap," I said.

Stan shook his head and threw up his hands as he said; it's all in the numbers, right here, the stuff you don't want to look at."

"Okay, okay, Stan, I'll talk to Frankie," I said.

Stan told me that Frankie would be at the Toad later in the afternoon to finalize the deal with Wei before he started his shift at Roma's at four p.m. After going over the courier billing for the next few hours I finally headed over to the Toad and was greeted by a smiling Apri who told me Frankie was in Wei's office.

After several drinks at the bar Frankie emerged from the back office dressed in his trademark pimp attire consisting of a white suit, white shoes, red shirt with white silk tie and his long black hair in a pony tail held in place with a diamond studded clasp.

As soon as he saw me sitting at the bar, he broke into a big smile, held out his hand, and said, "Mr. John, I hear you are one of my bosses? Remember I work on a commission basis. There are no free samples."

"Frankie," I laughed, "I've always overpaid you. Now I get to see you screw other people and I get a piece of the action. How many girls are you going to bring with you?"

"Not sure," replied Frankie, "maybe 10 or 15, but I need to 15 to 20. I'll have to find a few more."

"Frankie, I want you to hire a girl I know. She will do a good job. No question," I said.

"Where has she worked before?" asked Frankie.

"One of the bars," I said.

"You mean that she's never worked in a fishbowl before? How do you know if she is any good?" Frankie asked.

"I can vouch for her, Frankie," I said. "I got a free sample last week. She's good-looking, young, and her name is Nicha."

"Okay, boss, but here's the deal. I'll take her on, but if she doesn't make me money, I'll dump her back in your lap. I make a commission on every customer. If a girl does not handle enough guys, I replace her with someone else, just like that." Frankie snapped his fingers.

"Okay, Frankie, I'll have her ready for the first day of business," I said.

Frankie nodded, turned, and headed out the door. I looked down to the far end of the bar and saw Apri staring at me. I held up my thumb and mouthed the word, "Okay." Apri winked and continued washing the bar glasses. As I stepped out of the bar and headed to my hotel I suddenly realized I had just become a pimp, and I didn't feel bad at all about it.

It was just a few minutes after seven p.m. as Al and his driver pulled up in their dark blue Toyota station wagon with the dark tinted windows. As I jumped into the back seat Al held out his hand and wanted to know all about my trip to Vietnam. After relating the entire adventure and the killing in the market, Al turned to me and said, "That's war, all kinds of shit happens, especially in Asia. These people do not put the same value on life as Westerners; don't get upset about it, that's the way it is here."

"So Al, let me get this straight, man's inhumanity to man can always be justified by saying it's a war, right?" I asked rhetorically.

"Look kid, don't be an asshole. You've been out here long enough to know you're not going to change a fucking thing. Either accept it or go back to suburbia," he said. After an hour of dodging the dangerously overloaded trucks on the motorway, we approached the international passenger area and spotted Pera, my operations manager. His crew waited by their delivery vans for the documents to be clear Customs.

After about ten minutes the big green bags had cleared Customs and were dragged to the waiting vans where the pouches would be sorted by customer and delivery location.

I walked over to Pera and described the pouch that I wanted to see. In a few short minutes he emerged with the bag in hand.

I told him to hold the delivery vans until I returned with the pouch at which time he could place it in the designated van for delivery with the rest of the pouches. I walked back to the car and slid into the back seat. Al immediately grabbed the pouch, turned on his large flashlight, and sorted through the documents.

As he looked at the documents he placed some back into the pouch and others he carefully stacked into a pile next to him. Al was so absorbed in the task he didn't notice me at first looking over his shoulder. As he pulled his small camera with its built-in light from his briefcase, however, he turned to me, and said, "Kid, why don't you go for a walk somewhere, when I'm done I'll flash the headlights on the car."

"Okay Al," I said. As I opened the door to leave, I said, "Remember, we have a deal. Don't take any of the documents or add anything into the pouch." Ten minutes later I saw the flash of the headlights and retrieved the pouch. I gave it to a waiting Pera and his crew for delivery.

As Al and I drove back to Patpong I suddenly remembered what I needed from him. I couldn't believe that I had almost forgot to ask him as I said, "Did you get it, the address of the round eye chick?"

"Yeah, I got it. I thought you might have forgotten about her. Here's the address," he said, handing me a slip of paper. "It's a shop on the outskirts of Bangkok, near the botanical gardens, and it's a real tourist area. Guess that's why they're out there.

"So kid, what are you going to do, just walk up to her and ask her for a date? Shit, you told me you only met her once at a Patpong bar and you were drunk and she was with two transvestites. For all you know she could be ugly as hell or maybe she's a transvestite."

Al started laughing as he said, "Kid, you been out here too long. You're getting weird like the rest of us. You've got to call me and tell me what happens. Hell, you won't even know who's really screwing you in this deal."

He was still laughing as we pulled up to my hotel. As I started to slide off the back seat toward the car door, he stopped laughing and with a serious look said, "You kept your end of the deal; I'll let the General know that. Let's keep in touch. You never know when we might need each other."

It was the next morning when I gave Steven the hotel doorman the crumpled piece of paper with the address of Vina's workplace that Al had given me the night before. Steven blew his whistle and signaled for a cab as he told me that the address was a well known tourist area near the zoo and botanical gardens.

As I sat in the cab and bounced through the roads and side streets of Bangkok, I thought to myself, maybe this is not such a good idea. What am I going to say to her, that I just happened to drop in; it was some kind of coincidence. What if I ask her out and she just ignores me, or worst yet, rejects me in front of a bunch of American or English tourists?

Maybe I should just go back to the hotel and take the chance of meeting her in Patpong some night, but what night and where? Hell, I need to have some guts and ask her out. If she shuts me down I'll just go back to the Toad, get loaded and then see Sonja at Roma's.

The cab made a right turn into an area that looked like a huge park and within a few minutes we had arrived at the entrance to the Botanical gardens, just to the right was a small wooden building with a curved roof similar to a Buddhist temple with a huge sign that said, Song's Teakwood Products.

I looked at the piece of paper with the address on it; this was the place she worked.

As I gave the driver the fare, I told him to wait. I walked up the gravel pathway to the entrance, opened the screen door, and walked into the building. Inside, I found a large room with rows of various teakwood carvings of all sizes and shapes, from Buddhist figures to intricately carved tables, furniture and doors.

I looked around for several minutes, walking between the various rows of carvings and suddenly heard a voice in a Thai accent say, "May I help you, sir?" I turned around and saw a young Thai fellow that looked as if he were in his late teens. He was about 10 feet away and wore jeans, a tee-shirt, and a wide smile.

"Well, yes," I replied. "I'm looking for a young white woman named Vina. I was told she works here."

The young man smiled, raised his eyebrows and said, "Yes, she works here. Do you want to see her? Whom may I say is asking?"

"Just tell her that I'm a recent acquaintance," I said. The young man nodded and disappeared. I continued to walk between the rows and rows of carvings that seemed to go on endlessly.

After about 10 minutes I heard a movement behind me and almost at the same time a soft women's voice say, "Do you wish to speak with me?"

I turned around and came face-to-face with a young white woman. Was it Vina? This woman looked so different than the Vina I had met in Patpong. Her blond flowing hair was wrapped into a tight pony tail. Instead of a tight fitting skirt with the low bust line, white nylons, and high heels with a diamond choker around her neck. She wore a plain loose fitting dress that covered her from shoulders to the barefoot sandals on her feet.

I just stood there staring at her for moment. Yes, it was her. She wore no makeup and she was beautiful. "Well," she said, with no southern accent. "Do you want to speak to me? I'm very busy."

Nodding, I asked, "Do you remember me?"

Raising her eyebrows, she tilted her head and said, "Yes, I remember you. Did you come to buy some teakwood or to see me? How did you know I was here?"

I replied, "A mutual acquaintance told me I might find you here. I want to take you to dinner this weekend."

She just stared at me for what seemed like an eternity and with a serious look said, "I don't do dinners."

I just looked at her for a long time. It was like she had taken a shovel and smacked me right in the face. What a cold-hearted bitch. She stood there and gazed back at me. Not even a thank you. Not, "I'm busy, how about a rain check?" or "No, I can't but thank you for the offer."

I felt like a rat that had just been cornered in the kitchen by the cook with a big butcher knife. All of a sudden her stoic face changed. She broke into a brilliant smile and said,

"There's a good chance I'll be with my friends at the Toad this Friday night. Maybe I'll see you there."

I was stunned. The woman enjoyed watching guys squirm. Shit, she didn't just wear that choker for looks. I'll bet she's really into bondage and discipline, B & D. Damn, I could hardly wait to see her.

She just stood there smiling as I announced, "I'll be there. You can bet on that."

"Great," she exclaimed. "Now what kind of teakwood do you want to buy? We have a great assortment and business has been slow." Before I could answer she looked at her watch and announced, "I have to get back to the office and finish my accounting. I'll get Michael and Alex to show you around. Stay here. I'll be right back."

Within a few minutes she returned with two young men in tow, the one on her left was the fellow that had greeted me when I first entered the shop, the other looked almost like his younger brother. Vina nudged the two young men forward and with a giggling smile said, "Don't you remember them? It hasn't been that long ago."

Mooncake Man

"What in the hell are you talking about Vina? I've never seen these guys before in my life? The three of them just stood there, smiling, giggling, and looking at each other. They all started to laugh."

"What's so damn funny, Vina?" I asked.

"Oh yes, you have met them. I introduced you to them at my table in Patpong when you asked me to dance. Their names were Alexia and Michele then," said Vina.

It was a little after nine-thirty in the morning as I stood in line waiting for my coffee and mooncakes at the Chinese bakery next to my hotel. I had promised Stan I would be on time for his 10 a.m. managers' meeting and the final inspection of the massage parlor prior to our grand opening the following evening.

A few days later, on another hot and humid day, I thought about the meeting with Vina as I walked the two blocks to Stan's place. I couldn't wait to see her again. She was naturally beautiful, dominant, and mysterious.

Al had said she had gotten into some trouble in the states. I wondered what it was. This girl had moxie, as if she came from New York City, not Louisiana. Besides, she didn't even have an accent.

And what was the story with the two guys? She worked with them by day at the shop and at night they turned into transvestites and she hit the bars with them on Patpong Street.

Shit, no wonder I was so worked up about her. Vina was beautiful and weird. I didn't know what I wanted more, to get into her pants or find out her story. Hopefully I could do both in that order.

It was almost 10 a.m. as I opened the office door to our new business venture and found Stan sitting at a large conference table surrounded by several people. Wei was there along with Frankie. Stan introduced me to several new employees he had just hired.

A young girl named Vicky would handle the books and an older guy named Billy would manage the facility and keep the place running, including the backup generator when the lights went out during the all too frequent power outages.

Stan called the meeting to order and after describing each person's responsibility, he turned to me as I was drinking my coffee and eating my mooncake said, "The best thing you can do is stay out of the way. But bring some mooncakes for everyone at tomorrow's opening."

"No problem, Stan," I replied. "So what's the name of the place?"

Stan said, "Wei and I decided to call it Yvonne's. A big neon pink sign will be going up later this afternoon." Stan described his plan for the grand opening the following evening. It would begin at six p.m. and there would be plenty of food and drink to go around.

All the girls would be ready for business. Handbills had been distributed outside all the tourist hotels and at the entrances to the American airbases just outside of town. The flyers declared that Yvonne's girls were the prettiest, G.Is were always welcome, and they would never get ripped off.

It was exactly six when I stepped into Yvonne's with three boxes of mooncakes. A large red carpet had been rolled out leading to the entry. The glass panes of the double doors reflected the overhead pink neon sign that flashed, "Yvonne's" every few seconds.

As I opened the doors I was greeted by floating balloons and confetti in a dimly lit room that with a rotating crystal chandelier. In the center of the room stood numerous young women dressed in low cut burgundy gowns. Each woman had a numbered white disk pinned to the left shoulder of her dress.

In the middle of the crowd was a beaming Stan, dressed in a black tux and tails. His bald dome lit up with each turn of the chandelier directly above his head. Portable wet bars were set up on each side of the room. As I approached the one closest to the door, I recognized several guys from Stan's nooner crowd at the Toad.

A large table had been positioned directly in front of the large window called the fishbowl. It was laden with an array of cheeses, dips, Thai satay with various spicy sauces, and numerous platters of fresh tropical fruits.

As I opened the boxes and placed the mooncakes on the table, I felt a hand on my shoulder and turned to find a smiling Nicha dressed in a low cut gown with a large number eleven pinned to her dress. She said, "Thank you for getting me this job. You are a nice person to help me."

'No problem, Nicha," I replied. "I hope everything works out." She grabbed a mooncake from the table, smiled, and made her way toward several guys at the bar.

Gee, I thought to myself, what a nice guy. I get the girl a job as a whore like it's some kind of waitress job. And I feel good about it? Shit, I'm going nuts out here.

The mooncakes were going fast as all the girls came by and grabbed one or two and as I opened the last box I looked up and saw a smiling

Sonja. She was one of my favorite girls from Sophie's and introduced me to the world of Bangkok massage the first day I had arrived from Korea.

Sonja became a regular at Roma's before Frankie recruited her for Yvonne's. With a mooncake in one hand and champagne in the other, Sonja stood up on a chair grabbed me by the arm and proclaimed to the crowd, "We have a new name for the John. From now on we will call him, 'Mooncake Man'"

She raised her glass as did Frankie, who stood next to Stan. The crowd followed as Stan announced, "To the Mooncake Man."

The crowd roared back, "To the Mooncake Man." Stan walked over the large glass windows called the fishbowl which had a huge red ribbon fastened from one end to the other. Out of his pocket he pulled a pair of scissors and motioned to the photographer to take his picture. Cutting the ribbon he proclaimed, "Yvonne's is now open for business."

Stan just stood there proudly beaming from ear to ear in his black tux with tails as the photographer snapped pictures. It was like the grand opening of the Hilton Hotel, not a whorehouse in the seedy district of Bangkok called Patpong.

Chapter 18 The Horny Toad

itting on a bar stool at the Toad, I checked my watch. Given that it wasn't quite 9:30, I ordered vodka, and tapped my fingers. I didn't want to miss Vina when she showed up. As Tony the bartender placed the drink in front of me, he said, "Don't worry boss, I'll spot her as soon as she steps in the place."

Hell, the whole place would notice her. Where else in Bangkok would one see a tall blond with plenty of cleavage, dressed like a dominatrix, and followed by two tiny Thai transvestites. She and her friends were a circus act. "You're right, Tony. The weirder it gets the more crazy I am about her."

Looking around, I felt as if I had been in the place a hundred times before. The same band played the same songs to the same crowd every Friday and Saturday night. The Toad always filled up with a few locals, American G.Is, and tourists.

When I felt a hand on my shoulder, I turned and saw Tony smiling as he nodded toward the main entrance. "Look boss, there she is with her two little friends, right on time."

Vina stood in the entrance waiting to be seated by the hostess. She was stunning, not the plain dressed shopkeeper I had seen just a few days before. She wore a low cut black satin dress that clung to every curve of her body and revealed her ample breasts. She wore stiletto heels, black nylons, and the hemline of her dress rested several inches above her knees.

Her long blond hair covered part of her lovely face and flowed down to her shoulders and on to the black dress creating a striking contrast.

She wore a gold necklace attached to a large jade teardrop that was surrounded by huge diamonds on each side.

Shit, I thought to myself, how the hell did she get that piece, who gave it to her?

This girl was hot, smoking hot; every guy and girl in the place including the band was staring at her as she followed the hostess to a table adjacent to the dance floor, the one I had reserved for us a few hours earlier. Once seated the hostess took the drink orders from the three, then looked in my direction as she told Vina and her friends that the drinks were on my tab. I could see Vina looking in my direction and when she spotted me sitting at the bar, stood up and waved me to her table.

God, it was like Christmas morning. I bet every guy in the place is jealous as hell.

I nearly tripped as I stepped down from the bar stool. Within a few seconds I stood at Vina's table as she said, "See, I told you I would be here, and I knew you would be waiting for me."

Shit, what a confident, conceited little bitch. She knew I would be waiting for her. I hate being under anyone's control, but with her, I can't help myself.

Vina smiled and started laughing as she looked over to her tranny friends, Alexia and Michele and said, "Aren't they just gorgeous, and sexy too? I want you to dance with all of us tonight."

"Whatever you say, Vina." I held up my hand for another drink, and said, "This is going to be an interesting night." As my hand came down Vina grabbed me by the wrist and led me out in to the dance floor. She danced through three rock and roll songs, gyrating non-stop. Her energy amazed me.

She led me back to the table where my two drinks waited. No sooner had I poured them down my throat, Vina put Alexis the tranny's hand in mine and sent us out onto the dance floor again. Meanwhile, she ordered several straight shots and drank them while I was dancing.

This rotation went on for about an hour and as we were caught our breath at the table, Alexis whispered something into Vina's ear. She nodded, turned to me, and said, "I'm told that you live in a penthouse suite at the Montien Hotel just down the street. Let's all go over to your place and continue our party."

With my head still spinning, I motioned for Vina to come close as I whispered in her ear, "Why don't just you and I go there? I'll pay the taxi fare for your friends."

Vina wiggled her index finger and with her head bobbing declared in a firm but slightly slurred voice, "Fuck you! My friends go with me or I don't go." I sensed she was getting higher by the minute.

"Okay, okay, Vina, I'll just grab a couple of bottles of booze and then we'll all walk down to my place."

Alexia shook her head as she said, "We don't need the booze. We have some better stuff. I'll show you when we get there." With that we all staggered to the exit, holding on to each other and as I looked over at the bar, Tony shook his head as he said, "Boss, I don't want to know how this story ends."

The two blocks to my hotel seemed like two miles. Vina and I were both drunk. She leaned on one tranny and I rested against the other. When one of Vina's high heel shoes slipped off, I leaned over to pick it up, and fell flat on my face. Vina laughed and yelled, "Fuck it." She threw the other shoe in the street and then yelled back at me, "Now you can buy me a new pair."

As our merry band approached my hotel, Steven the doorman rushed over and asked if I needed any help getting to my room. I waved him off as he kept asking me, "Do you know these people?"

As we all tumbled into my hotel room my three companions wandered into every room with Michele finally announcing, "Shit, you must be a rich guy: three bedrooms, living room, a kitchen, and big bathrooms all on the 20th floor overlooking Patpong Street.

Alexia motioned me to sit next to her and Vina on the couch. Michele wandered over and sat at my feet as Alexia starting digging through her purse and came up with four dark brown sticks and then declared, "Thai Sticks for everyone. this is God's nectar." She lit one, put it in my mouth, and commanded, "Inhale and you will go to heaven."

After several draws on the smelly stick I felt a rush of calmness and a sense of well being that I had never felt before. I looked over at Vina, her eyes were closed, and she seemed to be in a trance as she periodically inhaled the brown stick. I turned to Alexia and almost shouted, "What the fuck is in this stuff? What is it?"

Vina turned to me, kissed me on the lips, and said, "This is Thai cannabis, dipped in opium. You'll love it." She continued to kiss me on the lips and I felt her tongue deep inside my mouth and then the sensation of several hands loosening the belt on my pants as she whispered in my ear. "Just relax and enjoy this, you're about to have the best sex of your life."

Oh my head, my goddamn head, it feels like It's going to explode. I just lay in the bed motionless and looked around the room; thank god it was my bedroom.

Are there any sounds in the apartment? Is anyone next to me? I quickly looked to my left. No one slept next to me. Silence filled the apartment. Great, they had all left. God, what happened last night?

I vaguely recalled Vina kissing me and her tranny friends all over me, but not much after that. It must have been the dope, the hash and opium really knocked me on my ass. At least with booze I remembered most of what happened. God I can't do that opium thing anymore, it scares the shit out of me. I don't want to end up in some dirty flophouse addicted with my life drifting away, like that depressing place I saw in Macau.

I looked over at the clock on the bed stand; it read 10 a.m. I didn't even remember how I got back to the hotel, what time I passed out, and if someone helped me into my own bed. I needed some coffee so I slowly got out of bed and headed for the kitchen. As I passed the living room I notice several open condom packages on the coffee table. Thank god we used some protection but I don't remember putting anything on.

After making coffee I sat down on the couch and promised myself from now on I would only drink booze. No more drugs and I wouldn't let anyone talk me out of the commitment. At that moment I heard the unmistakable sound of the shower getting turned on in one of the bathrooms. Who the hell is here? I walked into the bathroom and looked through the glass shower door. Vina who was pouring shampoo over her beautiful blond hair. I knocked on the steamed door and shouted over the noise of the shower, "What the hell are you still doing here Vina and where are your little friends?"

Shampooing her hair, Vina yelled back, "Make me some coffee. I'll be out in a minute."

I placed the coffee pot and a cup on the table next to the couch. Within a few minutes she appeared with a towels wrapped around her body and her head and as she stirred in the cream and sugar Vina said, "I kicked them out early this morning. Saturday is a busy day at the teak shop, always a lot of tourists. They need to mind the store. I didn't go with them because I decided to spend the weekend with you."

"Gee, thanks, Vina, for letting me know. What if I have other plans?" I asked.

She tilted her head, smiled, and said, "Then you would cancel them to be with me."

"You know what, Vina? You're a conceited, spoiled brat," I said.

"That's right and if you're nice, I'll let you spoil me. Now I need some clothes. Give me some of yours and then after breakfast we'll go shopping for some new ones. You had better bring a lot of cash because they don't take credit cards."

"Vina, I've got news for you. Your ass and tits are too big to fit into my clothes, the biggest clothes I have is a stretchable gym outfit, but it's not big enough to handle all that ass."

"You love every inch of that ass. Don't you remember last night? Now go and get me those clothes or I'll go downstairs and eat breakfast at your hotel in my birthday suit." She then turned and headed for the bathroom saying she needed some time to look for something.

I gathered up the gym outfit and some sandals and threw them into the bathroom where she was brushing her hair. I sat back down on the couch. God she remembers what happened last night, I don't remember anything and I don't want to ask. Twenty minutes later she sat down next to me on the couch, even in the baggy gym clothes with no makeup she was radiant and beautiful.

Vina smiled as she held my head with her two hands and gently kissed me on the lips. "Let's be tourists this weekend. I'll plan everything. Now have you ever been on the sewer tour?"

"I don't know even know what you're talking about, Vina."

Laughing and putting her hands on my shoulders, Vina looked into my face said, "The sewer tour is a trip along the Cho Phraya, the river that runs through the middle of Bangkok. Tourists get on a narrow river boat with a powerful engine and you go up and down the river. All kind of shit happens on the river: floating markets, restaurants, and prostitution, just name it. You'll see how the locals live their entire life on the river. We can go inside the golden Buddhist temples along the river. It's an awesome experience.

"If we stay on the river, toward the outskirts of Bangkok, we can catch the mongoose and cobra fight. It's unbelievable. The locals go nuts. There will be a couple of hundred people there, all betting like crazy, vendors selling food and fruit, it's a spectacle, like the Roman gladiators. Then after that I'm going to take you to my favorite place for dinner."

"Vina, how do you know about all these places? I've never heard about any of this?"

She finished putting her hair into a pony tail with a thick rubber band and said, "That's because all you do is work, drink, and go to the whorehouses. Hell, for all you know I could be living on Mars. I'll me get my purse than we'll go downstairs for breakfast."

As I sat on the couch I looked out the open patio door to the bright blue sky, a flash of light, a reflection of something caught my right eye just under the curtain. It was a bright gold color, all balled up into a golden heap. I walked over and picked it up, it was Vina's necklace. I looked at it closely, it was real Burmese jade, I had priced jade all over Asia and this was the best money could buy, it was a large piece skillfully carved into a teardrop surrounded by huge diamonds, with opals in between.

Suddenly I heard Vina's voice behind me. "There it is. I've been looking all over for that. I was starting to freak out thinking that I may have lost it last night." I held the necklace in my hand and let it dangle to it full length, the huge jade piece slowly turned and as it hit the light from the patio window there was greenish white flash of diamonds and jade.

"Where the hell did you get this, Vina?"

She grabbed it from my hand and in a terse voice said, "That's none of your business."

"Hell, Vina, that piece must be worth fifty or sixty thousand U.S. dollars. Did someone give it to you?"

Her face hardened like the stone of the necklace and as she stuffed it into her purse she said, "Don't you understand English, or do I need to say it in Thai? It's none of your fucking business. Now let's forget about it and go to breakfast."

It was Saturday morning and breakfast at the Montien Hotel was always crowded. The hostess recognized me and seated us ahead of everyone. The waiters called me by my first name. Pierre the Manager spotted me and came over to our table to say good morning but he really wanted a close up view of Vina. He kissed her outstretched hand then turned to me and whispered something in French. As I looked up at him with a puzzled look, he turned his smiling face to Vina and said, "In English, it means she is very beautiful."

"Jesus, Pierre, you French guys just can't help yourself, can you?"

Laughing, Pierre replied, "It's in our blood."

As we looked at the menu, Vina put it down and said, "Everyone in this place knows you and likes you. I think that's neat."

"Yes," I replied, "that's because this is my home. I try and take care of all these people, and they take care of me. Isn't that how the world works?"

Vina looked at me for a moment and said, "That's the way it's supposed to work." After a healthy breakfast of eggs and ten different kinds of fresh fruit we wandered outside to the hotel entrance where Steven the doorman hailed us a cab. As we entered the cab Steven asked where we wanted to go so he could tell the driver in Thai our destination.

Vina waved him off and once seated in the cab started speaking rapidly in Thai with the driver nodding his head in agreement. As the cab entered the main street I turned to Vina and said, "I didn't know your spoke fluent Thai."

"Well unlike you, I need to know the language to make a living in this place," she said.

After about fifteen minutes of driving through the narrow one-way streets, we came upon rows of small stores that sold women's clothing. There were hundreds of them, block after block, and street after street. Vina explained that it was common in Bangkok to have many stores grouped together by their specialty, women's clothes, baby clothes, and so on. As the cab approached a corner, Vina said something in Thai and told me to give the driver 50 baht. Then she grabbed my hand and pulled me out of the cab.

"Vina," I said, "there must be 300 stores here. How long is this going to take?"

She just looked at me and shaking her head said, "Oh you poor thing. You don't know much about women, do you? I'll just have to teach you."

Vina grabbed my hand again and led into one of the stores where we were greeted by several Thai women that seemed to know her. She told me to sit on the large couch opposite the fitting mirrors as she disappeared into a maze of dress racks, shoes and women's undergarments.

Thirty minutes later she reappeared followed by several clerks holding armfuls of garments that they placed on a table next to the couch. Vina would pick out an outfit, disappear into the fitting room and then several minutes later emerge in front of the mirrors. She always asked the same question, "Do you like it?"

And I always answered the same way. "Sure," I said. Each time it was as if Vina didn't even hear me. She disappeared into the fitting room and started the process all over again.

When Vina found something she really liked, she squealed, jumped up and down in front of the mirror, and told the attendant to put it in the pile next to me on the couch. After about two hours the clothing reached higher than my head. She told the attendant she would wear the last selection and to box up all the rest. Speaking in Thai she pointed to me and the clerk gave me the bill for 45,000 baht, about $800 dollars.

A smiling Vina kissed me on the check and said, "Thank you Sugar Daddy."

"My God, Vina, you're expensive," I said. "I've never spent this kind of money on any woman before."

"Yes," Viva winked and said, "but I'm not any woman." She spoke briefly to two clerks and one of them walked over to the dresses stacked on the couch and began counting them. Vina turned to me and said the dresses would be delivered to her shop. She said we needed to get going to the river if we were going to hire a boat for the day.

In the heat and humidity it seemed to take forever to get to the river. It was Saturday afternoon and most people were off work and driving or walking around. Thais filled the streets and sidewalks-- shopping and socializing. After about thirty minutes we arrived at an old dilapidated wooden pier and Vina jumped out of the cab and began negotiating with several boat drivers.

Within a few minutes she waved to me and we climbed down the pier ladder and on to a long narrow wooden boat. What a strange craft it was, about twenty feet long, sitting low in the water, only four feet wide with three sets of flat plank seats with moveable back rests. The boat would hold six passengers side by side with a driver in the stern operating the engine.

The engine looked like it belonged in a lawnmower and had an attached tiller that extended toward the bow. A ten-foot long aluminum shaft protruded out the stern attached to propeller blades barely submerged in the brown water behind the boat. We were the only two passengers in the boat and as we sat down Vina told me to pay the driver 3,000 baht, the price for the afternoon tour.

John R. Fischer

The driver was a skinny old fellow missing most of his teeth and wearing a beat up sport shirt and shorts. As soon as I gave him the money he nodded, wadded it up and stuffed the bills in his front pocket. In what seemed like one motion the driver pull a rope to start the engine and as soon as it ignited slipped the propeller shaft into the water and made a hard left turn and within seconds we were in the middle of the river.

The boat picked up speed rapidly and as the bow started to plane it kicked up a foam wake at the stern that looked like white cream in a vat of brown hot chocolate. As we sped down the middle of the river, the heat and humidity fell away, and it seemed as if a magical air conditioner has been turned on.

On both sides of the river, wooden Thai houses stood on stilts, packed closely together. Stilts elevated the structures some fifteen feet above the water and featured open porches that extended over the river. Wooden ladders led to the river below; several small open boats were tied to each one.

Young children were everywhere, shouting and chasing each other on the porches or throwing various objects to their friends in the water below. Periodically they would jump in the river, swim back to a ladder, and start the sequence all over again.

Everyone in those houses, the old people sitting on their bamboo chairs, the children, and the teenagers all smiled and waved as we sped by.

I looked at Vina who was sitting in the seat in front of me, her long blond hair streaming in the wind as she waved to all the people in the wooden houses. She turned to me and shouted over the engine noise, "Who says you have to have money to be happy? Look at these people; they are all poor, live in crappy little houses on a polluted river, and they're all happy as hell."

I nodded and looked at the passing scene of seemingly contented people living in river shacks. She's right. Happiness is a state of mind. It has nothing to do with material things. But the world I live in isn't like that. The boat started to slow down, the driver said something to Vina, and she told me the floating market was just beyond the river bend.

What a spectacle: a hundred small boats, floating barges, Chinese junks, and large pleasure craft all jammed into a small area just offshore. It seem like everything was for sale, the small boats were piled high with fresh fruits and vegetables, other boats had fresh fish, some served as floating restaurants and looked like they were on fire as the smoke from makeshift stoves rose lazily into the air.

Rows of clothes, toys, dishes, and sundries filled the large barges. Shoppers tied their boats to the sides and then scampered up ladders to shop. This rendition of the huge street markets found all over Asia took place on the water.

Vina hit my shoulder, pointed to one of the larger vessels and said, "Look over there. See that large boat, the one that looks like a Chinese junk? See how its sides are all covered?

I said, "Yeah, so what, there are hundreds of boats in here."

"Well," laughed Vina, "that one's a whorehouse. The customers just tie their boats to the side and have sex as they float down the river."

"Jesus, Vina, how do you know about this?" I asked.

Vina said, "Hey, it's part of the culture. Thais love sex, all kinds of sex, both men and women. Sex is a form of pleasure given from the Gods. Like good food, it should be found everywhere. It's the Westerners that get hung up on the morality."

Looking at the sun getting lower in the sky, Vina said. "It's getting late. We need to leave and head for the fight. After a few brief words with the driver he swung the boat back into the middle of the river and within seconds we were speeding toward our next destination, the mongoose and cobra duel.

As we headed out further from the center of Bangkok the river got wider and fewer houses dotted the banks. After about twenty minutes of high speed cruising we came upon a small island with numerous small boats lining the shore. The driver gunned the engine, pulled the long propeller out of the water, and glided the boat to the shore.

Vina and I jumped out and followed the driver up a hill and down the other side where a large crowd of people were gathered around a small circular cement pit about four feet deep. Several hundred men and women yelled, waved money, and placed bets with bookies jotting down numbers and giving receipts.

Food vendors hawked snacks from bulging aprons and pushcarts filled with fresh fruits. As we edged closer to the pit, I heard the deep chime of a metal gong and as the crowd started to close in I felt a tap on my shoulder. I turned to find a young guy speaking rapidly in Thai. Vina translated and said the fellow wanted us to bet or we could not stand in the second row to watch the flight.

I pointed to the caged mongoose that had just entered the ring and gave the man 500 baht. He quickly scribbled a number on a piece of paper and handed it to me. Vina looked at it and said it was a betting slip and the odds were three to one for the cobra to win. I told her to ask one of the Thais how the odds were set and after several minutes of conversation she explained that the cobra had won the last two matches and that's why it was the favorite.

A whistle blew and the crowd became deadly quiet. The first cage got lowered into the pit and after several seconds out came the mongoose. The creature had small legs, an elongated light brown body, a small head, and tiny ears. The mongoose slowly walked around the pit as innocently as if it were someone's harmless pet.

On the other side of the pit, a second large basket was lowered and turned on its side. The top was slowly opened and almost immediately a huge cobra stood erect. The hood on its head sprang out from both sides as a spitting hissing sound resonated throughout the pit area. The crazed crowd cheered the arrival of each animal, waved betting slips wildly above their heads, and shouted encouragement to their picks as the fight got underway.

The mongoose stopped the moment it spotted the cobra. Its elongated body slowly rose up on its hind legs to its full length, its ears folded back, nose flared as its huge teeth protruded from its open mouth and it let out a low growling sound.

My God, these are the two most frightening animals I have ever seen. The two edged closer to one another, the cobra swinging its head from side to side with its high pitched hissing sound. The mongoose walked on all fours and then suddenly stood erect less than a foot from the cobra.

The crowd froze, becoming eerily silent. Vina whispered in my ear, "Watch closely. It will happen so fast you won't believe it."

Bam! A brown blur mixed with a silver flash. The mongoose slung the cobra down as if wrestling lightening to the ground. It had won! Vina grabbed the wadded up betting slip from my hand and shouted, "Shit, you just won a three to one bet. That's 1500 baht. Now I'll think of a really nice place for dinner."

It was eight p.m. and almost dark as we pulled back into the boat dock that we had left in the early afternoon. We had had a long day in the hot moist air under the blazing sun, cruised the river, and watching the mongoose and cobra fight. Vina hailed a cab and after telling the driver our destination, she turned to me and asked, "So what is your favorite food, the first three, in that order?"

"I replied, Italian, Mexican and Japanese."

With a look of disappointment, Vina asked, "How about Indian?"

Shaking my head, I said, "That's not even on my list. God only knows what's in that food."

"Well," said Vina, 'Maybe you'll learn to like it because that's where we are going." We arrived at the restaurant of her choice after a short drive. Once seated, Vina studied the menu and talked about her favorites. Noticing that I had not opened the menu, she asked, "Do you know what you want to order?" she asked.

I shook my head and said, "I hate Indian food; I'll just have three vodka tonics and watch you." The waiter took our order and returned in a few minutes with Vina's first course and my drinks.

As Viva eagerly started eating some kind of mixed vegetable with green curry sauce I turned to her and said, "Okay, Vina, now that we've known each other for a while, tell me how you got to Bangkok. Where the hell are you really from? I don't believe Louisiana; you don't even have an accent."

She stopped eating and just looked at me and said, "You don't know shit. I've only been with you a couple of times. If you're referring to the sex, that's just recreation. Don't take it too personal. It's killing you isn't it? What's my story? Well, I'll tell you a few things, but let's just say how I got here was a twist of fate and leave it at that.

"You're right--I was not born and raised in Louisiana. I'm originally from Ohio. I met this guy during a college spring break in Florida. I fell for him; we got married, and moved back to his home in Baton Rouge. His family was rich-- oil money--but things didn't work out." She stopped talking as if she had told me her entire life story.

"What didn't work?" I asked.

She paused and added, "After he beat the hell out of me a couple of times I left him and turned up here. That's all I'm going to tell you. What about you? What's your story?"

I told Vina the short version of my life. "I was been raised in a military family and my father was a colonel. We moved every few years and lived all over the world. The longest time I ever lived in one place was in southern California. We lived close to the beach in a suburb of Los Angeles.

"I finished college and got drafted into the army right after graduation. I served my time and I returned to school for a teaching credential. I taught elementary school for a year.

During my first summer off I got a job as a route driver in a newly formed courier company.

"At end of the summer as I was about to go back to my teaching job the owner asked if I would help him open up an office in Singapore. After Singapore, I stayed in Asia and opened up offices in Indonesia, Malaysia, and now Thailand. I put out a few fires out along the way. That was three years ago, I never went back to teaching."

Vina shook her head and started laughing as she said, "You were an elementary school teacher? I would have never believed that unless you told me. And now you're the part owner of a whorehouse in Patpong. Shit, that's as funny as hell."

"Vina, how did you know that? I never told you about that. How in the fuck did you know that?" I asked.

"Hey, calm down John. I have a lot of friends in Bangkok. What the hell, there aren't many secrets here. But, I've got one question and it's killing me. When you want a piece of ass at your place, do you have to pay for it?" asked Vina.

"Hell, no, they work for me," I said.

"Yeah, that's just what I thought," said Vina.

"Vina, do you want to know the real truth?" I asked.

Smiling she said, "I'm listening."

I said, "Well, at our last meeting of owners and managers, they passed a resolution, especially for me. It's called Rule #8 and it says, 'Don't fuck the help.'"

Viva's laughter stopped. She turned to me with a stone cold serious look and said, "What the fuck are you doing here, John? A kid from suburbia, an elementary school teacher? Jesus, John, Patpong is one of the dirtiest armpits of the world."

I gazed at my third vodka tonic on the table and in one motion, picked it up and downed the entire drink. "I don't know, Vina. I really don't know what the fuck happened. It just happened."

Smiling, she leaned across the table, kissed me on the cheek, and whispered, "I'm just glad it happened. As soon as we're finished here, I'm taking you back to my place."

Chapter 19 Nicha

God, another Monday morning, and the sameness of the days struck me. As I waited for my coffee and mooncakes at the Chinese bakery next to my hotel, I felt tired of the routine. It was always the same, working during the week, and on the weekends, hanging around Patpong and seeing the whores.

The most exciting thing that had happened to me since I arrived in Thailand was Vina. What a fantastic weekend. The last thing I had expected was that she would take me back to her place after dinner at the Indian restaurant. She had a quaint little cottage just behind the teakwood store; it was a simple two room dwelling that looked similar to the store with its large temple like roof.

She was different in her own place, not the flashy, obnoxious sexy-looking chick at the Patpong bars, or the overbearing, bossy person she was at my apartment with her two transvestite friends. She had two personalities; in her own place she was sweet, considerate, and accommodating, and even the sex was different, much less demanding and more intimate. God, I 'm crazy about her, I would give up all the whores in Patpong just to be with her.

Stan and I spent the morning reviewing the books and the previous week's revenue of the courier service, and by the time we arrived at the Toad it was nearly noon. Stan headed for his usual seat in the corner booth by the door and raised two fingers signaling to Apri the bartender to serve his cold Amir beer.

As soon as Apri saw me she motioned for me to sit at the bar and after delivering Stan's beers, she leaned over the counter and said that

Nicha and Sonja wanted me to meet them in the lunch room just before their shift started at two p.m. at Yvonne's, the massage parlor.

"So, what's its all about?" I asked Apri.

"I don't know for sure, but I think it has something to do with her day off this week," she said.

"Apri, can I ask you something? Will you promise that you won't make fun of me or tell anyone?"

"Okay, I promise. What is it?"

"Well, I've been seeing this girl and we've been together only a couple of times, but I can't get her out of my mind. Shit, I was with her all weekend and the first thing I thought about this morning was her. What was she doing? When should I call her? When will I see her again? I must be going crazy. It's not like me at all. After screwing around with someone over the weekend I usually want to forget I even know her."

Apri just looked at me for a few seconds, shook her head, and started smiling as she said,

"Oh, you poor boy, I can see the stars in your eyes. You're in love with her. Her face turned serious as she asked, "Is it the white chick, the showboat blonde with the guy friends that dress like women?" I just nodded.

In a stern voice, Apri said, "I told you before, John, she's trouble. I think you should stay away from her."

"What the hell are you talking about? If you know something I want you to tell me. Or this some kind of jealousy because she's a beautiful white woman?"

"Okay, John, you want to know?" asked Apri, looking directly in my eyes. "Do you really want to know?" I nodded affirmatively. "Well, remember when I told you that Stan's silent partner was a Thai General, that he would come by the Toad every once in a while with his mistresses and transvestites in tow? Well, the last time he was here several months ago, your lovely white chick and her pretty 'girlfriends' were with him."

It couldn't be true. Stunned, I just sat there without moving. Speechless, I scanned Apri's face, hoping that somehow she would take back everything she had told me, but she just shook her head and said, "I'm not lying to you. Forget about her. Go see Nicha and Sonja, they have plans for you."

I felt a slap on my back and as I turned I saw the nooner crowd starting to come in and Rocky, the Air America pilot stood next to me. "How are you, kid? I haven't seen you for a while. Too many bad hangovers? Or maybe you spend all your time pumping those whores of yours over at Yvonne's. You better pace yourself or you won't even make thirty."

"Well, Rocky, to tell you the truth I'm getting bored as hell around here." Looking at Apri, I said, "Maybe I need to get away for a few days."

"Good idea," yelled Rocky. "I've got just the place--beautiful Cambodia. Every Friday morning we fly cargo into Phnom Penh. Hell, the scenery is great and you can sit with me up in the cockpit. Are you in, kid?"

"Hell, sounds good to me."

Rocky slapped his hand on the bar and said, "Done. Be there at 0530 sharp. Stan knows the place. It's his cargo we're flying."

After having lunch and a few beers with the nooners, it was almost two o'clock so I walked next door to Yvonne's to meet Nicha and see what was on her mind. As I entered the small room that served as a lunch room and lounge for the girls, I saw Nicha sitting on a sofa.

As soon as she saw me she jumped up and gave me a kiss on the cheek, took my hand, sat me down next to her on the couch, and said, "My best friend Sonja and I have the day off this Wednesday and we want to take you to the Loy Kratong Festival. It's our festival of lights where we float lighted and decorated flowers down the Chao Phraya River. Please tell me you will come with us. We will take you to our favorite restaurant afterwards."

"Nicha," I replied, "you are very nice but you don't owe me anything for the job at Yvonne's."

Smiling with adorable little dimples on her round face, she said, "I know that, but I would just like to be with you, okay? Say you will."

"Okay. Where do I meet you?"

Nicha jumped up and down as she said excitedly, "Meet us at the Hotel Oriental. The patio in the back overlooks the river. We need to get there early to get a good spot to watch the festival, so be there at six p.m."

Wednesday evening came quickly and as I wandered into the lobby of the Oriental Hotel a few minutes before six, I admired the scene. The Oriental was one of the oldest and nicest of the colonial hotels left in Asia, its architecture and character much the same as its sister hotels, the Raffles in Singapore, and the Peninsula in Hong Kong. As I entered the patio area at the rear of the hotel I saw Nicha waving at me from a table at the far end of the veranda. We would have a great view of the river.

I sat down in the empty chair between Nicha and Sonja and immediately noticed how different they looked. I had always seen them in the low cut dark maroon working dresses with the large white numbered discs on their shoulders. For the first time I saw them as young women, not hookers. They wore cut-off jeans with Western polo shirts and sandals with their hair down and over their shoulders instead of tight bun on their head.

Sonja was in her late 20's and stood 5 foot 8 inches, which was tall for a Thai woman and even after ten years of working in the bars and houses, she still looked good. Nicha was much smaller, short and stocky, her round face lit up when she smiled. Even though Nicha was nineteen, she didn't look a day over sixteen.

Nicha kissed my cheek, waved to the waiter, and ordered three Cokes. I looked at her in astonishment and said, "You know I like vodka. Why the hell did you order me a Coke?"

"Yes, we know," replied Sonja, "but tonight we are going to have fun without drinking."

I looked over at Nicha who just nodded and then went on to tell me about how the Loy Kratong festival was on of the oldest in Thailand. It originated from Buddhism when an offerings of flowers, candles, and joss sticks, a type of incense, were considered tributes of respect to the footprints of Lord Buddha on the sandy beach of the Narmaha River in India. She told me that as a little girl her parents would take her to this river to watch the beautiful lighted floats drift slowly down the river.

I never thought of Nicha and Sonja as little girls with families who loved them. I only thought of them as women who entertained men for money.

As the sun set a parade of lighted floats of all imaginable colors could be seen slowly drifting by the hotel patio amid the approving sounds of the hotel guests and staff. The floating parade continued for almost hour and when it ended Nicha and Sonja grabbed my hand and headed for the hotel taxi stand. After about fifteen minutes of traveling through streets I did not recognize, we arrived in an area of dense apartments with small shops and restaurants at street level.

Sonja pointed ahead, said something to the driver, and he immediately pulled over in front of a place with large water tanks containing fish, lobsters and crabs. The restaurant was small with only about ten tables and we were seated in the last vacant one. When the waiter arrived Sonja rattled off the order as she pointed to the assortment of live fish in the tank. After we drank several cups of tea, the cooked fish and shell fish arrived along with an assortment of vegetables and spicy sauces.

I was hungry and devoured several plates of the delicious food. As we finished I heard the thunderous sounds of rain hitting the roof and pavement. Sonja remarked this was the monsoon season. I looked at my watch. It was after 10 p.m.

As I turned to Nicha and told her it was late and I should go back to my hotel, she grabbed my hand and with her face pleading said, "No, you can't go. It's still early. You promised you would spend the evening with us. Let's go to Sonja's place. It's right across the street. She is going to make us some special tea."

"Okay," I replied. We dashed the short block to the apartment through the pouring rain. When we reached the elevator Sonja pushed the button for the fourth floor. Her place was small, neat, and clean with a large living room containing a small kitchen on the side and a small bathroom with a shower. The main room had tatami mats with only a few chairs and a long sunken Japanese table. Two glass doors opened up to a patio that overlooked the street below.

As soon we entered Sonja went to the kitchen to prepare the tea. Nicha turned on the overhead fan and we heard the fan blades swishing as they rotated. As soon as she opened the patio doors, the room filled with the thunderous sounds the hard rain.

Nicha placed pillows around the large sunken living room table, removed my shoes, and placed them by the door. She returned, smiling, sat very close to me, and started talking about how she was making enough money to move from Apri's place and get her own apartment.

Sonja returned with the tea and placed cups in front of everyone. Smiling, she slowly poured the hot liquid, then sat next to me, and asked, "John, have you ever made love to a woman?"

"Sure, all the time."

Shaking her head Sonja replied, "I don't mean having sex with a woman, like at the massage parlors."

"What are you getting at Sonja? It's all the same to me."

Nicha laughed and Sonja just looked at me with a serious face and said, "It won't be after tonight." She turned to Nicha and told her to take a shower and come back wrapped in a towel. Then she started to place the pillows in a neat row as she said to me, "Nicha is crazy about you and she is my best friend. I want her to know pleasure from someone she cares about. You only know us as women that pleasure men for money, but we are real persons. We want to feel love and pleasure, comfort and closeness.

"We are no different from other people; we just have two lives. The one where we give ourselves to others for money and the other where we want to be loved and protected. Tonight I'm going to teach you to make love to a woman and not a whore," said Sonja.

As soon as Nicha returned, Sonja pulled the towel off, revealing her naked body and told her to lie face down on the pillows. Sonja leaned over her and gently kissed her on the neck and slowly started to run her fingers lightly down both arms to her neck, then her back, butt, and down each leg.

Sonja took my hands and repeated the massage over Nicha's body several times as she whispered in my ear, "Do it slowly and take your time. You have all night." After numerous repetitions I started to hear the sounds of deep soft breathing sounds from Nicha as Sonja guided my hands to the warm softness between her legs. As Nicha started to moan and move her hips upward Sonja whispered in my ear, "Read her body. She is telling you what she wants."

"Jesus, Sonja. How long are we going to do this? When are we going to have sex?"

Sonja smiled, pulled my ear to her and said, "You are having sex. Let your mind be one with Nicha and then you will know the same pleasure that she is feeling. You will become one. Her arousal will be your arousal. Her pleasure will be your pleasure and when you climax it will be together. This is real love, true pleasure, the kind that will sustain you in this life. It's not the mechanical, selfish sex of the whorehouses, the kind that can destroy your soul over time."

Sonja then disrobed and told me to do the same and for the next several hours as the rain continued its relentless pounding and the overhead fan slowly rotated endlessly she showed me ways I never thought possible to pleasure a women.

It was one of those cool humid overcast mornings as I stood on the corner outside Sonja's apartment trying to flag down a taxi to take me back to my hotel. What an evening. I felt like I was the whore and they were my customers. After twenty minutes I finally waved a taxi over and gave him the business card of my hotel written in Thai with a little map and address on the back. I needed to shower and shave, change clothes, and meet Stan at his office for a 10 o'clock meeting to go over the activities of the courier service for the prior week.

As I sat in the back seat of the bouncing taxi I couldn't help but think about what Apri had told me the day before. I couldn't get it out of my mind. Was Vina really the mistress of a Thai General? Is this the same guy who is my silent partner in the massage parlor? Maybe she just knows him, what about her tranny friends, what the hell are they doing there, this whole thing is crazy. Was this the part of her story she wouldn't tell me about?

Maybe I'll just take this trip with Rocky to Cambodia and try to forget about her. I'll talk to her when I get back. As the taxi turned into the hotel, Steven the doorman opened the cab's rear door, and once he recognized me, smiled with a facial expression that asked,

"Had a good night, Sir?"

After a quick shower, shave, and a change of clothes, I grabbed my briefcase and as I headed to the door I spotted the blinking red light on the phone that indicated I had a message at the front desk. While I headed for the hotel taxi stand I stopped by the front desk and the clerk handed me the message in a sealed enveloped which I stuffed in my pocket. As the taxi drove me to Stan's office I opened the envelope, pulled out a letter, and found big bold print that read, "What are we going to do this weekend? Call me, Vina. I guess I can't wait until I get back from Cambodia after all. I'll call Vina this afternoon from the Toad. I'll ask her point blank if she's shacking up with the Thai General. And if she is? Well, if she is, then it's over between us.

It was almost 12 o'clock as Stan and I walked into the Toad. Several "nooners" were there and after a few routine greetings I sat on the bar stool opposite Apri who was busy drying glasses with a small white hand towel. When she saw me she looked up and with a mischievous smile said, "Hope you had a good time with those two young ladies yesterday. How was it?"

"Oh, yes," I replied. "They put me through my paces, I felt like a Kentucky stud horse."

Apri laughed as she said, "From what I've heard, you are a Kentucky stud."

"Look, Apri, I need an honest answer. It's important to me."

"Were you bullshitting me about seeing Vina and her friends in here with the Thai General? How many times did you see them in here?"

Apri set a dried glass on the bar, leaned over, placed her hand under my chin and said,

"I told you before, that's what I saw. I only saw her once. The next month the General came in he was with two young Thai women."

I thanked Apri and headed to the back private office, picked up the phone, and started to dial Vina's number at the teakwood shop. What if she tells me she's the General's whore, would I ever want to see her again? Maybe I should just stick with the Patpong whores. Those are clean encounters: no emotional attachment, no remorse, just simple sex with no complications. Suddenly the sweet young voice of Vina answered and I immediately said, "This is John. You left a message?"

"Hi sweetheart," she blurted out. "So, what are we going to this weekend?"

"Well, Vina," I replied, "I'm leaving for Cambodia tomorrow and won't be back until late, maybe even the day after."

"Okay," she replied, "let's just plan on Saturday night then."

"Vina, I need to ask you something and I want an honest answer."

"Okay, big boy, no problem. What is it?"

"Apri, the day bartender at the Horny Toad, said that she saw you and your transvestite friends with a high ranking Thai General there a couple of months ago. Are you his mistress?"

The phone was silent for a few seconds and I had my answer. Then in a raised, shaky voice she said, "I'm nobody's mistress and that includes you. I have some acquaintances in this town; a few influential people helped me out when I first got here. You can believe what you want to believe, but I don't owe you or anybody a fucking explanation of my life.

"With me you get what you see, so if you're pissed off at my answer, or if it upsets your moral dignity that's too bad. Yeah, you, the guy who owns a whorehouse and fucks everyone in Patpong. Fuck you, I never want to see you again."

I looked at the phone for a few seconds expecting her to hang up as I finally said, "Vina, I'm not trying to judge you, I just want to know the truth. I'll call you when I get back from Cambodia."

A long silence followed and I waited until I heard Vina's stern voice saying, "I won't be holding my breath," and then the line went dead.

Chapter 20 Flying with Air America

*I*n Bangkok's Duong Muang International airport, the hotel shuttle driver delivered me to the cargo area opposite the passenger terminals. When I told the guard that I was with Air America, he nodded and waved us through without looking inside the van.

The cargo area consisted of numerous old army Quonset huts on the road that ran adjacent to the tarmac. Rows of pallets stacked high with cargo and draped with various colored plastic sheets for protection from Thailand's unpredictable rain lined the runway apron.

As the van traveled down the gravel road, I looked at Stan's directions that indicated the Air America buildings were at the end, but as we approached the area I saw no lights or cars in the parking lot. I told the driver to return to the first two lighted huts and as I walked to the door I could see a large sign above the entrance that read, "C.A.S. Operations."

Upon entering I saw a young Thai fellow behind a desk and after explaining my situation with the Air America buildings he told me that they would not open until eight a.m. as no flights were scheduled in the morning. Frustrated with his response, I asked, "Who the hell is C.A.S. and why was I told a cargo flight would be leaving at 7 a.m.?"

The Thai told me in perfect English that C.A.S. stood for Continental Air Services and it provided cargo flights for USAID government shipments, American consulates, and also handled commercial freight for various trading firms and oil companies throughout Southeast Asia. Air America crews routinely flew C.A.S. aircraft for various missions and scheduled routes.

After about ten minutes, Rocky arrived, and seeing me standing near the door, held out his hand and said, "Glad you showed up. We're one guy short this morning and we can sure use your help."

"What the hell are you talking about, Rocky? I'm here just for the ride, remember?"

Shaking his head, Rocky said, "No big deal, kid. All you have to do is help push out some cargo when the green light goes on? Here's Melvin now. He's our loadmaster."

I turned and saw a tall, lanky American in his mid 30's wearing a brown oil-stained flight suit with a blue Yankees baseball cap. Rocky announced, "Mel, I want you to meet the kid. He'll be your kicker when we get over the drop zone."

"Kicker? What's the hell is a kicker?" I inquired.

"Don't worry, kid, Melvin will show you everything. Now let's get some coffee and check the weather report. The aircraft was loaded late last night so we should be ready to go." Rocky walked over to the teletype machine, ripped off the top section, and after a few minutes declared, "Should be a good flying day. No bad weather, but we can't predict the visibility near the drop zone. The Laotian tribesman uses an agriculture method called slash and burn to rotate their crops and the smoke from the fires can obscure entire hillsides."

Looking at Rocky, my body froze. I was speechless as I finally blurted out, "Laos! Laos? Are you shitting me? Christ sakes, that place is crawling with Pathet Lao. Those fuckers support the Vietcong and NVA. They'll shoot our asses down in a minute."

With a smirk and then a friendlier smile Rocky said, "Take it easy kid. We do this every Friday. Were not landing in Laos, just dropping a few sacks of rice to the tribes, supporting our guys. That goddamn Agent Orange killed all their crops and animals and now we have to feed them.

"The U.S. government is so fucked up. We recruited these Montegard tribesman to fight the communists. Then we sprayed Agent Orange over their land to defoliate the jungle so we could see the Viet Cong infiltrators. That chemical killed everything and now we end up doing food drops to keep these guys from starving. Another well thought out strategy. Shit, this war is so fucked up I'll be here forever making good money."

Rocky pointed to a parked jeep and told the young Thai to drive us to the plane. The sun was just rising above the hills as the jeep headed for a silver speck at the end of the tarmac. As we came closer I strained my eyes to recognize the aircraft, confident that being raised as an Air Force brat I could identify any plane that ever flew.

"Shit, I don't believe this Rocky," I yelled over the engine noise of the jeep, "you've got to be kidding; this is a C-46, a two-engine plane that flew in WWII. Hell, I thought you were flying modern aircraft like C-123s or C-130s."

When the jeep stopped next to the plane, we jumped out. Standing beside the open cargo door Rocky said, "Listen kid, this aircraft is well-maintained. I'm not risking my ass in a piece of shit. Our payload today is 30,000 pounds and this is the most efficient plane for the job."

"Shit, Rocky, there is no lettering on this plane whatsoever; it's pure silver from nose to tail. I don't even see a registration number."

Rocky shook his head as he said, " Its there, you just don't see them. Kid, you can't be flying around Laos and Cambodia dropping shit with logos and big numbers on your plane because that would be embarrassing to some people. You know how it works here in Asia. Everyone knows but no one knows. Now get your ass into the plane. We gotta go. There's nothing to worry about it's going to be just another milk run."

I followed Rocky into the airplane and had to pull myself up to the cockpit through a narrow passage between the cargo and the left side of the fuselage. The nose of the plane was fifteen feet higher than the tail due to its tricycle landing gear configuration. Once inside the cockpit Rocky introduced me to his copilot Frank and sitting directly behind him at a folded out desk with gauges and switches everywhere was the flight engineer Perry. Both these guys were American in their mid-30s, wearing wrinkled brown flight suits and baseball caps.

Rocky pointed to the folded jump seat directly behind his pilot's seat as he adjusted his headphones and said, "Okay, kid, we're going to do our pre-flight checks so don't talk to the crew until we're up in the air. Put on your seat harness and if there is an emergency on takeoff and you need to get out of the aircraft quickly, the side window kicks out and there's a rope right above your head. Throw it out the window climb down like you're a monkey."

As I settled back into the narrow jump seat, the chatter of the crew checking off their preflight list started to fade from my mind as I thought about our destinations of Laos and Cambodia. Along with Vietnam these countries had all been a part of French Indochina, a part of the

French colonial empire for over a hundred years founded during the reign of Napoleon. For most of its history the region had experienced almost constant conflict, from the early days of the twentieth century and the revolt against French Colonial Rule to the invasion by the Japanese in 1941.

After WWII the French tried to reclaim Vietnam and their colonial empire but they met stiff resistance from the Viet Minh, a communist-backed army that defeated the French at the battle of Dien Bien Phu in 1954 and expelled the Europeans from the country. The U.S. had backed France during the conflict and in 1955 Vietnam was divided into North and South Vietnam. The U.S. supported the South and helped form the Army of South Vietnam, the ARVN, to counter the communist threat of North Vietnam.

Meanwhile, Cambodia and Laos had formed their own countries. In 1964 in an undeclared war the U.S. became involved in armed conflict against the Viet Cong, the communist guerrilla army that operated in the south and was supported and backed by the Army of North Vietnam, the NVA, and the People's Republic of China.

Supplies for the war in the south were funneled along the Ho Chi Minh Trail that wound its way through Laos and Cambodia thus drawing those countries into the bloody conflict. In Laos the United States backed central government was in a civil war with the communist led Pathet Lao. And in Cambodia the government of Lol Nol, also backed by the U.S., fought the Khmer Rouge, a communist army that controlled sixty percent of the country.

In 1969 while the American government tried convincing the world it had defeated the communists in South Vietnam, the Viet Cong staged the now infamous Tet Offensive, a massive and well-coordinated attack on every large U.S. installation in the country. By 1970 the war had become unpopular in the States and elsewhere in the world. The U.S. started withdrawing troops, but continued its support of the ARVN and its allies, the tribesman in Laos and Cambodia.

In this open wound of history, I found myself sitting behind an Air America pilot in August 1973. As we roared down the runway, the co-pilot named Frank shouted out the airspeed then yelled, "Rotate."

Rocky pulled backed the yoke and the airplane leaped into the air. After about twenty minutes, when the plane attained its cruising altitude of 10,000 feet, Rocky turned to Frank and said, "Go back and get some sleep with Melvin. I promised the kid that I would teach him how to fly this crate."

I could hardly wait for a turn at the wheel. The co-pilot's seat was still warm as I crawled into it and waited for instructions from Rocky. For the next twenty minutes he let me hold the controls and under his command showed me how to turn the plane and change altitudes. We flew at about 8500 feet and cruised about 180 miles an hour. All I could see as I looked down through the side window was the bright green landscape, a thick blanket that ran endlessly toward the horizon.

Rocky looked straight ahead and periodically looked through his binoculars until he announced, "There it is, the smoke from the slash and burn. It's thick as hell. Take her up to 11,000 feet and we should be able to fly over it. Any higher and we'll need to go on oxygen."

As the plane emerged from the smoke-filled area, I turned to Rocky and said, "You can't see shit down there. How in the hell do you make an accurate air drop? It's nothing but a sea of green with smoke almost everywhere."

"In about 10 minutes you'll find out. Go wake up Frank and tell him we're about 25 minutes from the drop zone. Then sit in the jump seat, put on the earphones, and don't say a damn thing. Just listen."

After a few minutes I returned with Frank in tow, took my place in the jump seat, and put on the headset. Rocky held up his hand as a clear American voice came over the earphones, "Red Rover One. Do you read me? This is Cinderella?"

Rocky replied, "This is Red Rover One. Over."

"This is Cinderella. I'll be taking you into the drop zone. You are 90 miles out. Turn 60 degrees northeast and hold for 10 minutes."

Rocky leaned slightly toward me and said we were 20 minutes from the drop zone. "Go to the back and help Melvin prepare to drop the cargo," he said. As I crawled through the narrow space and approached Melvin I could feel the plane starting to decrease airspeed and altitude. Melvin told me to stand still near the cargo door as he fastened a large belt around my waist. The strap was attached to an overhead anchor point.

When Melvin finished, he yelled in my ear, "This is so your ass doesn't fall out when we open the cargo door." He turned, unlatched the door, and slid it into its locked and open position. We felt cool refreshing air rushing into the airplane and heard the thundering engines. Melvin yelled in my ear that we needed to get behind the cargo pallets and get ready to push.

"When the light over the door turns yellow we have five minutes to the drop zone. When it turns green it will flash on and off and then we push the cargo out the door," he explained. As we crouched behind the cargo pallets, Melvin removed the C-clamps that secured the pallets to rollers and pointed to the light that had just turned yellow. I could feel the airplane continue to reduce speed and altitude as cool air and wind rushed through the open cargo door.

Suddenly Melvin hit my shoulder and pointed to the green flashing light above the cargo door. I pushed with all my might and the first pallet disappeared out the door, Melvin nudged me on the shoulder and pointed to the second pallet and we pushed that one out within seconds of the first.

Melvin closed the cargo door and immediately the roaring sounds of engine noise disappeared and the noisy of rushing air became quiet and calm. I leaned over and asked "How come no parachutes on the cargo? Don't those sacks of rice exploded when they hit the ground?"

"Hell, yes," smiled Melvin, that's exactly what's supposed to happen. After all, this is a hard rice drop. You don't know what that means, do you kid?" I just shook my head.

"Well, hell, that not unusual. Rocky never tells us everything either. Those burlap bags that had rice stenciled all over them? Well, its rice all right, but in the middle are M-16's and ammunition. Can't use parachutes. The Pathet Lao would see them coming down. Our friends, the Montengard tribesmen, wait at the drop zone, gather up the weapons, and split. If there are no commies around they'll scoop up the rice and take that too."

I unfastened my safely harness, made my way up to the cockpit, and sat down in the jump seat. Rocky turned around and said, "Good job, kid. I saw the drop out the side window. Right on the money."

"So Rocky, who were those guys on the radio with the Cinderella call sign? How did they know where we were and how could they guide us to the drop zone?"

Rocky nodded to Frank, the co-pilot, that he should take over the controls and as he turned from his pilot seat, he said, "Listen kid, what I'm going to tell you is supposed to be classified, but since you've already seen everything, well, I guess it's not classified in your case.

"Those guys on the radio with the Cinderella call sign are part of a top secret deal. They're U.S. Air Force people operating sophisticated radar equipment on a jungle mountain top somewhere in Laos. They see all the air traffic coming into Vietnam, Laos, and Cambodia. They guide in all the fighters and bombers to their targets, coordinate all the in-flight refueling, and tell guys like us where and when to drop our loads. They know where we are because we have a transponder on this airplane that identifies us and tells them our exact position. They coordinate the drop with the CIA boys on the ground.

"Every goddamn commie gook in Southeast Asia is looking for them; the Khmer Rouge and the Pathet Lao have huge bounties on their heads. No one knows exactly where they are, but I've heard they're on some mountain top in southern Laos where only helicopters can supply them.

"The official U.S. propaganda is that we have no military personnel in Laos or Cambodia, but that's all bullshit. Without these Air Force guys we couldn't stop the flow of supplies down the Ho Ching Minh trail. This is how we break the supply route to the Viet Cong, the guys killing our troops in South Vietnam."

Rocky told me we would be turning due south and heading for Phnom Penh, a two hour flight. We would land there and unload the rest of the freight which consisted of Stan's cargo of USAID food, medical supplies, and commissary items for the U.S. consulate.

We would be met by a U.S. consulate security detail that would be waiting for us on the tarmac at noon. As soon as the aircraft parked, an empty truck would pull up to the cargo door, and the freight would be transferred into the truck within twenty minutes. Rocky looked at me in the co-pilot's seat, shook his head, and added, "The quicker we get out of there, the better.

"Phnom Penh is getting dangerous. The country is in a civil war; it's pure chaos. The communist Khmer Rouge control 60 percent of the country and it's getting stronger every day. The central government of Lol Nol is totally corrupt; government troops are deserting everyday and going over to the other side. No one seems to know who's on whose side as it seems to change every day. It's a big fucking mess."

I settled into the co-pilot's seat as Rocky turned on the auto-pilot and looked out the side windows to the green fields that flowed beneath us. A huge brown ribbon intersected the endless emerald carpet. I pointed to the earth below Rocky said it was the Mekong River, the largest river in

Southeast Asia, a waterway that flowed south through Laos, Cambodia and into Vietnam, and finally out to sea.

I looked over at Rocky; he was slouched back in his seat with his head tilted toward ceiling of the plane as I said, "How long have you been doing this, flying cargo to these asshole locations? Don't you want to work for the big airlines some day, make some good money?"

Rocky straightened up in his pilot's seat, turned to me, and with a crooked smile said, "Kid, let me tell you something. I've been flying to these shit cities for the last three years and I've made more money than Pan Am pilots will ever see in their lifetimes. Hell, the company doesn't pay me the big bucks because it likes me. They have to. No one is going to do this for chicken shit money.

I just shook my head as I asked, "What are you talking about Rocky? I can't believe you make more than the guys with the big airlines."

He threw up his hands, looked up to the ceiling of the plane and said, "Jesus kid, what do you think will happen if we get shot down, or have a forced landing in Laos? Do you think the U.S. government will send in a rescue team? Hell no, they'll deny that we exist. We're not supposed to be here kid, get it? That's why I make the big money. That's what this war is all about, making money. And I don't give a shit who wins."

I closed my eyes, settled deeper into the co-pilot's seat, and listened to the unchanging drone of the engines. This place where I live in must be the absolute bottom of the world. It's a deep, dark abyss where easy money, drugs, whores and war are considered normal. Everything about this world is a contradiction of my previous life. My values are slowly slipping away. I medicate myself with alcohol and drugs to ease the pain of living, to escape my fears, and forget about the chaos.

I felt a hand shaking my shoulder. I must have dozed off. The co-pilot said we were about twenty minutes outside of Phnom Penh and he needed to help Rocky land the airplane. I moved back to the jump seat behind the pilot and put on the headphones as Rocky radioed the airport tower for permission to land.

Silence followed. With no response from the tower after several repeated attempts, Frank suggested trying another frequency. Still no response. Frank took off his headphones, turned to Rocky, and said, "What the hell is going on?"

"I don't know," said Rocky. "I've never seen anything like this before. We're only about ten minutes out. We should be seeing the airport just off to the right. We've got to go in; don't have enough fuel to land anywhere else."

The pilots prepared for the landing by decreasing the airspeed and lowering the flaps and the landing gear. As Frank continued making attempts at communicating with the tower, he met Rocky's eyes and shook his head to show he wasn't getting through.

Rocky nodded to acknowledge Frank and then looked back at me as he said, "Kid, you look out the side window to your left. Frank you do the same on your side and tell me if you see any airplanes trying to land or taking off. Jesus, no ATC, no tower, something is really fucked up."

As our aircraft started its approach to the Phnom Penh airport I could see several planes parked on the tarmac but no people or activity around them. As the plane landed and settled back on its tri-cycle landing gear with its nose high in the air, I looked out the side window at the passenger and freight terminals and saw no ground crews or vehicle movement. The entire airport looked deserted.

Rocky taxied the plane to the cargo terminal, feathered the engines, and said, "Something is wrong-- no consulate security detail. It looks like everyone has split. I'll stay at the controls in case we have to get out of here quickly; we only have enough fuel to taxi to the other side of the field. Frank, go find a fuel truck.

"Melvin, you take the kid back with you and arm yourself with the weapons and stand guard outside the airplane. If you see anyone approach, fire in the air. I'll start up the engines and we'll get out of the area. In the meantime, I'll try and contact the consulate and the security detail on the walkie-talkie handset to see what's going on."

Melvin led me to the rear of the aircraft and pointed to a steel metal footlocker bolted to floor. He slipped a chain with a key attached from around his neck and opened the locker. Looking up at me, he said, "Rocky said you were in the army, so you shouldn't have any problem with the M-16 rifle. Take one and a 45 pistol, the ammo, then lock and load and stand guard in front of the airplane. I'll load up the M-60 machine gun and stand by the cargo door.

"Fire in the air if you see anyone coming, even guys that look like soldiers, no one knows who's on whose side. If anyone fires on you, shoot their asses, and keep firing until the engines start and we can get the hell out of here."

I loaded a clip into the pistol, stuck it my belt, grabbed a vest containing 10 clips of ammo for the rifle, and walked to the front of the airplane. It was a hot, blazing day with no shade directly in front of the aircraft so I moved underneath the left wing just behind the engine. Dead silence surrounded us.

God, I might not get out of here alive. If we're killed, no one will know what happened, not my folks back home, not Vina. I wonder if Vina would care. Would she try and find out?

And why do I care about her? One day she's a whore and drug addict and the next a sweet young girl running a tourist store. Maybe I'm crazy about her because I'm crazy.

Instantly my mind jerked back to reality with the staccato sound of rapid gunfire in the distance, then the sight of thick black smoke slowly rising several miles away at the far end of the airport. More silence followed. Then I heard the sounds of heavy weapon fire, a deep intermittent thud every few seconds. I heard Melvin yell from the cargo door,

"Get ready kid. That's a fire fight going on. God only knows who's coming down that airport road."

I pulled the charging handle back on the M-16 and loaded a round into the chamber and switched on the safety, it was something I had done a thousand times on the ranges at Fort Leonard Wood, but never in combat. What was I doing here, how in the hell did this happen, finding myself in another stupid, unpredictable situation?

Shit, I'm not even in the army and I'm guarding a non-existent CIA airplane, in the middle of a bloody civil war in an airport and country I've never even seen before. And it's all because I was getting bored in Thailand and pissed off at Vina. Shit, if I get out of this in one piece, I'll never get into a situation like this again. Never again. Never again. God damn it.

Suddenly Rocky stuck his head out the pilot's side window and said he had just reached the consulate security convoy and learned that they had been attacked by Khmer Rouge forces on the airport road. The firing and smoke we saw just north of the airfield was the convoy under attack. The communist forces had been beaten back and the security detail should arrive to unload the plane in about fifteen minutes. Rocky said that the communist forces had attacked many government installations and once the airport workers found out what has happening they all had abandoned their posts and were hiding in various parts of the terminals.

Just then I heard the faint sound of a vehicle and spotted a fuel truck in the distance. As it drew closer I saw our co-pilot Frank at the wheel. Thank God. Now we can get the hell out of here.

Rocky stuck his head out the side window and yelled to Frank at the top of his lungs. "Get the fuel in the plane as fast as you can." And then he turned to me and said, "Kid, you stay right where you are, that security convoy should be coming right down that road directly in front of you. They told me every vehicle would have a large orange banner on the front bumper and one on the roof. That's how we tell the good guys from the bad guys today. If that lead truck or jeep has no orange banner, then start firing and I'll crank these engines up. Melvin will cover you from the cargo door with the machine gun so you can get your ass back to the plane."

God, I felt like a sitting duck. What if the Khmer Rouge had won the fight? What if they were the guys coming down this road right in front of me? My mind strained to detect any sounds from the road, but I heard nothing, just the low hum of the fuel being pumped into the airplane's empty wing tanks. Then I heard the faint sound of a truck, then more of the same. As the volume got louder, I peered down the straight dirt road beyond the wire fenced gate of the airport cargo area to figure out who and what was heading our way. They were military trucks, all brown, and then I saw the colors I longed to see. Thank God. Orange banners on the bumpers and on the tops of the vehicles. They must be our guys.

The lead truck stopped at the locked gate, but the airport security guys that usually guarded it had abandoned the post, so no one was there to open it. One of the soldiers wielded a large pair of vice grips, snapped the lock, and waved the three trucks to drive forward onto the tarmac.

The lead truck stopped in front of the aircraft and then backed up to the open cargo door of the airplane and almost immediately several bare-chested soldiers jumped into the airplane and started tossing boxes into the empty bed of the truck. I stood guard watching the process, clutching my weapons.

After ten minutes, a jeep drove up and parked underneath the nose of the plane and out stepped a young white guy with blond hair, wearing sunglasses, dressed in khaki shorts and an open Hawaiian shirt. He packed pistols on each side in a black holster slung around his waist.

The man nodded toward me before he yelled to Rocky in the pilot's seat. "Hey, Rock, don't worry; it was just another firefight on the airport road. Pol Pot's gang; they just hit and run, but they sure scare the hell out of the locals. The airport guys seem to know what's going on. They lock this place up tighter than a drum even before the firing starts. When it's over they crawl back out of their holes like nothing happened. Wish we could give you guys some warning, but hell, we don't know when or where they're going to hit us."

The blond guy walked over, smiled, and with his eyes hidden behind his sunglasses, he said, "Are you new to the company? I haven't seen you before."

"No," I replied, "I'm just a stupid tourist along for the ride."

"Oh, that's a good one. Well you stay close to the Rock, he's the best."

I looked back toward the rear of the airplane; the second truck was almost full of cargo. Melvin yelled for me to get back into the airplane. Without any hesitation I ran back to the aircraft and scrambled into the cargo bay and flung myself onto the floor. Melvin closed and locked the door. I remained flat on my belly in the empty cargo space as the starter on the left engine commenced its whining sound and within seconds the roar of the engines and vibrations of the engines came to life. I'm never going to do such a stupid thing as this ever again.

Melvin motioned for me to give him the M-16. I unloaded the weapon, cleared the chamber, and handed it to him. When he asked for the 45 pistol I said, "I want to keep this one, I'll pay you for it."

"Keep it as a souvenir," smiled Melvin. "Just don't tell Rocky. And unload the damn thing or you might shoot your dick off."

"Thanks," I replied as I took out the clip. I stuck the pistol in my belt underneath my shirt, made my way up to the cockpit, and slipped into the familiar jump seat behind the pilot.

Rocky turned on to the runway as Frank looked in all directions for other aircraft. As soon as Frank uttered "Clear," the engines roared to their maximum power and we blasted down the runway. The empty aircraft leaped into the air.

After a few minutes of steady climbing, Rocky looked back at me and said, "Kid that was more fun than I expected. I'm getting too old for this kind of shit. You did good kid; you hung in there and didn't freak out."

"Gee, thanks Rocky, but you'll never see my ass on one these ghost flights again. By the way, that American guy on the tarmac, the one with Hawaiian shirt and the Roy Rogers gun set? He asked how long I had been with the company. What company? What's he talking about?"

Rocky shrugged as he said, "The company? The company is the CIA."

Chapter 21 A Yo-Yo with Vina

It was Friday night at the Toad and a month to the day since my crazy trip with Rocky and his crew to Laos and Cambodia. I ordered another drink from Tony the bartender and as he set the double vodka and seven in front of me he said, "You know, Vina has been asking about you. She comes in every Friday night with her little band of ferries, dances with a few guys, and then hits the rest of the bars on the strip. Instead of leaving before the band starts, why don't you stick around and talk to her?"

"Cause she's a bitch, a whore, and a drug addict, that's why," I said.

Tony laughed, shook his head, and said, "Well, you just described most of the women in Patpong."

I downed the drink and ordered another. Vina is not good for me. If I stay here and she shows up, I'll fall prey to her intoxicating sexuality, like the fairy tale, the spider and the fly, I will be helplessly enmeshed. Damn it. Why can't I forget about her?

I looked at the band members setting up their instruments and microphones. At 10 p.m.--in just a few minutes--they would start playing and Vina could arrive anytime after that. I finished the drink and ordered another. If she shows up, I'll be sitting here at the bar in a drunken haze trying to pretend I don't notice her.

At exactly ten, the band began playing my favorite songs, the Rolling Stone's "Satisfaction," followed by the Doors' hits, "Riders in the Storm" and "Light My Fire."

By 10:30, the usual assortment of tourists, G.I.s with their Thai girlfriends, and a few locals filled the place. Tony the bartender slapped me on the shoulder and nodded toward the door as he said, "There she is boss, with her two tranny friends in tow."

I looked toward the front door and the hostess station. It was Vina. Damn, she was stunning. Her long blond hair flowed over a black low cut dress and her large breasts highlighted the diamond necklace that hung around her neck sparkling just above the center of the cleavage. The tight satin dress clung to her body, revealing every curve and ripple. It stopped several inches above her knees exposing the beautiful contours of her legs in black silk stockings and high heels.

No wonder I can't forget about her. She looks like a goddamn movie star.

Vina dutifully followed the hostess with her two trannies to a table in the far corner just a few feet from the band. I tried not to stare, but I couldn't take my eyes off of her. Then it happened. Our eyes met. I just stared at her and she sat there, motionless, with no expression, just staring back. If I'm going to leave I'd better do it now.

I was paralyzed, surely any second she would look away. Instead, she smiled that big beautiful sexy smile of hers. God, I'm done now. I'm not going anywhere. I watched helplessly as she got up from her table and walked toward me. As Vina approached the bar, she pointed to the empty stool next to me and said, "Hey, big boy, is that seat taken?"

I motioned for her to sit down and as she slid on to the bar stool next to me the sweet scent of her beauty and sexuality brought back the memories of our previous liaisons. She turned to Tony the bartender and said, "Give me a rum and Coke and put it on Mooncake Man's tab."

Laughing and smiling, she turned to me with her lovely face a few inches from mine said,

"So, where have you been, hiding from me? How come you never call anymore?"

With a surprised expression I replied, "Don't you remember? After our last conversation, just before I flew to Cambodia, you told me never to call again. I figured it was over between us."

"Oh, that," said Vina, smiling as she placed her hand on mine. "I must have been in a bad mood. Just forget about that. I've missed you. I've missed all the things that we did together-- the river, the restaurants, the shopping, especially the shopping.

"Well, why didn't you call me?" I asked.

Vina kissed me on the cheek and said, "Sorry, there were some things that came up in my life, some difficulties from my past, but that's all behind me now. Can't we start over? Can we have fun together again? Let's go over to your place, I'll dump the trannies and it will be just you and me, like before."

I just shook my head and said, "So you think I'm that easy, that you can just come in here and flash that smile and body at me and I'll just roll over and let you kick my ass?" She smiled her little girl smile and perked her lips into a kiss waiting for my final answer. Vina, being with you is like being in heaven and hell at the same time. You're a broad that busts men's balls, but I love it. Let's get out of here."

As I waited for Vina to tell her friends that she was going with me, I felt the glaring stare of Tony the bartender. When I glanced over at him, he was standing behind the bar slowly shaking his head as he said, "Boss, that didn't take long. Be careful she doesn't take any prisoners."

As Vina and I slipped out of the club and headed for my hotel down the street I couldn't help but remember that first trip with her and her trannie friends when we were all so drunk it took us twenty minutes to walk just a couple of blocks. Once inside my hotel apartment Vina settled in on the long plush couch in the living room and immediately started rummaging around in her purse finally announcing, "Found it."

Vina pulled out a long, cigarette-shaped, brown roll that I knew was a Thai stick, hashish laced with opium. She lit it up and inhaled deeply as she closed her eyes and reclined into the soft pillows of the couch. After a few minutes of taking in the drug and holding it in her lungs, she let out a low murmuring sound as she exhaled. Opening her eyes, Vina said,

"You want a hit?"

"No thanks, Vina. Why do you smoke that stuff, anyway? It's bad for you?" I said.

She dragged a long hit into her lungs, slowly exhaled, and said, "Probably the same reason you get so fucked up on booze. That's really bad for you. This stuff calms me down and makes me mellow. I like to take it just before sex. It gets me in the mood and magnifies every sensation. You should try it without the booze."

Vina propped up her beautiful legs across my knees on the couch and lay down with her head slightly elevated by a large pillow. The silver necklace with the large diamond pendant lay on her breast and flashed its reflective brilliance from the light of a corner lamp as she inhaled and exhaled the drug every few minutes. I just stared at the diamond; it was huge and must have been worth a fortune. "Where in the hell did you get that diamond, maybe the same place you got that huge piece of jade?"

She opened her glazed eyes, with no expression and said, "I have friends that appreciate me. Don't concern yourself with that now, come over here and make love to me. I'm ready now."

For the next eight hours we intimately enjoyed ourselves. She was the most exquisite and sexually fulfilling woman I had ever been with and she seemed insatiable. I remembered all the massage and pleasure techniques Sonja had taught me that rainy evening in her apartment with Nicha. Vina responded by rewarding me with multiple episodes of pleasure throughout the night and into the early morning.

As the dawn light beamed through the opening of the bamboo drapes in my bedroom, I heard the shallow breathing of Vina next to me and I looked over at her. Am I falling in love with her?

What was love anyway? I was only twenty-six. Was it like the time I thought I was madly in love with Pamela in high school? I was so freaked out about her I couldn't sleep for two weeks after our first date, but then after a month I got tired of her and found someone else.

I once thought I loved Wendy, the cute little blond I dated in college. Going out with Wendy tied up my stomach in knots every time, but I still could not remember breaking up with her. Then I fell for Jenny in Hong Kong, but she was just another infatuation, a fantasy complicated by my feelings of competition, the desire to win her over from her wealthy and obnoxious fiancée.

And, of course, Mieko in Korea. I was crazy about her and missed her terribly when I first got to Bangkok, but after several months she became just another memory.

But Vina, she is different, the first time I saw her that evening at the Toad something clicked in my brain. I was driven to find out where she worked so I could see her again. When I found the store where she worked, I asked her out on the spot, and that was not like me.

I thought about her in the morning, in the middle of the day, and at night. Sometimes little things reminded me of her and I actually cared about what might be happening in her life. When she told me not to call her anymore before my trip to Cambodia, my pride kept me at bay for a few weeks, but I knew I would see her again.

And when I was standing out there on that stupid tarmac in Cambodia with the M-16 rifle and not knowing if the Khmer Rouge would be coming down that road and it could be my last day on earth, I thought of my parents and Vina. My last thought was of Vina.

I looked over at her soundly sleeping next to me; I gently kissed her on the forehead and rolled over for a few more hours of needed sleep. Maybe she is the one.

It was almost ten in the morning when we sat down to breakfast at the hotel coffee shop. Vina wore one of my loose fitting shirts and khaki shorts with sandals. She remarked that it must be time to go shopping again as she only had an evening dress from the night before. "So," I said, "now I know why you're such an easy pickup from the Patpong bars. The next day I get to take you shopping for clothes."

She kissed me on the cheek and said, "Oh, you love it. You know you do."

I just looked at her. She was stunning and more radiant then I had ever seen her. When I told her so she replied, "Don't you know that women glow and sparkle when they have good sex? Most men can't tell, but women can, and we had good sex last night, so I 'm going to reward you by taking you someplace special, a place you've never been, the cobra milk farm."

I rolled my eyes and asked, "What the hell is that? Do you have some kind of thing with cobras? The last time it was a cobra and a mongoose."

"Yes, but this is different." Vina explained that the cobra farm was set up next to the Red Cross building in the center of Bangkok and the public was free to watch the venom being extracted from the captive cobras twice a day, late morning and afternoon. A handler selected a cobra from one of the cages, placed the snake's fangs over a receptacle, and the poison flowed into a small glass cup. The poison would be used to make anti-venom to save the lives of hundreds of farmers who were bitten by cobras that inhabited the rice fields of northern Thailand.

After our late breakfast we caught a cab and with Vina's directions we arrived at her favorite shopping area. And even though I had been there before, nothing looked familiar in the dizzying array of women's dress shops.

The routine was the same--Vina tried on garments, asked my opinion each time, and then decided for herself what she liked. The rejects went in one pile and the keepers in another. After about an hour and half when the keeper pile was twice as high as the rejects she signaled the attendant for the bill and then pointed in my direction. As I dutifully handed over my American Express gold card having no idea of the final amount, Vina was busy writing the delivery address in Thai.

Wearing the last outfit she tried on, a beautiful pearl colored silk dress and sandals, we flagged down a cab and headed for the Red Cross Building and the cobra farm next to the government buildings. It was early afternoon as our taxi slowly wound its way through the maze of one way streets. It was a hot and sticky Saturday and there were crowds, cars, motorcycles, and bicycles everywhere as most people had the day off.

As we approached the main street, several hundred yards from our destination, the traffic came to a dead stop. After about ten minutes, I got out of the taxi and looked ahead; nothing was moving as far as I could see for about five or six city blocks. Vina spoke to the driver who seemed to know nothing.

While we sat in the cab listening to the labored hissing sound of the little fan mounted on the dashboard, the same kind every cab driver in Asia had, I started to hear the faraway sounds of drums beating, and yelling coming from loudspeakers.

Vina said something to the driver in Thai. He replied quickly and she turned to me and said, "It looks like some demonstration at the government buildings. The streets have been blocked. I'll bet it's the college students, I heard this might happen."

"Really?" I replied, "I haven't heard anything about this."

Vina turned to the taxi driver and after a few minutes of conversation, she faced me and in a concerned tone said, "The driver wants to leave. He'll take us back to the hotel, but he doesn't want to stay here. What do you want to do?"

"Hell, since we've come this far. Let's check it out and see what's going on," I answered.

I gave the driver fifty baht and we started to walk on the sidewalk toward the sound of the loudspeakers. As we were walking, Vina told me that Thailand had had six coups in the last ten years. There seemed to always be a power struggle between the rich and privileged classes and the military generals that ran the country.

This student demonstration was nothing more then a pretext to trigger another power grab between the generals and the wealthy few. The only real stable force in the country was the revered King and the royal family. They tried to stay out of politics unless things got bloody and out of control. When that happened his royal highness simply walked out on his royal veranda, spread his hands out over the kingdom, ordered his subjects to stop, and they did.

"Jesus, Vina, how in the hell do you know all this shit? Who the hell have you been talking to?"

Smiling, she put her hand in mine, and said, "Friends, just some good friends." As we approached the government buildings, the yelling and drum rolls got louder. And then we saw the demonstrators. They were all young students who were lined up about 20 feet opposite the police in their blue helmets, face masks, and shields.

The police stood their ground as the students threw rocks, glass bottles, and other objects at them. Suddenly, without any warning, the police charged the demonstrators, wildly swinging their clubs, and firing tear gas canisters into the crowd. The demonstrators produced baseball bats and waded into the blue line of policemen.

When I heard the unmistakable rat-tat-tat of shooting, I grabbed Vina's hand and pulled her toward me. Instinct, or perhaps, military training, told me that we had to move quickly. "Let's get the hell out of here. That's gunfire." She stared at me, frozen in place from fear. I jerked her hand again and she followed me as we ran down the street and to where we had left the cab some 20 minutes before.

People were running everywhere. I could hear the bullets whizzing in the air around us, the cars stuck in traffic had been abandoned, and everyone was trying to get off the streets. As we turned the corner into another side street I spotted an abandoned motorcycle on its side, still running. I righted the bike and motioned for Vina to get on the back.

Driving slowly between all the parked and abandoned vehicles we finally made our way out of the area and onto an open road. Since Vina's place was closer, I told her we would go to her apartment. For the next 20 minutes she yelled directions in my right ear and by the time we arrived I was almost deaf.

It was dusk when we got to Vina's place. I hid the motorcycle in the back of the building away from the road and walked into her apartment. Vina had turned on the news and they were talking about the demonstrations we had just witnessed at the government buildings.

Several people had been killed and about a dozen wounded and each side blamed the other. The military had imposed a curfew on the entire city and anyone caught outside after dark would be arrested. I shook my head as I said, "The Thai people are beautiful until they get pissed, then anything can happen."

She nodded her head, "Yes, they get very violent, but I don't think this will last long. It could be over by tomorrow."

"Why do you say that, Vina? You knew in the cab it was a student demonstration before we even got there. Where the hell do you get your information?"

"I told you, I have friends and acquaintances that care about me."

I closed my eyes and tried to control my anger as I said, "Cut the bullshit, Vina. Are these the same friends that give you expensive jewelry, just because they like you? You're telling me that you don't have to do anything for them?"

Vina got up from the couch, and with her face bright red rage, she blurted out, "What the fuck do you want from me, John, my goddamn life story and the names of every man I've ever fucked?"

"Yes, I do," I shouted back.

"Okay, charming asshole," she yelled back. "Sit down on the couch and pour yourself a drink while I light up a joint. You'll probably die of jealousy right before my eyes." I poured a double vodka and seven and sat on the large stuffed chair opposite the couch.

Vina was stretched out on the sofa with her head propped up on pillows and was deeply inhaling a joint and staring straight up at the ceiling. She dryly said, "Are you ready?" without looking at me.

"I was born in Ohio, the youngest of three sisters into a strict and religious Methodist family. My father was a farmer and an elder in the church and could be a mean person like he was on the day I was born when he said to my mother, "Another goddamn girl." All the children went to religious schools and we were always model students.

"In high school, I did well, but was not allowed to date until I was a senior, and only when my parents had met and interrogated the boy on a previous occasion. As a result, I only had three dates the whole time in high school. I wanted to become a teacher and enrolled in a private Christian college some fifty miles from home and lived on campus in a girls' dorm.

"In my junior year my crazy roommate Maggie talked me in to going to Fort Lauderdale for spring break. I made up a story to my parents that I needed to stay at school for some special project. My God, the things we did there. It was the first time I had ever had alcohol and I got drunk. And by the end of the week I had slept with three different guys.

"That's where I met Steve. He was a senior at LSU and I fell in love with him at first sight. He came from a wealthy oil family in New Orleans, and to make a long story short, I ran off with him that summer against the wishes of my parents and got married in the French Quarter.

"Things were great for the first year, but then I got pregnant, and Steve started screwing around on me. He didn't even try to hide it. When I confronted him one night over his infidelity he beat the hell out of me and I miscarried.

"I left the bastard and went to Los Angeles to try modeling. After a couple of crappy jobs and several disappointments, I decided to go to Honolulu and ended up working at one of the strip joints on Hotel Street.

"I did private parties on the side and that's where I met Mr. Ma, the "Teakwood King" and his associates. They were frequently in town negotiating to buy several pineapple plantations. They were very nice to me."

"Cut the bullshit. Vina. Private parties. They were nice to you. My ass. You were a whore. Right?"

Vina didn't move on the couch or even look at me. She just stared at the ceiling for a few seconds and finally said, "Yes, you're goddamn right. I made fucking great money at it, too. My clients were mostly businessman. Monday was always my busiest day. After being with the wife and kids over the weekend, going to the church socials, and all that bullshit on Sunday, they couldn't wait to see me. What a bunch of fucking hypocrites.

"But why am I telling you all this shit? You know the business better than I do; you own a whorehouse in Bangkok."

"Okay, Vina, you made your point. How did you end up in Bangkok?"

She finally looked over at me and said, "Mr. Ma liked me or maybe he felt sorry for me and he got me a student visa to attend college in Bangkok. He supported me and I studied business for a year and learned to read and write the Thai language.

"After that I started working at one of his teakwood stores. I've been doing that for the last couple of years. She turned and looked up at the ceiling as she inhaled the drug and said, "So, does it piss you off that I sold my ass for money?"

I just looked at her smoking the joint, the pale peach silk dress was pulled up above her knees exposing her beautiful legs. I never figured her for a hooker. She looks too clean, too beautiful.

She stopped looking at the ceiling, sat upright, looked me in the eyes, and said, "Well?"

"Well what?" I shot back. "What do you want me to say, that I'm happy about you being a prostitute? No, I'm not happy about it, but that was in the past and you did what you had to do at the time. What I need to know now is whether you're still a whore. Are you taking care of the General and his friends? Are you Mr. Ma's whore?"

"Shit, John, I told you before, I'm nobody's whore. I know these Generals and their rich friends because they are acquaintances of my boss. He is a very powerful man and must protect his interests. I go over to his house for dinner every week. That's how I know these people and what's going on this country. That's how I knew about the protest march."

"And what about the jewelry, the expensive stones, where do they come from?" Vina explained that when she went to the weekly dinner at Mr. Ma's place, he allowed her to pick out one piece from his collection to wear but it had to be returned before she could pick out another.

When she finished her explanation she sat silent for a few moments then looked directly at me and said, "So now that you know about my past, do you still want to see me?"

I just looked at her sitting on the edge of the couch with her hands folded in front of her, like a little girl waiting to find out if she can go on her first date. She didn't have to tell me all this stuff. She took a gamble that I would not get all pissed off and reject her. I hope she's telling me the truth.

I finally said, "Vina, as long as you're honest with me now, I'm okay with everything. I'm still crazy about you."

Smiling, she patted her hand on the couch, I moved next to her and she gently placed her hand on my neck and pulled me closer to her as she whispered in my ear, "John, you are a kind and considerate person. I don't use the word love anymore, but I like you, I like you a lot."

It was another Monday morning as I jumped into the cab for Stan's office, coffee in one hand, and crumbling mooncake in the other. What a great weekend with Vina, I finally got the straight story. For the first time I felt like I really knew and trusted her.

Stan was already at his desk when I arrived and as soon as he saw me called me into his office and told me to take a seat as he said, "Kid, I'm worried about this demonstration bullshit that happened over the weekend. I've heard from several reliable sources this is really the start of a right wing military coup. This student bullshit is just the start of it. They have allied themselves with the conservative rich people and factions of the military and are expected to target immorality and foreign influences on their culture.

"That means us kid--the red light district bars, massage parlors and whore houses could all see student demonstrations and police right on our front doors. Needless to say, it's bad for business, our customers; especially the foreigners and G.I.s won't come around. And if things get really ugly the cops might not protect the clubs. Let's head down to Patpong and get the crews together and start preparing to board the place up, not only Yvonne's but also the Toad."

So for the next few hours Stan and I spent time with the staff at Yvonne's and we all agreed that Frankie would be responsible to close the place up and get all the girls safely out if demonstrators showed up. All the windows and the glass door entrances would be covered and sealed with plywood.

It was almost two p.m. when we finished at Yvonne's so I walked next door to the Toad and ordered a cheeseburger and a beer for lunch. The place was almost empty and as I looked for the bartender I spotted Apri eating her lunch in one of the corner booths. She motioned for me to join her and as I sat down across from her she poured me some tea from a small pot and said, "Stan said you were at the student demonstrations yesterday. Did you see anyone killed?"

"No," I said, "Vina and I got out just as the bullets started to fly."

Apri starred at me and her smile vanished as she said, "So, you're back with her again? I thought you broke up with her."

"Well, we're back together again and this time I know it's going to last," I said.

Apri straightened her back, leaned forward, and with a deadly serious look she said, "Listen to me, John. That woman is no good for you. She's a whore and an addict. You need to find a good Thai woman."

"Oh, okay, Apri, I got it, like your cousin, Nicha, or maybe Sonja, or some other nice upstanding Patpong Thai lady?"

Apri sat back in her chair and slowly shaking her head said, "No, I don't mean them. You judge all Thai women as either whores or gold diggers, but that's not the case. Do you know that only two percent of Thai women are prostitutes? But you, like all the foreigners, either live or hang out in these little gutters like Patpong and you think our entire culture is like that. It's not.

"Straight Thai women are much more conservative than you think. Most are virgins when they marry. They are loyal, loving women and they expect the same from their boyfriends or husbands. These women are shy, they are very sensitive to things that effect their reputations and status, and they would never be seen with a foreigner who publicly surrounds himself with prostitutes.

"You may not believe this but most straight Thai women marry for love and not for money. John, you live in a subculture of Thai society, a place where the lust for money, power, and immorality are considered achievements and normal behavior. If you stay here long enough you will never know the real culture of Thailand, the heart and spirit of its people."

"Okay, Apri, so I live in a sewer and so do you. You make a living here just like I do, why are you still here? Because I have little choice. I have no real job skills. I was a whore and a drug addict. I was one of the worst kind, a person with no conscience.

I am saving my money. One day soon I will leave here and never return."

Apri placed her hand on my arm and with her face pleading said, "This place will devour you, John. You're young and already an alcoholic. Where will you be in three or four years from now? And that girl, Vina, she will destroy you. Get out now, while you can, leave this place. Tell your company to send someone else here."

Apri gently folded up her cloth napkin and placed the empty tea pot and cups in her lunch bag, as she got up from her chair said, "Have you seen Nicha lately? She hasn't been home for three days. She usually calls and let's me know what's going on. No one seems to know where's she's at. Can you go next door to Yvonne's and ask some of the girls? I'm really starting to worry about her."

"Okay, as soon as I finish my lunch," I promised.

It was almost 3 p.m. as I finished my second beer. Looking at my watch and I thought how the girls at Yvonne's would start arriving any minute to start their late afternoon to early morning shift.

Suddenly I heard the boisterous voice of Stan as he entered the building and approached the bar yelling at Apri and me, "Shit! They're coming! Those goddamn bastards are going to try and close us down tonight.

"I just shut down Yvonne's and told the girls to go home. We're boarding up the place now. We need to do the same here. God only knows if the cops will protect us."

"Hell, Stan," I stammered, "Patpong is quiet as hell. No one is freaked out but you."

Stan angrily looked over at me as he said, "Kid, don't argue with me. I got this straight from the top, from our silent partner. The student demonstrators will be right on our doorstep in a couple of hours. They'll be yelling about how foreign devils like you and me have corrupted their society and turned their women into whores."

Stan spoke to the several workmen who had followed him into the bar and started giving them directions on how to board up the windows. He turned to me and said, "If I were you I would hole up in your hotel until this thing blows over. From your third story penthouse you'll have a ringside seat."

The muscles in Stan's face tensed as he said, "Listen to me kid. Stay off the street. The Patpong locals know who you are. This could get ugly real quick."

Chapter 22 The Coup

Workers nailed lumber over the windows and the front entrance of Yvonne's, scrambling to board up the place. It was few minutes before three when I entered through the back door and spotted several of the girls putting clothes in their bags and getting ready to leave. When I asked about Frankie no one seemed to know where he was.

As I was about to go back to my hotel I spotted Sonja in the lunchroom and asked if she'd seen Frankie. "He left with several of the girls," she told me. When I asked her if she knew where Nicha was she stopped putting items in her bag, turned to me with tears welling in her eyes said, "The last time I saw her was three days ago, right here, at the end of her shift.

Yesterday I asked Frankie about her and all he said was, 'She broke the rules. Forget about her.' When I asked what he meant, he screamed at me, and said, 'Forget about her.'"

The workmen had finished so I motioned for all the girls to leave and told Sonja I would speak to Frankie later. As I walked back to my hotel I wondered what rules Frankie was talking about. Girls came and went at Yvonne's and I seldom kept track of who they were or the reasons. That was Frankie's job. But Nicha was a young kid and I was the one that got her the job, and Frankie knew that. Why hadn't he said anything to me?

Nicha loved the place and the money. I had to find out why she left and where she was.

As I settled into the large couch in my hotel living room with its view of the city, I sensed a strange calm in the Patpong District. Almost no one walked the streets; the normal bustle of people and the constant sounds of traffic and car horns was gone. An eerie quiet blanketed the neighborhood.

As I poured my third double vodka tonic I felt the alcohol numbing my brain and then the distant ringing of the telephone. After countless rings I finally got up and answered the phone and heard Stan's booming voice, "Christ kid, answer the fucking phone. Are you drunk or what? This is important. I forgot my ledger book at Yvonne's. I took the cash from the safe, but I forget that damn book. It's got the cuts for the partners and all kinds of shit in there that would not be good for us if it fell into the wrong hands.

"You're only a few blocks from there. Use your back door key and get into my office. The ledger is in the cabinet under the safe, the third drawer from the bottom on the left side. It's locked so get a hammer or a crow bar from the maintenance room, rip off the lock, grab the book, and get the hell out of there as fast as you can. I heard the students are loading into buses right now to demonstrate at all the bars and whorehouses in Patpong. Call me when you get back to your hotel room."

I told Stan I would try and get the book, but if the demonstrators stormed the place or started throwing shit I would be out of there in a hurry. I looked down at the streets below. The place was still quiet. Everyone who cleared out must have been waiting for something to happen. If I got caught on those streets by the demonstrators and one of the locals told them I was the owner of a whorehouse it could be over for me real quick.

As I considered heading downstairs for Yvonne's, I poured yet another double vodka. A drunken rage overwhelmed me. Fuck these guys. If they screw with me I'll blow their heads off. I walked back to my bedroom, pulled open the bottom drawer, and there it was, the 45 automatic I had taken from Rocky's Air America crew. I jammed a clip into the pistol butt, put another in my pocket, and hid the loaded gun under my shirt. I pulled on my sports jacket and headed out the door.

The lobby was deserted except for Steven the doorman who stood against a back wall. He had locked the front door and when he saw me begged me not to go outside. I shouted, "Unlock the damn door," and as I left the hotel I could hear him calling after me, yelling that the streets were not safe for foreigners, urging me to return to the hotel.

Mooncake Man

I ran down the several blocks to Yvonne's past bars, restaurants and massage parlors, all locked and boarded up. No one was on the streets, not even the cops.

At the street that ran adjacent to Yvonne's on Patpong Street I turned into the narrow alley and ran the last half block to the back entrance. I inserted my key into both locks and opened the door. It was dark inside except for a small light in the hallway leading to the back offices but I didn't need much light. I had been there so many times that I knew the layout like my own hotel room. As I approached the offices at the end of the corridor, I froze. Someone was in the building. The sound came from Stan's office, I heard a clicking sound, a clicking dial, like the unlocking of a safe.

I stopped, slowly pulling the 45 automatic from my belt underneath my jacket. The clicking sound continued as I inched closer to the open door of Stan's office. Edging toward the opening, I slowly peered inside. In the dim light I made out a figure stranding in front of the wall safe frantically turning the dials in one direction and then the other. The tumblers of the safe's lock made clicking sounds. After the third time that the man turned the dial, he pulled the handle on the safe, but it failed to open.

I moved closer to the figure whose back was to me as I shouted, "Put up your hands and turn around." The man stopped and slowly turned around to face me. It was Frankie, the head pimp at Yvonne's, decked out in his usual white suite and red tie.

His wide eyes showed panic as he said, "What are you doing here boss? Stan told me to empty the safe before the cops and demonstrators get here."

I stuck the gun in Frankie's chest and leaned forward so I stood a few inches from his disgusting face. "Bullshit. Stan already emptied the safe, and, besides, it looks like you don't even have the right combination." Frankie pleaded with me to let him go and claimed he was only doing what Stan told him to do.

"You're a fucking liar, Frankie. Now I'm going to ask you one more question and you better fucking tell me the truth, I'm a crazy drunk and I'll blow your head off if you don't start singing."

Frankie fell to his knees begging me not to shoot him and said he would tell me anything I wanted. "Okay, Frankie, where is Nicha?"

Silence filled the room for a few seconds, then Frankie jumped up and started yelling at me, "You son of a bitch. You got me on my knees begging for my life and then you ask me about a fucking whore, a mother fucking whore. I don't believe this shit. Those girls are nothing, nothing."

"Well, Frankie, she means something to me." I swung the pistol with all my force against his head. He screamed and fell face first to the floor. I kicked him and told him to get up and as he slowly rose to his knees I put the gun barrel into his forehead and said, "Okay, mother fucker, this is your last chance, what happen to Nicha?"

Frankie started wiping the blood from his face and whimpering. "Okay, okay, don't hit me anymore." After a few seconds he muttered, "She broke the rules. She rode bareback for a couple of extra bucks and she got the clap. The doctors told me a couple of days ago when they did their weekly exams. I had to let her go."

"So, you threw her out in the street, like some piece of garbage? You're a real piece of shit."

Frankie pulled himself up to a chair, wiped the blood from the side of his head, and screamed, "Me, me? She agreed to the rules. She knew the penalty for getting the clap in here. Shit man, you own this place. They're your fucking rules, not mine."

The combination of alcohol, adrenalin, and stress of finding Frankie breaking into Stan's office made my head spin. I stopped and stared at Frankie, trembling hard, and the blood that streamed freely down his face onto the collar of his white shirt and sports coat. His face had puffed up and his left eye had nearly swollen shut.

What a pathetic creature. He has absolutely no feeling or compassion for anyone. How does someone become this way, so callous that human life means nothing to him? Am I any different? What a stupid little fucker I've been, so stupid, so naïve, I didn't even realize the consequences of my actions. Am I any less culpable than Frankie? Apri told me this place would destroy me, or did she mean I'll destroy myself?

I pointed the gun at Frankie and said, "Get out of here; I never want to see your face again." Saying nothing, he slowly backed away toward the office door, abruptly turned, and broke into a full run toward the back entry and out the building. I located the drawer with ledger inside, and found it locked as Stan said it would be. I hurried down the hall to the maintenance locker, grabbed a crow bar, returned to the office, and sprung the lock. I turned the desk light on and opened the book; it contained pages of accounting details with amounts, dates, and names.

I folded the ledger under my arm, turned off the lights, and left the building, locking all the doors behind me. As I entered the alley I heard the faint sounds of trucks and buses several blocks away breaking the silence of the night. It must be the demonstrators.

I ran the last few remaining blocks back to my hotel. After pounding on the main entrance, Steven finally recognized me. He opened the door and as I heard him locking it behind me, I bolted up the stairs. Once I secured my hotel room door, I looked down to the streets below. Three buses had arrived and parked directly across from the Horny Toad and Yvonne's. Student demonstrators streamed out in all directions.

The occupants of several police cars parked several blocks away waited inside their vehicles while two more buses arrived. More demonstrators exited the buses, this time yelling into bullhorns, waving signs, and assembling the demonstrators into ranks on the deserted street.

I made myself another double vodka tonic, took the loaded pistol from my waistband, and laid it on the coffee table. I sat down on the couch overlooking the street and saw at least a hundred demonstrators shouting and waving banners. I turned on the light next to the sofa and opened the ledger. I scanned page after page listing every detail about what went on behind the scenes at Yvonne's: how many customers they served, the room numbers, the times in and out, the payments made by clients, and the commissions due the women.

The back section of the ledger listed the total amount grossed per shift, daily operating expenses, commissions paid to the pimps and the girls, and the net daily amounts. The last two pages showed the monthly net payouts to the partners. The partners? I was one of the them. There was my name, then Stan's, and then Gen. W. Sukumvit. So that's his name, the name of the silent partner, the guy that never puts in a dime but gets a full share.

I looked closer at the entries in the ledger, it showed a payout of five to six thousand dollars per month to each partner. The most I had received since the starting the whore house six months ago was 10 thousand. Was this bullshit accounting or was Stan holding out on me? The phone rang and as soon as I picked it up Stan wanted to know if I had his ledger book. I told him I had the book and had caught Frankie in his office trying to open the safe.

"Doesn't surprise me," quipped Stan. "Never trust a pimp, kid." Stan said that he had been contacted by the secretary of our silent partner.

The General wants to meet with us tomorrow at the Dusi Tani Hotel. "I don't like this," said Stan. "I don't want to talk on the phone. It's hard to find a taxi with all these damn demonstrators so I'll pick you up at noon with my car and driver."

"Okay," I replied, "by the way, Stan, I looked through your ledger. The book said that my cut should have been five K every month for the last six months. Most I've ever got from you was 10K so you owe me 20K."

There was silence on the phone, and then Stan said, "You're right kid, but it's not as bad as it looks. I was going to talk to you about it. I had to put some money back into the place. Don't worry about it. We'll settle up later. We've got bigger problems now. I don't trust our General."

The main street of Patpong was vacant as I waited for Stan and his driver to pick me up the next morning. I had fallen asleep or passed out the previous evening after watching the demonstrators march up and down the street carrying banners and yelling into bullhorns in both Thai and English about the corrupt and immoral red light district. By 10 p.m. it was all over. The students filed back into their buses in an orderly manner, as if they had completed a military maneuver, and disappeared into the night.

I spotted Pierre in the lobby and he told me most of the tourists had left the hotel and were at the airport trying to leave the country. Almost all of the international airlines had canceled their flights into Bangkok and the national carrier, Thai Airways, had ceased operations, leaving aircraft stranded throughout Asia.

Pierre wiped his bald head with his silk handkerchief as he said in a thick French accent,

"Mr. John, this could be a bad one. The prime minister fled the country last night and the generals have picked sides. No one is giving in. This could be a bloody power struggle between them. No one knows who's going to win. Be careful my friend."

Stan's black Toyota turned into the circular hotel driveway and as Steven opened the back door he said, "Take care of yourself."

As I slid into the seat next to Stan he became animated, gesturing, and telling me about all the coups he had lived through in his 13 years in Thailand. He told me all the other coups were a result of a group of ambitious generals, politicians, and wealthy families who formed alliances to further their interests. It seemed that every five or six years it happened and most of the time there was little if any bloodshed. But this time things were different.

There had been a falling out among the generals, each had support from their own Army units which had modern weapons, tanks, and even armed helicopters. They could turn on each other at any moment. After pausing, Stan said, "And you'll never guess who one of the key generals in this coup is."

"Okay, Stan, let me take a guess, Gen Sukumvit?"

"How the hell did you know that kid?" asked Stan.

"Jesus, Stan, it's in your book, the ledger," I replied.

"Oh that's right," said Stan, shaking his head. "Forgot about that. Now you know why I had to get that book. It's best not to know any generals right now, at least not until we see how this thing turns out."

What a strange experience, driving through Bangkok with so little traffic or noise. Here and there I saw pedicab drivers, but all the taxi and bus drivers had abandoned their vehicles. Civilian traffic was nonexistent and only few people walked on the streets. The trip by car from my place to the Dusi Tani Hotel normally would take forty minutes; we arrived in half the time.

It was a little after noon when Stan and I walked into the bar at the Dusi Tani Hotel and a small, bald, middle-aged Thai fellow seated in a corner booth waved us over. As we walked toward the booth Stan said he knew this guy. He was the personal secretary of our silent partner and took care of all his business and non-military affairs.

When Stan ordered beers for the two of us, the Thai guy rolled his eyes. The man put on his glasses and introduced himself as Mr. Wong, special assistant to General Sukumvit, Major General of the Thai Army.

Stan said, "Yes, we know who he is. What do you want from us?"

Mr. Wong said, "These are uncertain times in Thailand. The civilian government has exploited and abandoned the Thai people and several corrupt and immoral Thai generals are trying to take control. But General Sukumvit and his followers will prevail and restore order and human rights to the people of Thailand."

Stan interrupted and with an agitated voice said, "Cut the crap. I've lived here for 13 years and heard all this shit before, what do you want?"

The little man took off his glasses and gently started wiping them with his handkerchief as he said, "It is not wise for the General to be directly associated with your business during these troubled times. As you know his relatives have extensive business interests in this country and they have authorized me to offer you $50,000 for your establishments, 25K for Yvonne's and 25K for the Horny Toad Bar."

"Fuck you," roared Stan. "They are not for sale, especially at that price."

"Don't be so quick to reject my offer," responded the little man. "These are very uncertain times. The students will undoubtedly become more violent and unpredictable. They have vowed to burn down all the whorehouses and bars patronized by foreigners. I don't know if the General and the police can control them, they are very determined and many Thai people support them."

Stan slammed his fist on the table as he yelled at the little Thai man, "You little worm. Let me get this straight. You want to buy me out for chicken shit money and if I don't sell, the Army and the cops will look the other way as the students burn me out. Well, fuck you, fuck the General, and fuck his family." Stan's face burned bright red and he said, "Let's go, kid," and he flung his half-filled beer glass against the wall.

As we entered the hotel lobby we found the staff gathered around a television in the lobby watching pictures of soldiers firing their weapons in the street. The commentator spoke rapidly in Thai and after a few minutes, I asked Stan what was going on. He said that rival army units had begun firing at each other in various parts of the city.

Sniper fire had been reported a few miles from where we were and the civilian government was telling everyone to stay off the streets and foreigners not to leave their hotels. As we left the hotel and started to descend the marble stairs to the main street below we heard the unmistakable sound of gunfire a few hundred yards up the road. Stan stopped and said, "Kid, I told you this could get bad. Let's get the hell out of here." After looking in both directions he exclaimed, "Where the hell is my driver? Shit, there's no traffic. Where the hell could he be?"

I looked up and down the street; there was no one on the street except for two people sitting on wooden stools buying fruit from a street vendor with a wooden pushcart directly across from us. I stopped for a moment and listened. I thought I heard the distant sound of a diesel engine. It became louder and then came a noise like a thousand hammers hitting steel plates. The engine roar became louder, the clanging of metal intensified; I strained my eyes in the direction of the noise but didn't see anything.

Mooncake Man

Stan turned to me and asked, "What the hell is it?"

I shook my head, the sound got louder, the metal clanking noise and diesel engine became a roar then it hit me. I had heard that sound before, in the army. I turned to Stan and yelled, "It's a fucking tank."

As I said those words, the tank emerged around the corner, engine screaming, thick black smoke gushing out the rear, and metal tracks squealing. The vehicle churned up the asphalt from the street and tossed it some 20 feet up into the air. The tank suddenly stopped. Its gun barrel waved up and down because of the sudden maneuver. In a thunderous roar, the turret-mounted 50 caliber machine gun exploded, hitting the shoppers, the fruit vendor, and his cart. Bloody body parts and shattered wood fell to the sidewalk.

Stan and I looked at each other with incredulity as we watched the turret of the tank slowly swing in our direction. I grabbed him by the arm and pulled him down the stairs and we dove behind a concrete planter box that lined the entrance to the hotel. At the same instant I heard the roar of the machine gun and the whizzing sound of huge projectiles over our heads hitting the marble steps that we had been standing on seconds before.

Bullets and marble chips flew everywhere as Stan let out a scream and grabbed his leg. Blood came gushing out of his lower leg. I pulled up his pant leg up and saw a piece of marble lodged in his calf. I took off my belt and tied in around his leg below the knee to stop the bleeding. Stan tried to get up and kept yelling, "They shot me. The mother fuckers shot me."

"Stay down, Stan," I shouted. "You didn't get shot. You were hit by a shard of the marble staircase. "Get down Stan," I repeated. "If you had been hit by that 50 cal, you wouldn't even have a leg. You've got a flesh wound. Once we stopped the bleeding you'll be okay." We huddled behind the huge concrete planter box, grateful that we had the protection. The tank remained some 20 yards away. It did not move but we heard the electrical whine of its turret swinging from side to side like a giant eye looking for its next prey.

The engine roared again and we heard the metallic chatter of the beast rumbling away. After a while, when the sound had faded almost completely, I looked over the planter box and sighed with relief. The tank was blocks away, almost out of sight.

Stan could barely stand so I enlisted several of the hotel staff to carry him back into the hotel where we found his driver and car parked in the underground garage. His driver explained that he had seen the tank approaching and decided to park underneath the hotel for safety. Stan told his driver to take him to his private doctor close to his home on the outskirts of town.

I paid another driver who had holed up in the garage a highly inflated fee to take me to my hotel. As Stan was helped into the back seat of his car, he paused, turned to me, and said, "Kid, thanks for throwing me behind that planter box. I owe you. Don't worry about our investments. I'll have the places ringed by guards if the demonstrators show up tonight."

It was late afternoon by the time I returned to my hotel where I discovered Steven still guarding the entrance like it was Fort Knox. As I headed to the elevator the front desk clerk motioned that he wanted to speak with me. As I approached he leaned over and whispered in my ear, "A woman has been waiting in the lobby several hours to see you."

"Well, who the hell is it? You know I don't want whores around here," I said.

"I don't know, but she's sitting directly behind you." I swirled around and came face to face with Apri.

She looked at me with a solemn face and said, "We need to talk. Can we go up to your room?" I nodded and pointed to the elevator. When the lift started moving I scolded her for being out on the streets and asked her why she hadn't called before coming to the hotel.

"All the phones are down. None of the lines in my apartment complex or the neighborhood have worked since the evening before last. It has something to do with the demonstrations."

Once we were inside my suite I made myself a drink and gave Apri a cold soda. As I sat down on the couch next to the coffee table I saw her staring at the loaded 45 automatic pistol on the table. She turned to me and asked, "What is that for?"

"It's for protection in case things get out of hand," I answered.

As tears filled her eyes she sipped on her soda. With her voice cracking she looked at me and said, "Nicha is dead."

"What do you mean? Dead? How do you know that?" I asked. Apri told me that an old Thai man had appeared at her apartment in the morning with a handwritten note addressed to her and stating a reward would be given if he delivered it. Apri knew from the familiar childish Thai handwriting that the note came was from Nicha.

The old man said the note was found lying next to the lifeless body of a young Thai woman in a cheap hotel. He thought she died of a drug overdose because there were several empty pill containers and syringes on the floor.

Apri started crying as she said, "I want to give her the proper Buddhist funeral rites. If I leave her at that place the authorities will dump her body in a mass grave on the outskirts of town where they put homeless and nameless people. That's where they put people when no one cares about them. In the Buddhist funeral ceremony, the monks will chant the sutras and then her body will be cremated. Please help me. I cannot afford the 5,000 baht."

"Okay, no problem. I'll give you the money," I said.

Apri started wiping her eyes with her handkerchief and said, "I want you to hear what she wrote me." She reached into her purse, pulled out the note, carefully unfolded the white paper, and read the message.

My Dear Sister.

You are the one who has loved and cared for me. My life on this earth no longer has meaning for me. The one I love has no love for me and my sickness is incurable. I cannot burden you any longer. Please forgive me and think of me often.

Nicha.

I poured another double vodka and said, "That's sad, really sad. Who is she talking about, '"the one I love has no love for me?'"

Apri stared at me with cool steely eyes and said, "You."

"Jesus, Apri, I only tried to help her. I never encouraged that."

Apri shook her head and said, "Don't you know how life is? We always fall in the love with the wrong person."

"What happened is over and done. I'll go get you the money," I said.

When I returned from the bedroom with a roll of Thai bills, Apri was pouring another soda into her glass as she said, "Remember when I told you that I would leave some day? Nicha's death is a sign that I must leave Bangkok for good. I will live with my relatives in a small village up north, the place I lived as a young girl.

"Come with me John. It's a simple life and a chance to forget about this cesspool of Patpong. You need to get away from here, to stop using addictive drugs and alcohol. It will be a good, pure, life and your salvation." She paused for a few moments and asked directly, "Will you come with me?"

I looked at Apri sitting erect on the couch with her long black hair flowing over her shoulders and her thin brown eyes pleading with me as I said, "I can't go with you, Apri." I tried to soften my words by adding, " I can't do that right now."

She stared at me for several seconds and her face turned to stone as she said, "It's her, isn't it? Vina the white whore."

I felt the blood pumping hard in my chest and my face getting hot as I blurted out, "You hate her, don't you, Apri? You fucking hate her."

Apri moved her body to the edge of the couch only a few inches from where I sat. Her face contorted into an angry snarl as she raised her voice and said, "You're so in love with her that you are completely blind. Don't you understand? I'm trying to save your life. Come with me. Forget about her. She's using you. She's not an honest person and she's a whore."

I stood up and pointed my finger at Apri as I angrily shouted back, "Fuck you Apri. She's not a whore."

Apri stood up and I did, too, so that we faced each other. I looked down at her she jabbed her finger into my chest and shouted angrily, "Don't tell me about whores. I was one for fifteen years. When that ugly corrupt general that is Stan's partner came into the Toad with your white virgin girl friend and her tranny friends he had his hand up her dress within the first 10 minutes. The transvestites told everyone that they go out to one of his country villas and have a foursome. Don't you ever try and tell me about whores, John."

I felt a wave of anger sweep over me as I grabbed the money off the table and thrust it in her hand. "Take the money. Take it. Go away and leave me alone. I never want to see you again."

She said nothing, wiped the tears from her eyes with the back of her hand, put the money in her purse, and walked toward the door. She slowly turned around, looked at me one more time, shook her head, and then walked out the door.

At the wet bar in the living room I poured a water glass half full of vodka and then added a small shot of lime juice. This would be a good night to get drunk and pass out all by myself. I sat on the couch and looked down at the streets below. Several buses had pulled up and were uploading demonstrators who filed into orderly ranks in the middle of the street. The police and Stan's security guards no where in sight.

As I took my first hit of the potent drink my mind wandered back to Nicha, this simple little girl who felt so hopeless that she took her own life at nineteen. I remembered the night we were together with Sonja at the Oriental Hotel watching the festival of lights, how excited she got watching the lighted flowers slowly float down the river. They both looked like young girls then, happy, carefree, and naturally beautiful, not prostitutes who worked their trade 12 hours a day, six days a week.

How did it happen that her life ended the way it did? Was I responsible for her death? I was the one who had got her the whore job. I had indulged in sex with her at Sonja's place and then rejected her numerous invitations. And lately, hell, I had completely ignored her.

Was it because I felt she was beneath me, a common Thai whore, rather than someone who had real human feelings? And when she got sick she didn't come to me. Why would she? Maybe I did have some responsibility for her death.

I poured another drink. Booze never let me down, it relieved the pain and let me forget about everything. There was only one thing more permanent. I looked at the loaded pistol on the table.

What would it be like? Would it be a flash of pain then silence or would it be an agonizing, slow pitiful pain as I drifted off into death? I wonder how it was for Nicha.

I stared at the gun as I finished the half filled glass of vodka. A sudden explosion in the street below brought me to my senses. I watched as Yvonne's erupted in flames.

Chapter 23 That Sexy Smile

I heard the soft patter of rain on the veranda as I slowly open my eyes. My head was aching and my mouth felt like it was stuffed full of cotton, the familiar vodka hangover. The smell of burnt wood hung heavy in the air and brought me back to the night before. I had sat on the couch, drank from tall vodka-filled water glasses, and watched the student demonstrators torch the street below until I finally passed out.

An entire block of Patpong street was non-existent. My place, Yvonne's Massage Parlor, and Stan's Horny Toad Bar, were just smoldering piles of rubble. Stan's security guards had never showed up, and the cops and fireman were no where to be seen. The plan had been well-executed, just as the little Thai man who was the General's secretary had proposed. Sell me your establishments at my price or your places will be burned to the ground.

I guessed that was the way things were handled in Thailand when people didn't get what they want. My first shocking experience with it was when I retuned from Vietnam and found Sophie's, my favorite massage parlor, in ashes.

I felt sorry for Stan. He had lost everything. I wondered if he had insurance and did it have the standard clause that stated losses were not covered if they resulted from civil disobedience, strikes, or coups. My original 30K investment was gone, but I was still ahead, I had gotten back 10K from Yvonne's profits. The courier service had turned out to be a cash cow, covering all of our expenses with a nice profit every month. I had taken out 20K in cash from the business and with the money from Yvonne's, stashed 30,000 U.S. dollars in Pierre's hotel safe.

Mooncake Man

I had learned in Asia to never trust the banks. They could be taken over at any time by the government and getting your money out was a problem in a time of civil strife or coups. My thoughts proved correct, every local and foreign bank in Bangkok had been locked up tight.

I had called Po in Hong Kong at the start of the demonstrations and told him the courier service was suspended as our business customers had locked up their doors. Nothing had changed in the last six days so I called him again. I said I would be leaving Bangkok until we could operate again. Stan and his crew could start the service up once the coup was settled and businesses opened up.

It was late morning and I didn't feel like breakfast so I poured myself a glass half full of vodka and a chaser 50 milligrams of Valium. As I sat on the couch overlooking my burnt out whorehouse and the rubble that used to be the Horny Toad I thought about everything I had lost.

Gone was the courier service and there was no guarantee it would start up again. A new government could demand new permits. Once they realized how successful it had been they could take it over or demand some ridiculous percentage of the business. It could be another Korea with negotiations going on for months.

And there were my friends and acquaintances. Stan was in the hospital with a badly infected leg he got from the tank incident. Nicha was dead. Apri was the only true friend I had that really cared about me. And I had thrown her out in a fit of ego and drunken rage.

But there was still Vina. Our relationship was all over the place, from love and good times to vindictive fights over some insignificant episode or stupid act. Deep down I still didn't know if I trusted her, but she was all I had left. I had to convince her to leave Thailand with me; we could both get a new start on life and forget about this place forever.

But how could we get out? All the passenger flights were suspended in and out of Bangkok. I took another hit of vodka from my water glass and thought things over. Then it hit me. I could call Rocky.

I'll bet he's still flying. The Thai generals are not going to mess with the CIA and their airline. If anyone can get me out of this place it's the Rock. I picked up the phone and dialed Rocky's direct office number. As it started to ring, I thought, "Thank goodness that the phones are still working but that could change at any minute."

After the sixth ring I heard a deep American voice say, "Rocky here."

"Hey Rocky, this is the kid. I need a favor, I want to get the hell outta here."

There was a laugh on the other end and then, "Hell kid, we all want to get out of here. Want to go to Cambodia again? Can't get enough action, huh kid?"

"No way, Rocky. Hell, that place is worst than Thailand. I remember you guys saying you fly to Saigon once a week to pickup some military cargo."

Rocky replied, "You're right kid, every Wednesday morning we leave at 0600 hours.

"Can you take me? One way?" I asked.

"Okay, kid. I owe you one for the Cambodia deal. Be here at no later than 0530 tomorrow morning."

"Okay! Thanks Rock. One more thing. I have a friend. A woman needs a ride, too."

"Shit, kid, I only have one jump seat, and besides I can't be seen having some girl in the airplane, especially a local. That would raise all kinds of questions."

"Rocky, she's not a local, she's a round eye."

"Jesus, kid that's even worse. I can't be hauling around some goddamn white ass chick. She's a civilian and doesn't even have a security clearance. These are really goddamn military flights and you know it. What the hell would I say when she climbed out of the aircraft at the U.S. Air Base in Saigon?"

"What a bunch of bullshit, Rock. I'm a civilian and I don't have a security clearance."

"Want to make a bet kid? You think I just let anybody on my aircraft, especially a snot noise kid who owns a whorehouse and has no fucking idea of where he's at? I checked you out with my buddy Al. Remember him? He and the General got your ass into Thailand through the back door. We all work for the same company. Kid, they got a file on you and your stupid company six inches thick."

"Okay, Rocky, I'm in a bind. I'll make it worth your while. How much do you want to take the girl"

There was silence on the phone. I braced myself for an abrupt rejection, then I heard,

"One G, a grand in U.S. dollars, small bills."

"Okay, Rock, its done. My girlfriend and I will be at your place at 5:30 a.m. tomorrow."

"One more thing kid. Dress her up to look like a guy. Put an overcoat on her and make sure all her hair is underneath a baseball cap."

As I hung up the phone I thought, "Once we get to Saigon we can catch any number of flights to Hong Kong and Taiwan. Hell, we may even be able to catch the daily Pan Am flight to San Francisco."

I settled back on to my couch and finished off the last of my water glass of vodka. Now all I had to do was to convince Vina to go with me. I dialed her number and all I heard was a steady buzzing sound. I hung up and tried several more times with the same result. I called the hotel operator and she explained the steady buzzing sound meant the phone was out of order because of the street demonstrators and rioters pulling down phone lines and destroying relay boxes throughout the city.

There was no way to determine what phones were working unless you called, and no one had any idea of when service would be restored as the telephone workers were not reporting for work. It was almost five p.m. and I decided my plan would be to keep trying to reach Vina until around nine p.m. and then if I couldn't reach her, I'd drop by her place on the way to the airport and try and convince to go with me in person. I would enlist Steven to drive the hotel van to Vina's and then on to the airport and I would give him a good tip and make sure he got back to the hotel before the midnight curfew.

I rang the hotel manager Pierre and told him I needed to speak with him. It was after five when I walked into his office and I could see he was getting ready to leave for the day. I told him I would be leaving Bangkok for good and needed to get my money out of the hotel safe. As he opened the safe and placed the bills in front of me he said, "Where will you go? What will you do?"

I looked at Pierre in his usual tailored white suit and shoes and his always sweating bald head and realized he had been a true friend. When I first arrived in Bangkok he went out of his way to help me and always told me the truth, his positive attitude toward people and his business professionalism were in stark contrast to the Patpong red light district that surrounded him. Pierre was a class act and I would miss him.

I handed him an extra month's rent, shook his hand and said, "I'm not sure where I'm going. Maybe I need to go home. I'm leaving tonight; you can have anything left in my suite."

As I entered the lobby, I spotted Steven the doorman and told him of my plan. After I mentioned a U.S. hundred dollar tip he assured me the hotel van would be ready and waiting for a nine p.m. departure. As soon as I got back to my room I called Vina again. The phones were still out of order.

I made myself a tall vodka tonic and turned on the television. It was the same old story, one politician after another talked about saving the people of Thailand. It was still a dangerous and unpredictable place as street fighting between Army units broke our sporadically throughout the city. As in prior coups and insurrections, when things got bloody enough and out of control, the king would step in, mediate a cease fire, and impose a solution. The question was when that would happen.

I pulled my largest suitcase from the closet and stuffed it with as many clothes as I could fit into it. Pierre would inherit a lot. I put a fifth of vodka into my brief case. It would be a long night until I flew out in the morning. I needed something to numb my brain.

It was almost nine p.m. when I hear Steven's knock and voice outside my door. "It's time to go," he said. I made one last phone call to Vina. The line was still dead. I took one final glance at my place, grabbed my loaded 45 automatic, and stuffed it under my shirt. There was no way I was going to be cornered by some Army guy or crazy demonstrator without protection.

Once inside the hotel van I gave Steven the directions to Vina's place. When he saw it was near the Botanical Gardens, he assured me he knew the way. As we drove through the city, the streets were darker than normal and several traffic lights continually flashed red to indicate they were out of order. Traffic was light and almost non-existent in some areas. Small groups of people could be seen in front of the few shops that were open, quite a contrast to a normal night when throngs of people lined the streets and packed the night markets.

As we made our way through the narrow dark streets of Bangkok I asked myself how would I convince Vina to leave with me. I had mentioned going on a short vacation trip to Malaysia several months back and she responded with indifference. I couldn't figure that one out. Most women would love to go to a five star hotel on one of Malaysia's beautiful beaches. There had to be something else. Maybe she had some kind of Visa issue. Hell, she might not even have a passport.

I'll tell her leaving Bangkok does not have to permanent, just until the riots and demonstrations are over. Besides, she's not doing any business. All the tourists have left.

She can stay at one of my company's Singapore apartments or I can get a room at the famous Raffles hotel in downtown right next to the Jockey Club. She'll love the place, the night markets, the great restaurants. She wouldn't have to work, I'd take care of her as long as she wants.

Steven jolted me out of my thoughts when he told we had arrived. I looked out the window and recognized the large sign that said, "Bangkok Botanical Gardens." I told him to turn right down the gravel road and as we approached Vina's cottage I noticed a large dark colored American sedan in front.

Steven pulled up next to the car and I looked over at the vehicle. It was olive drab with Thai Army markings on the door. Then I saw it, I froze and my heart sank, on the front bumpers were the small little flags of a Thai General.

What was he doing here? Maybe she is in some kind of trouble, or maybe Apri was right, she is the general's whore. I told Steven to wait for me. As I approached the door my hand unconsciously felt my gun to make sure it was still hidden under my shirt. Slowly, I inched my way to the cottage entrance and knocked on the door. Silence. I knocked again, only this time harder.

Suddenly I heard Vina's shout something in Thai in an agitated voice. After a few seconds she said in English, "Who the hell is it?"

I replied, "It's me, John. I've been trying to call you all day. I need to talk to you."

Immediately she replied in an angry voice, "Go away John. Not now."

"Damn it Vina," I yelled. "I'm leaving Thailand and I want to talk to you now."

"Shit John. Not now. I don't want to talk to you. Go away."

"Okay, Vina. If you don't come out I'll break the fucking door down."

Suddenly there was the deep voice of a man yelling in English with a Thai accent. "If you do not leave immediately, I'll have you arrested."

My mind went blank as rage instantly overwhelmed me. I kicked in the door and was confronted with the spectacle of Vina lying naked on the living room couch and sitting next to her in his underwear was the fat old Army General named Sukumvit. Vina's eyes grew wide and the General rose from the couch and started to say something just as I crashed the automatic pistol into the left side of this face.

He went down instantly with blood flying in all directions as Vina started screaming, "Don't. Don't."

221

"Don't what?" I yelled at her, "kill your sugar daddy?"

I looked at her, she was sobbing uncontrollably, and next to her on the table was an empty syringe. She was a junkie, a mainliner shooting heroin. I heard a noise behind me; it was the General starting to get up. I look down at him and realized he was the SOB that gave her the dope in return for sex.

I reached over and grabbed him by the hair and slowly pulled him up to me. He was still bleeding and grasping for air as I put the pistol in his mouth and pulled back the hammer I said, "Okay, you bastard, I'm going to blow your fucking head clean off."

The general began crying and Vina started screaming, "Don't do it John. You've been drinking, Please don't do it. It's me you should hate, not him."

I looked at her. Tears streamed down her face, she pleaded in a soft voice, "Please, please don't do it."

I looked down at the crying, whimpering old man hanging on to my leg and smashed the pistol to the side of his head that was not bleeding and he instantly crumpled into an unconscious heap on the floor.

I looked at Vina and said, "You lied to me the whole time didn't you? You're a whore and junkie, just as Apri said. What a fool I've been. I came over her to take you with me, to leave Thailand and go anywhere you wanted. I'm such an idiot I even fell in love with you."

She wrapped a sheet around her naked body and sat upright on the couch slowly wiping the tears from her eyes and said, "John, I'm not like you. I could never be committed to one person. I don't have enough love in me anymore, for anyone. This is way it has to be for me, I don't want to change my life. I just want to live it. Go find yourself someone who will love and take care of you."

She got up from the couch, the satin sheet flowing from her beautiful figure, put her arms around me, and gently kiss me on the cheek as she said, "They'll be looking for you. What do you want me to tell the General when he gets up?"

"Tell him that I'm leaving on the train for Malaysia tomorrow morning at the Bangkok Central Station." I wrapped my arms around her and felt the softness of her body against mine, the smell of her perfume overwhelmed my senses, but I knew she was slipping away, like someone slowly drifting downstream in an unseen current and disappearing into black cold swirling waters. I knew I would never see her again.

Mooncake Man

Smiling she placed both hands on my neck and drawing me close to her gently kissed me on the lips as she whispered, "Good-bye Mooncake Man. I'll never forget you."

The hotel van rumbled along the back roads to the international airport. Steven the driver looked into his front mirror and said, "Boss, I heard a lot of yelling in there. What was going on?"

"Some things are just not supposed to happen, Steven, and this was one of those things." As we drove along in silence on the dimly lit road I pulled the fifth of vodka from my bag and took a long gulp. I had lost everything, even my beautiful Vina.

I pulled the loaded 45 automatic from my waist band and laid it on the seat next to me and watched the pistol jump up and down with each jarring bump and crack in the road.

It would be so simple, one more drink, than bam, it would be all over.

I looked out the window, we were crossing over the Chao Phraya River bridge, I looked down at the muddy water below and remembered. It was her, sitting in the front of the boat, beautiful blond hair blowing in the wind as we raced to see the cobra and the mongoose fight; she looked backed at me and smiled, that sexy smile.

A calmness settled over my body and mind, an unexplained force grabbed the gun, and threw it into the river.

It was time to go home.

Epilogue

I did return to the USA and continue to work for DHL for several more years, selling the courier service to companies throughout the country. In 1979, I left DHL at the same time Adrian Dalsey sold his interest in the company to Larry Hillblom and his associates. A few years later my alcoholic lifestyle finally caught up with me and I entered a rehab program and shortly thereafter became a life long member of AA. Through my higher power and loving friends in the fellowship I have been sober for the last 30 years.

This year 2012 will mark my 40th year in the shipping business and I plan to retire and travel the country, writing and enjoying myself with my cat named "Bugs."